Age and Guile
Beat Youth, Innocence,
and a Bad Haircut

Also by P. J. O'Rourke

Modern Manners

The Bachelor Home Companion

Republican Party Reptile

Holidays in Hell

Parliament of Whores

Give War a Chance

All the Trouble in the World

Age and Guile Beat Youth, Innocence, and a Bad Haircut

P. J. O'Rourke

THE ATLANTIC MONTHLY PRESS
NEW YORK

Printed in the United States of America

FIRST PAPERBACK EDITION

Library of Congress Cataloging-in-Publictation Data

O' Rourke, P. J.
    Age and guile beat youth, innocence, and a bad haircut: twenty-five years of P. J. O'Rourke.—1st ed.
    Partial Contents: Juvenilia delinquent: "underground" press, 1970–1972—The truth about the sixties and other fiction—Days of wage: National lampoon, 1971–1981—Drives to nowhere: automotive journalism—Essays, prefaces, speeches, reviews, and things jotted on napkins—Current and recurrent events.—Bad sports.
    ISBN 0-87113-653-8 (pbk.)
    1. O'Rourke, P. J.   2. Journalists—United States—Biography
    I. Title.
PN4874.O58A38   1995   814'.54—dc20   95-16430

DESIGN BY LAURA HAMMOND HOUGH
ILLUSTRATION ON TITLE PAGE BY ALAN ROSE

The Atlantic Monthly Press
841 Broadway
New York, NY 10003

10 9 8 7 6 5 4 3 2 1

Acknowledgments

Twenty-five years of writing for a living leave me with a lot of people I need to thank—or a lot of blame I need to spread around. However the reader may feel, *I'm* grateful to those who helped me avoid a real job. First I would like to thank my cousin Dennis Loy, to whose memory this book is dedicated. Dennis became my friend, as opposed to relative, when I was in high school and he had just finished studying at the Art Institute in Chicago. He was the only person in my family to have read a book all the way through, for fun. Dennis was an enthusiastic audience and unpatronizing patron of even my most labored neophyte efforts. When I showed up in New York in 1971 with exactly fifteen dollars, he gave me a place to stay. I would have surely, and deservedly, starved (and frozen) that winter if it hadn't been for his help.

Acknowledgments

In college my first love, Bonnie Hall, had been equally generous. She actually thought I had something to say. She even went so far as to listen to me say it. There are no kinder or better people in the world than those who listen to you when you're eighteen.

Important, though less witting, assistance was given to me by the Woodrow Wilson Fellowship board. I had been nominated for one of these scholarship plums and went through the various rounds of elimination until I reached the final cut, an oral examination to be conducted in Columbus, Ohio.

I arrived in Columbus the night before the interview and went out beer drinking and pot smoking until all hours. I was supposed to be in the offices of the Ohio State University English Department at 9:00 A.M. I came to on somebody's couch at 9:15, pulled on my Stroh's-drenched jeans and a sweatshirt reeking of sinsemilla, and rushed, unshaved, unwashed, and unregenerate, to the campus. I was shown into a seminar room and placed on a hard chair facing a conference table behind which sat five or six middle-aged worthies with notepads. I remember only one of the questions.

WORTHY: Which literary critic has had the most profound influence on your thinking?

ME: . . .

I could not think of the name of a single literary critic. Not Roland Barthes, not John Crowe Ransom, not even R. P. Blackmur, from whom I cribbed my entire junior thesis on Henry James.

ME: Henry David Thoreau.

WORTHIES *(more or less in unison):* Henry David Thoreau wasn't a literary critic.

ME: His whole *life* was an act of literary criticism.

Well, it was 1969. Bullshit was an intellectual mainstay of the era. And I became a Woodrow Wilson Fellow.

This allowed me to get my M.A. in English at Johns Hopkins by attending something called "The Writing Seminar." It was a creative writing program of the way-creative kind run by a poet named Elliot Coleman. Coleman's distinction was either that he was Ezra Pound's only friend or that he was the only friend of Ezra Pound who wrote worse poetry than Ezra did. Maybe both. The Seminar possessed its good and bad points. I had, at age twenty-two, the complete luxury of writing anything I wanted with no worry about a paycheck and no thought of a public other than Professor Coleman (and, by extension, Ezra Pound). That was the bad point. The results were not as gruesome as having, at age twenty-two, the complete luxury of spending anything I wanted or screwing anything I wanted, but almost. The good point was that the Seminar's course work entailed reading only such high modernists as John Barth, Donald Barthelme, Thomas Pynchon, Jorge Borges, etc. A couple of semesters of this and even a twenty-two-year-old was cured of an interest in art.

But I seem to have digressed from the acknowledged purpose of an Acknowledgments page and wandered into autobiography or some other form of self-gratification. And it is others I mean to gratify if I can. Michael Carliner, who'd started a Baltimore weekly newspaper named *Harry,* gave me my first writing assignment while I was still at Hopkins. And my fellow Seminar student Denis Boyles started another newspaper and gave me a second assignment. My career was launched. That is, I had gained the privilege of getting a free handful of either of these papers and standing on street corners selling them for twenty-five cents each until I had enough money for beer.

I stayed in Baltimore, off and on, for two years, working with Tom D'Antoni, who managed to keep *Harry* going well into the 1970s, and with graphic artist Alan Rose, who has been my collaborator on such projects as the *National Lampoon High School Yearbook Parody,* the *National Lampoon Sunday Newspaper Parody,* and *The Bachelor Home Companion* and who drew the illustration on the title page of this book, which a certain significant other of mine won't let me get as a tattoo.

Some time about 1971 Bob Singer, a writer for the *East Village Other,* wandered into Baltimore and convinced me that I should try my hand at *EVO,* which was the grandaddy of the "underground" newspapers, dating all the way back to 1965. Poor Bob languishes today in a California prison for something to do with smokable substances, not—amazingly enough, considering Californian attitudes—tobacco. Another *EVO* writer, Ray Shultz, got me a job on a legitimate weekly called the *New York Herald.* I rose from messenger to features editor in six months, this having nothing to do with my talents and everything to do with the number of talented people who were leaving the *Herald,* which folded about ten minutes after I achieved my exalted position. A third habitué of the *East Village Other* and the best writer the "underground" press produced, Dean Latimer, took me with him to the headquarters of the *National Lampoon,* where the late Doug Kenney agreed to let the two of us do an article "on spec"—mostly, I think, to get us out of his office. I was entranced by the *Lampoon* and hung around the place making a pest of myself for over a year until the chairman of the company, Matty Simmons, broke down and gave me a job. The *Lampoon* was puerile, maybe, but with a finely crafted puerility undertaken by very well educated kids. I was not a good enough writer to work on the *Lampoon,* but I received patient encouragement from Doug Kenney, George W. S. Trow, Henry Beard, and the late Michael O'Donoghue (who kept the patient, encouraging side of himself a strict secret from the public).

While I was at the *Lampoon* I began to freelance for other magazines, notably *Car and Driver* and *The American Spectator. Car and Driver* editor David E. Davis, Jr., allowed me to try all sorts of things that aren't usually done in motoring publications, such as saying "shit" and admitting that I had shit idea how an automobile worked. And, at *The American Spectator,* editor in chief R. Emmett Tyrrell, Jr., Managing Editor Wladyslaw Pleszczynski, and Assistant Managing Editor Andy Ferguson gave me a license to violently fulminate which has not expired yet.

After I left the *National Lampoon, Rolling Stone's* then editor Terry McDonell convinced me to write a piece on "cocaine etiquette." This article would grow—perhaps metastasize is the better word—into my first book, *Modern Manners,* edited by (have I used the phrase "patient encouragement" already?) Susan Moldow, designed by Alan Rose, and given better illustrations than it deserved by Robert Neubecker. Terry McDonell went on to edit *Esquire, Sports Afield,* the back of the book at *Newsweek,* and his own magazine, *Smart,* giving me much-needed work at each.

Meanwhile I found myself in a quandary. (A wonderful name, by the way, for a Korean subcompact. Auto importers take note.) I wanted to go to various of the world's trouble spots and make fun of them—combining the silliness of foreign correspondence with the solemn business of mockery and slander. There were magazines willing to let me do this, but they didn't have the money to send me overseas. Other magazines had the money but thought my project was, as one (okay, more than one) editor put it, "stupid." *Rolling Stone*'s Carolyn White and her boss Jann Wenner (sterling fellow) came to the rescue in 1986, and ever since, when anything stupid is happening internationally I'm there being stupid about it.

The following year my old friend Morgan Entrekin began his own imprint at Atlantic Monthly Press (which company he later bought and then merged with Grove Press to create the corporation that made what you hold in your hand). Morgan purchased a collection of my magazine pieces, published it as *Republican Party Reptile,* then he purchased another collection, and another, and now I get paid twice for everything I write. Cool.

There are many other people I want to thank, who provided me with employment or helped make sure the fruits of that employment were unembarrassing or at least remunerative. I hope I'm not forgetting a whole bunch of them, but I am a scion of the 1960s and prone to—not "acid flashbacks" but whatever the opposite of that would be—"booze and coke flameouts." There are whole years for which I can't account. Dean Latimer used to tell the story of how he bought tickets for a Jefferson Airplane concert and the next thing he remembered he was standing in line at the Fillmore Auditorium. When he looked up at the marquee he saw that this was the Fillmore East, in New York. But when he looked at the tickets in his hand they were for the Fillmore in San Francisco.

Acknowledgments

Anyway, I'd like to thank Rex Weiner of the old *New York Ace,* Al Goldstein from *Screw,* Julian Weber, John Weidman, and Susan Devins of the *National Lampoon* and John Hughes and Jeff Greenfield, who were there, too, whether they care to admit it or not; Don Coulter at *Car and Driver,* Jean Lindamood at *Automobile,* David Hirshey at *Esquire,* Robert Vare, Bob Wallace, and Eric Etheridge of *Rolling Stone* and Patricia Cohen, my current editor there, and her (and my) invaluable assistant Tobias Perse; Shelley Wanger of *House and Garden*; Cato Institute President Ed Crane; John Fund, David Brooks, and Melanie Kirkpatrick at the *Wall Street Journal,* John Rasmus at *Men's Journal,* Silvo Calabi at *Fly Rod and Reel,* Michael Kinsley of *Harper's* and *The New Republic,* Hendrick Hertzberg of the latter, Bob Asahina of the former and the *New York Times Book Review,* Glen Gavin and Jack Shafer of *Inquiry,* Larry Smith, Gail McCarthy and Walter Anderson at *Parade,* John Rezek at *Playboy,* Elizabeth Beier and Bill Grose at Pocket Books, Wayne Lawson at *Vanity Fair;* Mort Janklow and Art Klebanoff, who gave various contract negotiations a needful kick in the pants; Jacqueline Graham, who has, under the aegis of Pan Macmillan, loyally published me in England (even though I barely speak the language), and Don Epstein, whose lecture agency, Greater Talent Network, paid my way through some lean years, or they would have been lean years if Elaine Kaufman hadn't kept me fed. I'd like to thank Bob Wagner, who took the recent photograph of me on the cover. Thanks also to whomever took the "1970" picture. I think it was Shelley Lustig. Give a call, Shelley, I owe you one of those princely publishing company dust-jacket art fees, fifty dollars or something. And I want, of course, to thank my agent, Bob Dattila. And, most of all, thanks and love and everything else to Tina Mallon.

P. J. O'ROURKE
Washington, D.C.
1995

A Forgotten Hero of the Trojan War

Thersites only clamour'd in the throng,
Loquacious, loud, and turbulent of tongue:
Awed by no shame, by no respect controll'd,
In scandal busy, in reproaches bold;
With witty malice studious to defame;
Scorn all his joy, and laughter all his aim.
But chief he gloried with licentious style
To lash the great, and monarchs to revile . . .
Spleen to mankind his envious heart possess'd,
And much he hated all, but most the best.

—from Alexander Pope's translation of *The Iliad*

Contents

Contents

Drives to Nowhere
Automotive Journalism

Essays, Prefaces, Speeches, Reviews, and Things Jotted on Napkins

Current and Recurrent Events

Contents

Age and Guile
Beat Youth, Innocence,
and a Bad Haircut

Introduction

There's a long-term problem with being a writer, and the problem is all the things that, over the long term, I've written. How would you like to have the twaddle and blather you talked twenty-five years ago preserved in detail, set down in black-and-white, and still extant someplace? I once had hope that the fashion for recycling would rid me of my printed past. But what artisan—however modest his art—can bear to think that his life's work amounts to no more than the 1/100th part of the local Boy Scout paper drive? So there's still a pile of it in my attic. Sooner or later somebody will find these manuscripts. I might as well publish them myself. Also, I'm being paid for it. The business of trading embarrassment for money is an old American custom, dating back to the murky beginnings of the Phil Donahue show.

Examining these works, I see evidence that I was once younger than anyone ever has been. And on drugs. At least I hope I was on drugs. I'd hate to think that these were my sober and well-considered thoughts. It is, I guess, interesting to watch the leftist grub weaving itself into the pupa of satire and then emerging a resplendent conservative blowfly. Also interesting is the career arc. I start out making cruel fun of a second-rate American president and wind up making cruel fun of a second-rate American president.

And that is all the interest I can summon. I wonder how many people in the so-called creative fields stand before their accumulated professional efforts and think that the thing they've been doing for the past quarter of a century is a thing for which they have no particular talent. Not enough, to judge by the too copious output of various mature painters, poets, and architects. Hardly ever do we hear these people exclaim, "My pictures don't look like anything," "My poems don't rhyme," or "This isn't a building, it's the box a building comes in."

Fortunately, I discovered journalism. Talent hasn't been a question since. But I didn't mean to be a journalist. I meant to be a genius. I was going to produce an oeuvre so brilliant, important, and deep that no one would ever understand it. Pooh on *Finnegans Wake.* "riverrun, past Eve and Adam's, from swerve of shore to bend of bay, brings us by a commodius vicus of recirculation back to Howth Castle and Environs. . . ." Anybody can read that. Here's a line from a play I wrote in 1968: "vIvAvIvAvIvA vIvAvIvAvIvA vIvAvIvAvIvA."

Unfortunately I didn't have the knack for literature. It seemed that a certain number of English professors had to have written brilliant, important, and deep Ph.D. dissertations on how no one would ever understand you. Also, it helped to be dead.

To tell the truth, I didn't even mean to be a writer. I meant to be a race-car driver, except I didn't have a race car. Or I meant to be a rock star, except I couldn't sing or play an instrument. (I know, I know, there are so many who haven't been stopped by that, but I was naive.) Or I meant to be a soldier of fortune except the entry-level job in that field was a stint in Vietnam and, jeeze, they were actually shooting at you over there. What I meant *not* to be was just a college student. How bourgeois. I did spend the summer of 1966 working as a railroad brakeman, and that seemed to me to be the coolest job that a fellow who knew all the verses to "If I Had a Hammer" and "Old Stewball" could possibly have. I wanted to quit college and stay a brakeman forever, but (this never seemed to happen to Neal Cassady and Jack Kerouac) my mother wouldn't let me. So I had to find something I could be while also being a college student and something that didn't require expensive equipment, difficult skills, or courage under fire. Writing was the obvious choice.

I decided that I would, over the summer of 1967, write a novel. I wasn't sure how long something had to be before it was considered a novel so I looked around for the briefest acceptable example of the type. I settled on Oscar Wilde's *The Picture of Dorian Gray*. In point of learning the craft, I would have been better off reading the book. Instead, I counted the words in it, multiplying the average per page by the total of pages to arrive at the figure 50,000. There were 130 days in my summer vacation. If I wrote 384 words a day I would be within 80 words of a complete novel by fall. And, so, every night after work and every noontime when I got up on Saturdays and Sundays, I would sit down and write 384 words. Oh, sometimes it was 380 and sometimes 390, but usually I was pretty close to my mark. And in September I indeed had something that was . . . just awful.

I have not been able to reread it, partly because of severe wincing but partly because I couldn't type and all 49,920 words are scrawled in longhand (also execrably spelled and punctuated with mad abandon). The text concerns, as much as I can determine or remember, being young in Ohio. Fair enough, since I'd never been anything other than young in Ohio (though I had visited Chicago and been to Florida twice). I believe the protagonist visits Chicago and goes to Florida twice. The problem with the book is that I saw being young in Ohio as a horror beyond telling and my prose proved the case.

When I got back to school in the fall, I gave my opus to Jerry Bovim, the only real writer I knew. Jerry, who appears as "Gary Ballow" in two of the stories in this book, hadn't actually published anything, but I could tell Jerry was a real writer because, although he was not yet thirty, he was already drinking himself to death. (I still have some of Jerry's fragmentary manuscripts, and the sad truth is that he *was* a real writer. Indeed, he might have been another John Kennedy Toole if only he'd killed himself after he'd completed something instead of before.) Jerry wrote a long critique, a largely charitable assessment in which he expounded upon the difficulties of the picaresque novel, the challenges of first-person narration, and the need for consistency in fictional point of view. He allowed that some of my characters were effective, was indulgent with my attempts at plot development, and even went so far as to say "the thing as a whole is rather likable." But at the end of his commentary he appended this postscript: "It has just occurred to me that there is, however, the dreadful possibility that your book is supposed to be serious."

Juvenilia Delinquent

"Underground" Press,

1970–1972

I began to write for pay in the spring of 1970, albeit that pay was mostly peanut butter sandwiches and mattress space. The mattress was not very clean. But neither was I.

This place of first employment was in Baltimore at a newspaper called Harry, which had been founded the year before by Michael Carliner, Thomas V. D'Antoni, and other members of Baltimore's "hip scene," such as it was. Baltimore was a depressed and seedy industrial town and the Sixties never really caught on there. A bunch of young people who stayed high all day and weren't working didn't make a huge impression on a city full of unemployed drunks.

Harry had a circulation of six or eight thousand and came out every . . . so often. Our publication schedule was determined by marijuana. Either we printed an issue whenever we had marijuana (looking at old copies of Harry tends to confirm this) or we printed an issue whenever we ran out of marijuana and hence got bored with the peanut butter sandwiches and mattress space. I don't remember which. The odd moniker was chosen by a two-year-old. In the spirit of the times, he was asked to name the newspaper. His grandfather was Harry, and the kid was calling everything "Harry" just then, and Harry it became. Oh, we were wild, creative, and free.

Editorially, Harry was opposed to war and capitalism and wanted to replace these with loud music and drugs. (Today, in America's inner cities, boom-box-carrying crack sellers have accomplished this very thing.) Harry was also in favor of Love. Here we staff members put our beliefs into practice. We didn't just talk about Love, we did something about it. Unsatisfied with being mere journalistic observers, we became true activists. Which was how the mattress got so dirty.

Why I Invaded Cambodia

by Richard Milhous Nixon

(as told to P. J. O'Rourke)

***Harry*, June 1970**
AUTHOR'S NOTE: Richard Nixon did indeed go out at some ungodly hour to speak to antiwar demonstrators in Washington. According to an article by Robert B. Semple, Jr., in the May 10, 1970, *New York Times:*

> President Nixon left the White House shortly before dawn this morning, drove to the Lincoln Memorial, and spent an hour chatting with young people who had come to protest his war policies.
>
> The extraordinary visit, which caught his staff unawares and left the Secret Service "petrified," was Mr. Nixon's first direct exchange with students massed here for a weekend of protest.

As he stood on the steps of the memorial and talked, the crowd around him grew from eight to thirty to fifty, and near the end of what appears to have been more monologue than dialogue, he asked the students "to try to understand what we are doing."

To understand where I'm at you've got to dig it that I've been into this very heavy political thing for a long time. In some ways this has done strange things to my head. But I've always felt that when you're really into something you shouldn't cop out on it. To be really out front, I get off on ego trips, power games. It's a speed-freak sort of trip, I admit it. But, like, that's where I'm at. . . . I mean you can put me down for kicking your ass but don't put me down for being an ass-kicker 'cause that's my movie. That's cool, I got to do my thing. I just want to make that perfectly clear.

I'd always been sort of into this kind of riff, but I never meant to get as strung-out on it as I am now. It was in '52; I was out on the coast to get my head together when Ike calls me on the phone. "Dickey," he said, "you won't believe the job offer I have."

"Tell me," I said.

"Dickey," he said, "they're going to make me president."

"Far fucking out!" I said, but he sounded troubled.

"Dickey," he said, "I'm troubled."

"What's the matter, Ike," I said.

"Dickey," he said, "if someone were to find out, *Time* magazine or someone, that all these years Mamie's been in drag . . ." I told him about the operations in Sweden. I guess Ike could see I had my head together about politics, because several days later he calls again and asks me to be vice president. I told him I wasn't up for that; I was just ready to split for Mexico City with Jack and Alan and Neil. But he came on strong and vibed me out about the whole thing—I've been into it ever since.

So like one thing led to another and I got to be president myself. Now being president is a really heavy thing. It's like being a very big dealer, like doing deals for five or six hundred kilos every day—guns out on the table and briefcases full of hundred-dollar bills. You have to deal with really heavy cats. This redneck that held the job before me had some fucked-up war going down. First thing I did was I called up the Pentagon and said, "This is the president, off that shit! I want every-body back in California by Friday night." Fifteen minutes later the chairman of the board from GM walks in with this weird cat in a sharkskin suit and sunglasses.

Well, there's a time to stand and fight and a time to cut and run. Being president is a bummer.

Not only heavy cats like that to hassle with all the time, but for a vice president I get a Yippie infiltrator who runs around the country saying the most outrageous possible things—trying to discredit the entire government.

I was really getting freaked out. All these frustrations and anxieties building—bad vibes. Like the Supreme Court. The whole country's making an ass of itself, pasting up American flags everywhere, shooting kids and spades, saying things like, "Leave loose the dogs of war!" So I figure they must want a Nazi for their Supreme Court. Give them what they want, I say. Two Nazis I give them, but no, no, they don't want Nazis; they want a liberal. A Liberal! There are only eleven liberals left in the United States. I had a hell of a time.

Like I said, when I first got into this trip I couldn't dig the war. But then I started getting to know Westmoreland and his buddies. They'd be walking up and down Pennsylvania Avenue wearing their colors and looking really bad. We got close. They're good guys once you can dig where they're at. I started going out on runs with them in their choppers, drinking beer. When I got behind it I understood they aren't really violent. They're for peace love and everything; they just like to stomp gooks. They gave me a set of honorary colors—a cutoff Eisenhower jacket with script lettering in an arch across the back say-ing, "JOINT CHIEFS OF STAFF" with "USA" down at the bottom and a big mushroom cloud in between. I'd got very tight with Westmoreland, Wes the Axe, so I laid it on him about the vice president and all that shit. Wes said, "Yeah, you got to be a badass in this world or you just ain't gonna make it." I thought about that, and when I found out Cambodia was hiding those gook Viet Cong I said to myself, "I'm gonna trash that country!" Jesus, I never thought anybody'd get all that uptight about it. But soon as I told Wes to do a number on the Cong the shit really hit the fan. I felt bad about it. I really did. First thing you know there are thousands of people planning to gather outside my house to vamp on me about it. Night before they were all to come I dropped a tab of sunshine and thought it over. I went through some weird changes. Early in the morning, when I was coming down, I decided to go outside and rap on it. Hardly anybody was there and I had to wake this cat up to find somebody to rap to. "Wake up," I said. "I'm the president. Wanna do some boo?"

"Oh, yeah, far out, hey, Fat Freddy, wake up, it's the president."

"Abbie?"

"No, no, their president."

"Oh, yeah, far out," said Fat Freddy. So they got up and blew some of my dynamite Laotian shit, and I sniffed some coke they had and laid it on them what I said here.

"Wow, man," said the first. "Where's your head at?" He told me my thing is really bad karma. That I'd be reincarnated as a Gila monster. I could dig what they were saying. That's the way people should be with each other, really out front. This is what America's about.

The Boxer Shorts Rebellion

An Exclusive Look at Sex Behind the Bamboo Curtain

Screw, March 1972

AUTHOR'S NOTE: The following was part of a semi-elaborate hoax wherein I claimed to have been a member of the press corps accompanying Richard Nixon on the epochal trip to China in February 1972. (Poor Nixon seemed to possess some pheromonal lure for pests like me—which may explain Woodward, Bernstein, Deep Throat, and the whole Watergate imbroglio as well as anything does.) The hoax began in an "underground" newspaper, *The New York Ace*, continued on radio station WBAI (then, as now, the Voice of Nonsense in Gotham), and culminated with this article for *Screw*.

The original editor's note is attached. Nothing in it except "available on four hours' notice" was true. Interesting to note that,

12

of the hundreds of publications founded in those exuberant days, only two—the self-explanatorily-titled *Screw* and my current employer, the pop music journal *Rolling Stone*—still flourish. What does this say about the intellectual, moral, and artistic contributions of the Sixties to present-day society? Practically everything.

The China hoax fooled whole dozens of people, and *Newsweek* almost did a story on "Our Hippie in Peking," except (for once) *Newsweek* checked its facts. When the penny dropped, some of my fellow lefty journalists were wroth. "You're just lying to the people," said one. "What's the point of this?" I guess the point was that the press coverage of Nixon's China trip was so shallow and predictable you didn't need to be there to write it. How green I was to think this notable.

P. J. O'Rourke was among the eighty-seven newsmen who accompanied President Nixon to Peking. Representing the Syndicated Collegiate Press Service (SCPS), twenty-four-year-old O'Rourke was the youngest member of the China trip press corps and the only one who, by any stretch of the imagination, could be deemed hip. His coverage of the Nixon junket has been syndicated to college and underground papers nationwide.

P.J. is a New York–based freelance writer who graduated from the University of Michigan with a degree in Chinese language and literature. His opportunity to go to Peking came as a result of Presidential Press Secretary Ron Ziegler's appointment of one representative from the collegiate press, Faye Levine, coeditor of the *Harvard Crimson* and SCPS Boston correspondent. But Faye, also a Chinese major, was hospitalized with hepatitis on the eve of Nixon's departure, and SCPS's editor in chief, Ed Dale, picked P.J. as an eleventh-hour replacement. Dale said he chose O'Rourke, even though P.J. is not a college student, because "he was the only young, experienced reporter we know who speaks Chinese and is available on four hours' notice."

nisex is the very first thing that hits you in China. Not that ersatz continental garçonette haircut business or high heels for men, but real *unisex*. The clothing that they wear—it's not masculine or feminine, nor is it as dumpy and sexless as it looks in those *Daily News* centerfolds, it's just the *same,* for *everyone, UNISEX!* And the effect of those millions and millions dressed alike without regard for age or station is more spectacular than any Ken Russell costumed outrage.

This is what they're talking about when they say culture shock. This is not what I expected it to be. I had this picture in my mind of the "identical masses"—lumpish, lumpen, flat-faced, neuter, homely, puritanical, and paramilitary. But Chinese clothes are too loose and wrinkled and casual to look "military" or "like a uniform." There's an impression of comfort, not regimentation. The colors are all very quiet—gray, green, and blue, but faded with that washed-out look it takes us stateside hippies years to achieve in our jeans.

Nothing flashy about these people, that's for sure, but right away that makes you look at their faces, look at them, not what they're wearing. And that's sexual, in a subtle way, even erotic. They don't care much about clothes, wearing them with baggy disdain—not all bound up like a bunch of latent bondage freaks the way we do. And this does fantastic things for the Chinese women, really sets off their beauty. The same as when some girl puts on your old flannel shirt about five sizes too big. All the Chinese women look cute and scruffy like that. Also, I noticed right away that no one is wearing underwear. Those loose cotton pants are always molding themselves fluidlike around Chinese ass cheeks and draping with a sort of spartan luxury into folds at the crotch. At the factories we visited girls would be working away greasy and adorable and determined in the drafty shops and nipples would raise welts in their khaki work shirts all around. I almost went mad with socialized lust.

The Chinese are so pretty, small and lithe, fine-featured, not a wasted stroke. They made me feel clumsy and hatchet-faced, these unpainted beauties of the Orient with their pert breasts and Lolita-slim hips. But it's all unisex, finally, so not just the girls or even the handsome young people but the unnumbered lot of them exude this sexuality—the body proper, naked and strong beneath the handiest and most democratic thing available to throw on the back.

Of lewdness, on the other hand, there is nothing. There's no nightlife that I could detect. Liquor is sold in some stores but there are no bars, much less nightclubs, fuck movies, sex shows, massage studios, or whorehouses. Nor are there any sex papers, sexy publications, or even cheesecake shots. The best I could do was a photo of some lady soldiers with their pants rolled up in the rice paddies in the *Move Forward with Firm Determination Red Women's Brigade Magazine*. I tell you, I couldn't figure it out, such sexy people and no visible sex.

I was sure I just wasn't getting the full story. Our guides and translators weren't giving us much rope. They had an endless fucking itinerary planned, touring this communal bakery, that collective steel mill, and some other People's Tractor Assembly Plant until I had buns, Bessemer, and detachable winch and stump-pulling units coming out of my ears.

I tried putting the make on our head translator but she immediately explained that she was going steady (literally: "attached with progressive fervor"), and showed me her boyfriend's Chairman Mao button. Now how the hell she could tell it from her own Chairman Mao button is beyond me but there it was, with some angora wool wrapped around the back. That was the end of that.

Back in the Hotel of the Nationalities, where the press party was housed, I had this young waiter on my floor. I could tell he really wanted to talk as soon as he found out I spoke Chinese, but the waiters weren't allowed any lengthy personal contact with us. Finally, the third night we were in Peking, when he brought the evening tea, I told him to tell the bell captain, or whomever, that the decadent American had got drunk and was sick all over the floor, then come back to "clean up" so we could talk. He was leery but he agreed to try, and rushed back with a mop and ten solid minutes of questions. He hoped one day to be a People's Intelligence Agent, he confided, and had to know about America in great detail. What was it like to ride in a Packard? Who was pitching this year for the Brooklyn Dodgers? Was Eddie

Fisher still going with Elizabeth Taylor? What was Judy Garland's latest hit?

My Chinese is not the best but I answered him as well as I could and then asked him about China. "Wow," I said (roughly translated), "is everything as uptight as it looks?" He gave me one of those "foreign devil" stares. "You know," I said, "what's a fellow to do for laughs around here?" He explained they had Ping-Pong matches every Sunday at the school where he went. All the girls and boys would go to the Ping-Pong game. I told him that wasn't what I meant.

"Well," he said, "after the game, on the way home, sometimes girls will hug and kiss one in a spirit of revolutionary comradeship." He admitted too that you get bare tit that way sometimes, if you were "resolute in proletarian unity." But progressive girls didn't *do it* until the imperialist-running-dog oppressor had been crushed or they were married—whichever came first. There were some girls, though, who really put out. You could tell them because they'd kiss you after your first Self-Criticism and Aloud Reading from the Thoughts of Chairman Mao Study Group together. They were fast and usually wound up in homes for unwed revisionists.

"Is there any prostitution in China?"

He said, "No! That would be capitalist exploitation and bourgeois decadence!" But he allowed as how there were some dirty acupuncture parlors. I asked about masturbation and he explained that the Red Book was very clear on that point, that it caused Trotskyism and made warts grow on your chin. He had never heard of dry humping or "hickies." A mention of pornography, however, produced an enthusiastic response and he pulled out of his wallet a faded and poorly reproduced playing card with a chubby peasant girl on the back. She was pulling up the front of her quilted jacket and her entire stomach was exposed. After that he had to leave.

The only other people I really had a chance to talk to were some students at Peking University who were completely flabbergasted when questioned about "deep" or "French" kissing, and would only say that whenever they got "hooligan urges" they took a cold shower.

Myself, I'm not fooled. Such is the deceit for which the Orient is famed. We haven't been hearing about Oriental women for the past thirty-five years just because they build good tractors. My dad was in WW II and I know. These Reds just know we're a bunch of regular softies for this wholesome hard work stuff. They're just making a play for our respect and admiration. You can't tell me they're a bunch of goody two shoes over there in China when we're not around to watch them.

In the first place, there're so damn many of them. You don't find babies under cabbage leaves.

And in the second place, the last day we were in Peking, when we were all visiting the Forbidden City, I was wandering around looking for a men's room in the Palace of Sublime Peace when I turned a corner and came upon Kissinger and Chou En-lai embracing behind an ornate pillar. Kissinger kept wetting his little finger and twisting it in Chou's ear while humming, sotto voce, "Chinatown, My Chinatown." Chou was smiling inscrutably.

Jets and Sharks Drop Acid, Read Marcuse

Harry, June 1970

AUTHOR'S NOTE: This was written shortly after the May 4, 1970, killing of four college students at Kent State University and was the first of a series of addlepated rants. My old high school girlfriend was enrolled at Kent and was standing, clueless, in the crowd of demonstrators when the National Guard opened fire. Struggling against abstract injustice was one thing, but now I battled a ruling-class power elite so depraved that it shot at Connie Nowakowski's adorable snub nose and cute butt.

In time my radical ardor would cool. I realized that the actual killing of senators, congressmen, presidents, and so forth—while doubtless a very good thing of its kind—would be a bad career move. I'd probably never win the Pulitzer Prize for addlepated rant, marry Connie Nowakowski, and turn *Harry* into a daily paper as big as *The New York Times* only more influential. Then I got a job. It wasn't much of a job. I was a messenger. But it brought in $150 a week and that was wealth as far as I was concerned. We were paid fortnightly. I waited greedily for my $300. But when my pay envelope arrived I found, after federal, state, and city taxes had been deducted and social security, health insurance, and pension plan payments had been made, only $160 was left. I began yelling. "I'm a revolutionary! I've been a revolutionary since I went to college! I've demonstrated! I've rioted! I've done everything I could to overthrow capitalism! And what do I find when I get my first paycheck from a capitalist company? COMMUNISM!!!" Of course, it was several years before the implications of what I yelled sank in. At that age I wasn't listening to anyone, myself included.

New tactics for new times in the belly of the pig. Time to abandon your bullshit liberal sensibilities and bring the revolution home—us white-child college kids got a lot to learn.

No time left for pamphleting and leafleting, picketing and petitioning, talking and walking and shitting around. Time to TRASH THE STATE! We've got a lot to learn—Armed Love. We'll learn that Armed, for us, implies Love and that Love necessitates Armed. If we don't learn how to fight we won't win. If we don't learn how to keep our love, in the nexus of that fight, we won't deserve to win. Forsake the old values we pretended to forsake before. Not only racism, capitalism, sexism, nationalism but—as important—gratuitous hatred, viciousness, and cruelty. We don't want to off the pigs so much as we want to off piggishness.

Righteous Rage! Just Anger! We've come to destroy the real origins of the horror we live in—individualist property, selfish values, hateful concepts—and to save the people. We are the nightmares of the bourgeoisie come to life in their own homes, as their own children.

When I was a kid in Chicago there were street gangs with beautiful names, Belairs, Top Hats, Vice-Joys, Corner Lords, Cobras, original homegrown American experts in urban guerrilla warfare. Admittedly they didn't have much consciousness, cultural or political, but one of these (Blackstone Rangers—largest and toughest of the black gangs) has developed into a revolutionary force of the first order. And another group, the Young Patriots, from uptown Chicago, came out of the same gang war and Blackboard Jungle scene to found the Patriot Party.

Street gangs and cycle gangs are two spontaneous and thoroughly American social developments—natural forms in American society and we should use these forms. Or, not use these forms—be them.

Discipline is organic and pressure from the peers. Emphasis is on street reality and autonomous local control. Politics are a function of community love, neighborhood beauty. Shit on polemics. Shit on "protest." . . . The gang is a national tradition given a new direction, a little piece of Americana intertheorized. . . .

[and much, much more in the same vein]

Harry Interviews a Grown-up

arry went to interview "Sam Jones," self-styled "adult," at his "office" in downtown Baltimore where he "works." We found Sam friendly & articulate, eager to explain this strange and little understood cult which is now so much in the news. He was dressed in the colorful attire typical of Baltimore grown-ups, blue shirt, blue suit, blue tie, blue socks, and brown shoes. We proceeded to ask him some questions about the life and beliefs of an "adult," why they dress and act the way they do and what they are trying to say in this changing world.

HARRY: I believe you refer to each other as "Mister"?

SAM JONES: Well, no, not exactly. Adult men call each other Mister. Ladies are referred to as Miss or Missus depending on whether or not they're married.

H: "Married"?

S.J.: Marriage is a ceremony, very common among adults, where a female adult swears to love and obey a male adult for the rest of her life. After such a ceremony is completed the two then live together . . .

H: Just the two of them?

S.J.: Yes, at least until they have children. Anyway, these two are then supposed to have . . . uh . . . sexual relations only with each other.

H: Really? This really happens?

S.J.: Well, frankly, male adults are permitted, in a de facto sort of way, to have relationships outside the marriage. Female adults never do.

H: Oh . . . far out . . . "Do your thing," as you "adults" say. But don't the women, how do you say it? "broads," ever object to such treatment?

S.J.: Never.

H: Well, "Mister" Jones, how did you happen to become an "adult"? Did you have an abnormal background? I mean, did you come from a commune that had broken up or a collective rent by political dissension?

S.J.: No, nothing like that. I came from a very ordinary family. My mother belonged to a wandering tribe of Yogi Mystics and my father was a Mexican cocaine smuggler.

H: How do they feel about your lifestyle?

S.J.: I don't see my father very often. When I do we hardly speak. I feel bad about this. He's a vigorous old man whom I admire in many ways. Right now he's fighting with a guerrilla band in the hills outside Indianapolis. I have to admire the way he sticks to his beliefs even though these are very different from my own, from my subculture's.

H: Could you go into that?

S.J.: You often hear that we adults are in favor of wars. My father used to call me a "war creep" and a "butch ignorant slob." We're not really for wars. We only support wars that are for really worthy causes, such as imperialistic conquest, exploitation of third-world resources, and aggrandizement of the military-industrial complex. Honestly, we don't want great big wars. We can conquer, exploit, and aggrandize with little bitty wars. Really, we can. Just tiny little wars that no one would mind.

H: How about your mother?

S.J.: She's adjusted better to my living the way I want to. She complains about my hair and dress. "Son," she says, "a grown man shouldn't cut the hair off his head like that. It's not healthy."

H: Just what influenced you to become an "adult"?

S.J.: It was when I was at college. The family didn't want me to go to college but for some reason I insisted. I used to sneak out and buy copies of *The Saturday Evening Post* . . .

H: Isn't that one of those "adult magazines"?

S.J.: . . . Yes, and the family was always angry when they caught me with it, said it was sexist and racist, reactionary smut. Anyway, it talked a lot about college in there and I wanted to go. After a while they said all right. I wanted to go to Brigham Young or Whittier but they wouldn't let me do that. It was Berkeley or nothing and they wouldn't let me work my way through.

H: So you went to Berkeley?

s.j.: Yes and it was there that I fell in with adults, young adults. There were lots of people around like my family, the kind I'd grown up with, but young adults were something new. A whole different world, a world I'd never experienced. Materialism, sexual hang-ups, the Republican party, uncomfortable clothes, engagement rings, car accidents, Pat Boone, competition, patriotism, cheating, lying, ranch houses, TV, and suicide—I was dazzled. Pretty soon I was drinking beer,★ eating meat, and acquiring possessions. I've lived that way ever since.

H: Perhaps you could give us some specific details about "adult" life. What about fucking, for instance? Do adults fuck?

s.j.: You're not going to use my name?

H: No, this is all confidential.

s.j.: Adults don't fuck. We have sexual intercourse.

H: You talk about fucking?

s.j.: No, I mean we fuck but we always call it sexual intercourse. It's different than fucking. Sexual activities of adults are different than those of other people. For one thing, adults often don't have any sexual activities at all.

H: Oh, wow!

s.j.: Those adults who do have sexual activity have it with a member of the opposite sex on Saturday night in a dark room, male superior position.

★"Beer" is one of a number of drugs commonly used by "adults" which contains the narcotic alcohol. Alcohol (known in its various forms as "booze," "suds," "juice," etc.) has been proven to cause liver and kidney damage and to result in serious character deterioration. Studies have also shown that alcohol usage often leads to indulgence in other harmful drugs such as tranquilizers, sleeping pills, caffeine, and tobacco.

H: That's disgusting.

S.J.: I know. We try not to think about it.

H: Do you have any other disgusting sexual practices?

S.J.: Young adults sometimes kiss.

H: On the lips?

S.J.: They're not supposed to.

H: Tell us something about what "adults" do. We hear you talk a lot about "work." As best as I can understand it "work" consists of doing something you don't want to do eight hours a day, five days a week. Could you fill us in as to why you spend all that time doing things you don't want to do?

S.J.: We work in order to get money, which is, among ourselves, a universal medium of trade, something like dope.

H: I've heard a lot about money, even seen some, but I've never actually had any. Is there any way you can smoke it?

S.J.: No, money has a strictly metaphysical importance to us.

H: How do you "work" to obtain money?

S.J.: We look around for someone who will give us a lot of things for a little money.

H: What kind of things?

S.J.: Any kind of things. Then we find someone else to whom we can give a few of these things for a lot of money.

H: You do this with perfect strangers?

S.J.: Yes.

H: "Mister" Jones, what do you mean to express? What is the message of "adulthood"?

S.J.: The message of adulthood is that message of Christian love which we adults have preached for centuries: that thirty pieces of silver was a good price in its day but times have changed.

Editorial from the "Bummer" Issue

Harry, August 1971

AUTHOR'S NOTE: What people forget about the hippie period is how serious it was. The clowning was all freighted with earnest concerns. We were terribly solemn about our frivolity. But, looking through back issues of *Harry*, I notice sometimes even we got sick of us. We longed to indulge, every now and then, in plain stupidity instead of the deep, metaphysical kind.

I t would be very difficult to postulate any meaningful order in the universe, as a whole. One can, of course, ascertain various regular tendencies for certain things to blow up and other things to collapse, but at the molecular level this apple-pie order breaks down into an atomic game of chance, Quantum Physics According to Hoyle. Many have attempted to refute this principle by quoting Albert Einstein's remark "God did not shoot dice with the universe." But they neglect to include his next sentence, "He did, however, play a fair hand of gin rummy." Frankly, scientific evidence cannot be ignored. And the scientific evidence instructs us conclusively that earth and its inhabitants enjoy that class of relationship to the cosmic whole which we formerly reserved for red ants and two-headed brine shrimp.

These facts might be taken as an imperative to seek understanding of the universe in mystic terms. But world religious leaders (acknowledged experts in the mystic terms field) agree that this is not possible. Archbishop Fulton Sheen has repeatedly stated that, "Unless you happen to win at bingo there's really nothing we can do for you." Maharishi Mahesh Yogi, the Indian meditation magnate, warns, "You can believe this stuff if you want to but it won't do you a fat lot of good when payday rolls around."

Though there *have* been holdouts on this mystic terms question. Notable among these was "Incomprehensible Positive Life Force" advocate Albert Camus, until he drove his expensive sports car into a tree at 120 miles an hour. Another dissident was Lee Ann Bellworthy, a retarded girl from Fall Bend, Kansas, who was accidentally eaten by pigs.

Despite Karl Marx's deathbed confession that he was "just kidding," some thinkers have attempted to find a rationale, or at least a poor excuse, for existence in the social intercourse of mankind. Suffice it to say, very little comment is needed on that endeavor.

Other philosophers such as Walt Disney, Marlin Perkins, and Sheila MacRae have turned to the animal kingdom in an attempt to establish a suitable role for mankind. Comparative zoological studies have proven that several other primates have, in the past, evolved to man's level of sophistication. However, they all committed ritual suicide shortly thereafter. The porpoise, closest in intelligence to man of any surviving mammal, was interviewed with particular thoroughness. It was discovered, among other things, that the porpoise is none too bright. Below is part of a transcribed panel discussion with Henry ———, a porpoise from the Catalina area:

ZOOLOGIST: Henry, could you tell us something of the average porpoise level of education and vocational training?

HENRY: We're dumb. Can't read or write or nothing. Yup. Dumb.

ZOOLOGIST: Well, what does a normal porpoise do on an ordinary day? How do you spend your time?

HENRY: Oh, we just swim around and around and bump into things.

ZOOLOGIST: Could you tell us something about the porpoise philosophy of life?

HENRY: Yup. Shitty deal.

ZOOLOGIST: But better than nothing, right?

HENRY: Nope. Lotsa times we just swim right into boat propellers on purpose. But most of the time we just swim around and around and bump into things.

Emotional bonds have also come to the fore as a metaphysical raison d'être, as has hedonistic pleasure seeking. Liver trouble and bad breath have been advanced as virtually airtight refutations of such romantic and neo-Epicurean arguments. As Bertrand Russell points out in *Principia Mathematica,* "Fucking would be all right except women smell bad and slobber." Edna St. Vincent Millay has noted the same characteristics in other sexes.

"Taking the Train"

In Three Acts

by the Penn Central Players

***Chesapeake Weekly Review,* June 1970**
AUTHOR'S NOTE: In 1970 Denis Boyles, a friend of mine from graduate school, started a second "underground" newspaper in Baltimore. Denis called his periodical *The Chesapeake Weekly Review of Literature and the Arts.* It was pretty much indistinguishable from *Harry* except that it was full of insane aesthetic views instead of lunatic political ideas. I said to Denis, "How can you give your paper a name like that? It's cornball. It's squaresville." And Denis said to me, "Twenty-five years from now your curriculum vitae will say 'writer for *Harry'* and mine will say, 'Editor of *The Chesapeake Weekly Review of Literature and the Arts.'* "

For his first issue, Denis convinced me to go to New York by train and review the ride as experimental theater. I don't know why.

Act I (In the Station): I was surprised by the ordinary and modern atmosphere of the first set. Penn Central indulges in ironic play with the idea that trains no longer exist in their traditional form. They're making the point that "Railroad" as a form of environmental art is in decay. Thus there were no red caps, no garbled train calls and little bustle in the station. The New York troupe, I understand, is more interested in cultural nostalgia and provides such things. The station scene was mostly well cast and beautifully sleazy in a current sort of sleaze. I have, however, some detail criticism. Not to be picayune, but detailing in productions like this is very important. The food at the lunch counter was too good. This lent a note and left a taste of unreality which then pervaded the whole act. But the woman behind the lunch counter was perfect; old, fat, made up in a disgusting manner with moles and warts and things, and affecting a violent phlegmy cough. I asked her if there were any french fries. "Hell no," she said, "don't wish that on me." The crowd scene in the station was not exactly right. There were too few nuns and soldiers for my taste and too many affluent-looking businessmen parts. I couldn't see any purpose in this. It didn't make a statement. However, the obligatory mass of seedy types dubious in age, sex, and origin was fascinating—oblivious yet unavoidable. These were so well played, so understated, that I don't remember the face of a single one. The train was on time—a clever surprise, I thought.

Act II, by far the longest of the three acts, is the ride itself. This has a certain intentional boredom and audience fatigue à la Warhol. I found even less attention to detail here and less authentic effect. This is a fault only because I felt throughout that authentic effect (with the exception of the scenery) was being sought. None of the errors within the train could be excused as concept-play. The train was too clean. The bathrooms lacked that special smell. And sound effects were poor. No "clickity-clack" was in evidence though there was an excellent "continual annoying squeak." "Passengers" in my car were too well groomed and their performance forced. The small talk and development of interpersonal relationships were banal. A boy and girl met, very unconvincingly. The conductor made a pass at two women seated in front of me but their conversation was unmemorable and their acting horrid. One of the women, especially, was completely distracted and unable to relate to her part. I thought, for a while, she was reading cue cards in her lap. I was disappointed by the whole waste of potential. Here was an opportunity for the playwright to have engaged in vigorous audience participation but he avoided it as though he suffered from some aesthetic schizophrenia, so that while possessing a radical theatrical concept, he was unable to conceive of it except in traditional terms of distance from his audience.

The sets (outside the train) were truly first rate and constructed with a sense of humor. The scenery was completely hyperbolic. The city scenes were a tangle of artistically arranged garbage, slums, and industrial confusion, each a parody of the real item. No garbage is that profuse. No slums are that squalid. No factory is that dirty and disorganized. Credits aren't provided but this work is very like Robert Rauschenberg's. From the slums, kids waved and played happily in the open fire hydrants—a satire on the "down and out with happy feet" kind of 1930s movie. The garbage was stereotypic trash: beer cans, Wrigley's Juicy Fruit and Baby Ruth wrappers, empty Lucky Strike packs, and rusted-out '53 Buicks. The set designer placed countryside between New York and Baltimore, where there is none. The grass was Day-Glo green and the cows were made of plaster. It looked like "The Farm" exhibit at the Chicago Museum of Science and Industry. The freight yards were incredible too. The open cars contained beautiful freight—scrap glass and rusted metal in David Smith forms. All the train crews were young men dressed in sport clothes, models for a Sears, Roebuck catalog.

Whoever cast and directed the show did not work closely with his set designer. The director, of course, had the greater opportunity to shape the total effect of the performance but he got carried away with understatement. He wanted to express not only the decay of the "railroad" act but also the idea that reality violates preconceptions. This is all very valid, but, in this case, very dull too. The sets were better theater than the performance.

Act III is a birth metaphor. The actors and audience rise together and are expelled traumatically into the Penn Station set. This act is short, all fluid rapid movement, and superbly choreographed. I was left with no time for aesthetic or self-conscious reflection. Yet the unity and spirit of this human rush were so positive that I felt no confusion. Move, move, move, move, move, that was really the end. Leaving the audience within a massive and grotesque environmental sculpture, "New York," which costs an additional $9.75 to return from.

Show Times

Mondays thru Fridays except Sept. 7

AM	AM	AM	PM		PM
x 1.26	. . . . .	x 2.10	3.58	. . . . .	4.45
t 6.20	t 6.27	t 7.25	n 5.10	. . . . .	n 5.50
6.59	. . . . .	7.50	6.09	. . . . .	6.50
t 7.05	t 7.12	t 8.02	n 7.44	. . . . .	n 8.30
8.48	. . . . .	9.30	8.53	. . . . .	9.35
9.39	. . . . .	10.20	10.00	. . . . .	10.55
11.18	. . . . .	12.00	10.40	. . . . .	11.20
12.48	. . . . .	1.30	12.37	. . . . .	1.35
1.51	. . . . .	2.40	. . . .	. . . . .	. . . . .
PM	AM	PM	AM		AM

g Sundays and May 30, July 4 and Sept. 7.

k Saturdays except May 30 and July 4.

n Runs May 29, July 3 and Sept. 4 only.

t Except May 29 and July 3.

x Runs Monday mornings except Sept. 7; will also run Sept. 8.

y Runs May 31, July 5 and Sept. 7 only.

Poems

AUTHOR'S NOTE: It was also through the good offices of Denis Boyles that I became a published poet, more or less. Denis convinced Bob Cobbing, an actual poet who ran a small press in England, to print *Nancy Adler Poems* (Writers Forum Quarto Number Eleven, London, 1970). Later, when Denis was running a small press of his own, he published a second booklet, *Our Friend the Vowel* (Stone House, Baltimore, 1975).

These poems require some explanation. But, at this late date, I'm not sure I can give one. The form or genre in which I was working was called "Concrete poetry." It originated in the late 1940s and early 1950s with the works of Eugen Gomringer in Switzerland, Carlo Belloli in Italy, Öyvind Fahlström in Sweden, and a number of other oddly named people in places such as Iceland and

São Paulo. Fahlström wrote a manifesto of Concrete poetry called—
seriously— *manifest for konkret poesi.*

The idea was to combine the visual arts with literature to make
something that you can't read and that isn't easy to look at either.
Concrete poetry had a brief vogue in the Sixties and then, merci-
fully for all concerned, petered out. Examining my own contributions
to the field, I would say that, as a poet, I had talent in the graphic
arts, and, as a graphic artist, I was quite the poet.

P. J. O'Rourke

#9 (the evolution of surprise)

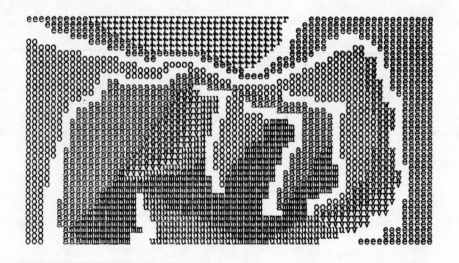

nemo

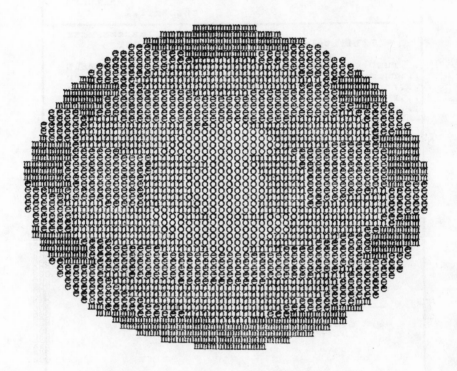

P. J. O'Rourke

<u>columbus</u> <u>circle</u>

```
    clink "one"   clink clink        click /thrunk/...
┌──────────────────────────────────────────────────────────┐
│    wait          wait          wait wait  waitwait         │
│        wait          wait wait        wait  waitwait       │
│      wait                    wait  wait    wait wait       │
│                     wait  wait  wait   waitwait            │
│           wait                    wait     waitwait        │
│                                            waitwait        │
│                              zzzzzzz...                    │
├──────────────────────────────────────────────────────────┤
│                                   ...zzzzzzzzzzz           │
│      (lililitelitelight light LIGHT LIGHT                  │
│            D    D   D D D  DDD D DD)                       │
│ ...rumblerumblerumblerumble rumble RUMBLE RUMBLE           │
│ ...rumrumrumrumrumrumrumrumrumrumRRUMRRUMRRUMrrr           │
│ ...rrrrrrrrrrrrrrrrrrrrrrrrrrRRRRRRRSCREEEeech             │
│ ...rrrrrrrrrrrrrrrrrrrrrrrrrrrrRRRRRRRRRRRR                │
│ ...wwwwwwwwwwwwooooooooooooooooOOOOSHHHhhh                 │
├──────────────────────────────────────────────────────────┤
│         step                      step                    │
│       step step                 step step                 │
│         step                      step                    │
│    pmrrrr step rrrrmp        pmrrrr step rrrrmp           │
│         step                      step                    │
│      stepstepstepstep step stepstepstepstepstep           │
│   step stepstepstepstep step stepstepstep step            │
│   step stepstep step  step   stepstepstep                 │
│        step      step   step step    step    step         │
├──────────────────────────────────────────────────────────┤
│        step       step    step step    step    step       │
│   step  stepstep step   step   stepstepstep               │
│   step stepstepstepstep step stepstepstep step            │
│      stepstepstepstep step stepstepstepstepstep           │
│        step                      step                     │
│ _____  step  _____               step  _____              │
│        step                      step                     │
│      step step                 step step                  │
│        step                      step                     │
│                                                           │
│       _____                                               │
├──────────────────────────────────────────────────────────┤
│   ...pmrrrrrrrrmp...        ...pmrrrrrrrrmp...             │
│ sit sit        sit sit sitsit   sit     sit sit           │
│   stand          stand            stand                   │
│                                            stand          │
│       stand            stand stand                        │
│ sit sit       sit sitsit sitsitsit    sit sit            │
├──────────────────────────────────────────────────────────┤
│ ...CLICKITTY-CLACK.....CLICKITTY-CLACK.....CLACK...        │
│ ...CLICKITTY-CLICKITTY-CLICKITTY-CLICKITTY-CLICK...        │
│ ...RRRRRRRRRRRRRRRRRRRRRRRRRRRRRRRRRRRRRRRRRRRRRR...       │
│ ...RRRRRrrrrrRRRRRrrrrrRRRRRrrrrrRRRRRrrrrrRRRRR...        │
│ ...DONDUNDONDUNDONDUNDONDUNDONDUNDONDUNDONDUNDON...        │
│ ...RRRRRRRRRRRRRRRRRRRRRRRRRRRRRRRRRRRRRRRRRRRRRR...       │
│ ...Kuh-Dunk....Kuh-Dunk......Kuh-Dunk...Kuh-Dunk...        │
└──────────────────────────────────────────────────────────┘
```

38

poem on nothing at all

```
O
OOOOOOOOOOOOOOOOOOO
OOOOOOOOOOOOOOOOOOO
OOOOOOOOOOOOOOOOOO
OOOOOOOOOOOOOOOO
OOOOOOOOOOOOOO
OOOOOOOOOOOOO
OOOOOOOOOOOO
OOOOOOOOOO
OOOOOOOOO
OOOOOOOO
OOOOOOO
OOOOOO
OOOOO
```

The Truth About the Sixties and Other Fiction

The generation did not jibe with the calendar any better than it agreed with its parents. When I say "the Sixties" I mean the years from about 1965 to about 1973 (a period roughly congruent with the Vietnam draft, in case anybody's still wondering why the kids were acting weird). It was an era of great self-interest. Everyone involved in the Sixties was fascinated by his own involvement and many of us remained so long after hipness had collapsed into disco.

I spent seven or eight years trying to write stories based on my experiences in the previous seven or eight years. The result was, I think, supposed to be a novel. I had an idea that these short stories would somehow get together on their own, perhaps while I was drinking at Elaine's, and arrange themselves into a plot. They failed to do so. In 1978 I became the editor of National Lampoon. I published the stories there because I was the editor and no one could stop me.

An Inquiry into the Nature of Good and Evil

was living in a middle-size city on the eastern seaboard in 1971, and for two years my best friends and I had been putting out a bimonthly newspaper called the *Community Underground Press*. It's interesting that we had the word *underground* on the banner. I can't remember what we thought this meant. The paper was, of course, sold openly. And though the police did raid the old row house that served as our home and office, it was illegal drugs that brought them there, not publishing. The "underground" was a matter, I believe, of self-dramatization—the one undeniable talent of my generation.

There were four of us who had been on the staff since the newspaper's inception: myself, Bob Vincente, Barry Hendler, and Corey Harrison. We spent almost all our time together, partly working but mostly sitting around, lying around, driving around, and talking constantly, all day and all night, as only very young people can, about everything that can be imagined, which is to say about nothing that can be recalled. Sometimes we even, though not for carnal purposes, slept all together in the same bed. And we shared everything we owned and a number of things that didn't belong to us.

The paper itself was owned, if that verb can be applied to something that consisted of ten thousand dollars in bad debts, by Bob. He'd been raised in the city's Italian slums, had put himself through college, gotten a good job, married, settled down, and then had thrown it all over, job, wife, and every possession, to become a hippie. He was a happy, plump, kindly person. Even the narcotics detectives were fond of him and would wave hello from their unmarked cars. Bob styled himself publisher, meaning that he took some concern with if and how our publication could be sold or, at least, given away and whether and when we'd pay the rent. I called myself editor, meaning I did not take any concern with those things. I was very politically minded in those days and spent most of my energy trying to think up new ways to call for the overthrow of organized government by some people whom I called "the people." It's hard to remember images that are not connected to real events, but I believe I saw these "people" as a couple of put-upon Negroes, some earnest college students, and one housewife with a nascent political sensibility—a group, come to think of it, not too different from the Carter administration of today.

More important to our daily—that is, twice-monthly—operation were Barry and Corey. Barry was a no-account rich kid, a couple of years older than Bob and me, who had been kicked out of several colleges and the Marine Corps. He was a professional photographer, supposedly, but really supported by an allowance from his family in Chicago. He wasn't a bad photographer, but he was lazy, and this particular city was not a venue for professional photography careers. The *Community Underground Press,* however, was a place where Barry could print whatever he wanted to photograph, and in return he did everything he could to make sure it continued to publish. Barry was more of a bum than a hippie or a radical. He preferred beer to dope and sex to socioeconomic discussions. And he couldn't be made to care much about politics beyond saying that election to office should be a felony crime. In fact, he sometimes claimed he didn't "give a shit about anything except naked women." Our acquaintances thought him "square," but we never goaded Barry for his lack of ridiculous clothes or social conscience. He had a sharper wit than we did, and, besides, he always had a few extra dollars, which we did not. And his car usually worked.

The car was important, because Corey would take it and drive around the city and actually do some work. Corey was our only staff member with any real journalistic capacity. For the rest of us, the newspaper was an easier thing to have than a job or a more concrete societal mission that might actually land us in jail. But Corey took the *Community Underground Press* quite seriously. She was the daughter of the city's preeminent, not to say only, left-wing lawyer. He was a man of substance with an extensive corporate practice who had seen the light or hit his head on something sharp a couple of years before and had abandoned his lucrative partnership to right legal wrongs, protect the poor from the depredations of capitalism, defend draft dodgers, and, I think, annoy his wife.

Mrs. Harrison was mystified not at all by what her husband was doing but by the speech, dress, manners, and hygiene of the people he chose to do it with. She did not understand, she said, why it was "necessary to have horrible mores in order to promote laudable morals." Mrs. Harrison and I had several sharp conversations about Corey staying overnight at the newspaper office. Corey had been only sixteen when she'd started working on the paper, and Mrs. Harrison had had every reason to be concerned. But I was a friend of her husband, and Corey was very stubborn (with me as well as her mother) about coming and going as she pleased. Eventually Mrs. Harrison conceded the issue and treated me thereafter with every kindness. I could never stand the woman. Looking back on it, I would say she was the only person of my then acquaintance who was wholly in her right mind.

That summer, Corey spent every day interviewing people or getting descriptions of things: be-ins, teach-ins, love-ins, sit-ins; nude, seminude, and completely clothed encounter groups; crafts festivals, music festivals, and festivals for which there was no apparent purpose; riots, demonstrations, and squabbles of every kind; and the innumerable cliques of pothead communards. She covered, indeed, the motley gamut of social experiments that had spread across the nation with the same speed and nearly as dreadful result as the Spanish influenza of some fifty years before. She was, by the lights of the time, a diligent career woman. And she was a formidable thinker for a person of her years. Corey loved theories, especially theories of human interaction. She herself had more theories than ever there were real things in the world to animate them all. And she was drawn to people whose theories of consociation were excessive—me, for instance. But her work brought her in contact with people whose theories were far more exciting, dangerous, and stupid than mine. Among these was a rented house full of student-age Trotskyites who called themselves the Rosa Luxemburg Collective. Corey rather liked these self-professed terrorists, or, at least, she was intrigued by them. And through her they became, more or less, friends of ours.

The *Community Underground Press* had voiced its share of radical cant. We were all, even Barry, in favor of a revolution. In fact, we had talked ourselves into a political position far to the left of anything that made sense. Bob, however, drew the line at killing anyone. He would gladly support, he said, a war of liberation, but not if anybody was going to get hurt. Gandhi never hurt anybody, he said. I was more radical than that. I suspected that even Gandhi had had a few rifles tucked away. I was perfectly willing, I said, to kill for the revolution, but only if it were very important. After all, that was why I wanted to kill people, because they were killing people in Vietnam and elsewhere and that was wrong. So it would have to be very important before I would kill someone too. (And I believe I secretly trusted that if it ever got as important as that, I would be able to talk myself into thinking it wasn't so important after all.) The people in the Rosa Luxemburg Collective, however, had talked to themselves a bit more than Bob and I had, and had talked themselves right out of any such bourgeois scruples, so that, they said, they stood ready to kill for the revolution whether it was important or not. In fact, they stood so ready to kill for the revolution that they were in something of a quandary as to why they hadn't done so, especially the collective's leader, or "chairman," a fellow named Red Lenny, whose real name was Leonard Feinermann and who was as extreme and committed a revolutionary as the minor hypocrisies and mild indignities of upper-middle-class suburban life have ever produced. Lenny was determined to kill a cop. Or to injure one. Or, at any rate, to do something bad to someone bad who held some sort of authority somewhere in this vast bad republic of ours. And cops were more widely available than, say, generals, and were easily identifiable by their uniforms, which congressmen, for instance, were not, and were much less protected than the president or someone like that. So, a cop it was. Thus I think went the reasoning of Lenny and his compatriots, though doubtless not even so clearly as that. I mean, they didn't really set out to assassinate a policeman. They were just burning with embarrassment at having called for so much mayhem without having committed any. And thereby they set in motion a little drama into which my friends and I would be dragged.

What got us in trouble was a newsreel. The four of us weren't satisfied with mismanaging a newspaper. We wanted something else to mismanage too. It was Bob who had the idea. We would film and record all manner of events that involved people like ourselves, or, at least, people with haircuts like ours. And then, every month, we would show this film at . . . Well, we'd find someplace to show it. People would doubtless pay a buck or so to see themselves as they saw themselves. Barry was enthusiastic. He wanted to expand, he said, his "arena of professional failure." And said he thought he'd meet more girls going broke in movies. So he volunteered to buy a Super-8 sound camera. Then we set about making a sort of ill-defined documentary of everything that was happening or, more often, attempting to be made to happen in what was then called the counterculture. Bob was director, Barry was cameraman, I forget what I was supposed to be, and Corey was anchorwoman. We filmed an interview with a coming (now gone) rock group. I remember the most interesting thing about them was their preposterous name, and I don't remember that anymore. We filmed the opening of a free university, which was something of a fizzle, since among the things this university was free of were campus, curriculum, faculty, and student body. We tried to film a natural childbirth, but Bob and Barry got sick to their stomachs. We filmed an "urban farm" where two hundred cubic feet of topsoil had been dumped on a tenement roof. Unfortunately, part of the roof collapsed and only the radishes sprouted on the rest of it. Bob pronounced the radish bread "delicious," and Corey told our viewers that the radish tea was "nice." And we had our weather report given by an authentic member of the Weathermen faction of SDS, disguised with a plastic wastepaper basket over his head. We had to stick the microphone up inside the wastepaper basket and the audio results were not very satisfactory. I do remember hearing the phrase "There's a shit-storm coming." All in all it was a pretty fair piece of work, we thought, but it lacked action.

There was a riot due in about a week, a Fourth of July demonstration against the war and everything else, in front of City Hall. I suggested we wait until then, when no doubt we would get plenty of action footage. Two months before, on the anniversary of the Cambodia incursion, someone had caught a tear gas grenade in a fielder's mitt and tossed it back into the middle of the mounted police, causing a police-horse stampede through the middle of the outdoor vegetable market and resulting in everything anyone could want, cinematically. We were hoping for something at least as good on July 4, what with the veterans' groups marching and all.

And it did turn out to be a good riot. A thousand of us gathered in the big square in front of the new City Hall building, which was cordoned off by rows of sweating, irritated police who had been restrained by decree of the liberal mayor from use of unnecessary force. And necessary force, I'm afraid, was not going to carry the day. We milled around, chanting and screaming and working ourselves into a lather, and then some inspired young strategist among us urged a feint at the veterans' parade two blocks away. There was no real leader to the crowd. More correctly, there were ten hundred would-be Frantz Fanons. But we knew a good idea when we heard one. Or maybe we didn't and just itched for a wild surge in some direction. So we surged for the parade, and the cordon of police went running, half-suffocated in their riot helmets, with all their police equipment flopping on their bodies, trying to head us off and keep us from being beaten bloody by VFW bandleaders and enraged packs of American Legionnaires. Our assault drew up about fifty yards from the parade. This was the tactic, of course; except, of course, it wasn't. It was the orderly rows of angry veterans that gave us pause, traversing our front line with their eyes turned toward us, with the intent of doing to us just what our fathers must have often considered doing. And the only thing that kept them from doing it immediately was the self-imposed dignity of their parade.

With both antagonists hesitating, the police were able to interpose themselves. This left the City Hall undefended, and it had been thoughtlessly constructed with an all-glass facade. Paving bricks, pieces of police barriers, and small items of landscaping went through the windows. There was that incomparably wonderful sound of much glass breaking, and then there was a rapturous wave of vandalism. Everything destructible was destroyed. Everything that could be smeared with paint, was. Members of the Rosa Luxemburg Collective were notably vigorous, but even those of us with less penchant for wreckage were having a good time. Corey and I ruined a picture of Vice President Agnew and unraveled a fire hose. Bob stayed outside. He really *didn't* like violence, and there was something of the poor childhood's good sense in him that did not want to see anything nice destroyed, particularly our movie camera. So he and Barry stayed out on the back fringe of the mob, standing on a park bench, with Barry filming the panoramic sweep of trampling fist wavers and Bob shouting against the war.

We later found out that Red Lenny was also on the outskirts of the demonstration, not twenty yards from Barry and Bob. There were few police on this side of the City Hall plaza. The only one visible was

standing in an intersection with his back to everything, calmly directing cars and trucks away from the ruckus. He wasn't wearing a helmet
or carrying a riot stick; he was just a traffic cop. Lenny sneaked up
unseen behind this man and cracked him over the head with a length
of two-by-four.

When we got home that night and had showered off the tear gas
residue, the traffic cop was already on the evening news. He was unconscious and not expected to live. We also heard, from sources of our own,
that Red Lenny was openly bragging about having done this. Or he
was until he got arrested for it the next day. Barry said he thought what
Lenny had done was "chickenshit." And Bob was outraged. He said that
this was just the kind of thing that gave violent revolutions a bad name.
He sat down and typed out a passionate editorial calling upon "the
people" to mete out "revolutionary justice" to the "assailant"—"You
know who we mean." I think Bob's idea of revolutionary justice was
that Lenny would get a real talking-to, probably from Bob, and would
be converted to a philosophy of passive resistance and would fast for a
while to "get his head together about things." Even so, Bob and I had
a bitter argument about the editorial. I said that no matter how much
we might personally disapprove of the "specific guerrilla action" that
Lenny undertook, we must still maintain "revolutionary solidarity with
the Rosa Luxemburg Collective," and that whatever differences we had
with Lenny could be worked out during "self-criticism," which was a
word we used to use to mean a bitter argument. Actually I agreed with
Barry, but "chickenshit" didn't have a ring of political correctness.
Corey was the closest to Lenny and the other members of his group.
She didn't like what he did either, but she didn't know what to think
about it, the less so after her dad took the case.

Mr. Harrison was sure he could get Lenny acquitted. The prosecution
wasn't thought to have any eyewitnesses, and a number of people stood
ready to swear that Lenny had been urinating on the mayor's desk at
the time of the attack. Then, the day after the arrest, the traffic policeman regained consciousness and was pronounced not to be dying after

all. Bob gave in and said that as long as the cop was going to be okay the editorial didn't need printing. And the case slipped our minds.

We went back to work on the newsreel. The demonstration movies returned from the developer and the four of us pulled the blinds and watched them. They were not spectacular examples of filmmaking. Bob and Barry had been too far away, and when they weren't, people had been bumping them and getting placards and Viet Cong flags in front of the lens, causing a series of surreal camera jiggles and color swirls punctuated by long shots of frenetic denim wearers dashing in one direction and darker blue policemen chasing them back the other way. It was like a pair of thousand-man soccer teams viewed from the cheap seats. We were about halfway through the last of three reels and talking about how, after all, maybe we could use more of the film we already had on a fellow who had been the town's first and last nude panhandler, when something caught Bob's eye. He rewound the movie and ran it again until we came to one of the broad crowd vacillations, where Barry had been following a flight of young radicals across the plaza. But as Barry panned along the hippie retreat, he panned too far and swung the lens all the way past the crowd's rear guard. And there for a few seconds was the back of a traffic cop, standing out of the path of the riot, obliviously directing traffic. And into this frame scurried the perfectly clear form of Red Lenny, two-by-four in hand. Lenny smacked the cop on the head, and before the man could fall, the camera had swung back to the frenzied demonstration. "What was that?!" said Barry. *"What was that?! I never saw that in my life!"* And he hadn't. The crowd was being gassed and Barry and Bob were blinking and crying on their park bench, which is how Barry had happened to pan past the running protesters. But it was there on film, Lenny braining the traffic cop.

Now here is a part of the story that I don't understand. We did not destroy that piece of film. Not even the little section that could be counted as evidence. And that was the only rational thing to do. Instead, we put it in the safe. We had an old safe in the office. Only Corey, Barry, Bob, and I knew the combination. I don't know why we had the safe. There wasn't anything else in it. Even the narcotics cops, when they raided our office, didn't bother to look inside. But we put that reel of film in the safe, and I believe the reason that we did so was in order to have something secret and important to put in there. A momentary thrill could have been had by burning the film in an ashtray and burying the ashes in the yard or something, but a much bigger and more tingly kind of thrill was provided by having it and keeping it and repeatedly swearing each other to secrecy. It gave us something to whisper importantly about for a month.

We finished the newsreel (without *any* demonstration footage), and it was shown somewhere and not actually greeted with hoots. And we started on another, which I can't remember if we ever finished. Then there was the paper to put out, which became all the harder when Corey went back to school at the end of August. And life proceeded with its ordinary proliferation of small concerns and long mescaline interludes. Summer became fall, as it usually does, and the Red Lenny case slipped our minds again.

I was spending as much time as I could with Corey. I'd hitchhike out to her family's house in the suburbs in the afternoon, about the time school let out. And we'd sit outside on the lawn and talk or shoot baskets on the driveway apron. When we were alone, sometimes, we'd make love in Corey's bedroom, which was at the southwest corner of the house and brightly lit at that time of day. I remember lying there one afternoon with my head by her side and looking at the sunlight on the fine line of down that ran up the middle of her little belly and thinking that I might never be as happy again. And I haven't.

Usually we *were* alone on those afternoons because the Harrisons, at the behest of Mrs. Harrison, had adopted a seven-year-old autistic boy named Kevin. And Mrs. Harrison had to drive into the city each weekday at four to pick him up at the special school he attended. Kevin's autism was severe, and he would stand in a room with his arms flapping up and down like a child playing bird, which perhaps he was, but for hours at a time. He could not talk. It was something to watch Mrs. Harrison that fall as she made the slowest and most patient progress with him. Just as she had made the slowest and most patient progress with me—by October I was appearing at the Harrison household a little cleaner, and my language in their home was now not quite so free and profane. Kevin was beginning to pay some attention when speech, which he evidently understood, was addressed to him. And though he would not talk, he had begun to think and act. He showed, for instance, great facility at taking apart clocks and other mechanical objects and putting them back together again too. But even then, I confess it, I didn't like Mrs. Harrison. It's hard to forgive someone when you're beginning to agree with her.

Corey, too, was kind and understanding with Kevin, almost as patient as her mother. She thought that Kevin performed his unceasing motions because he could not distinguish between sensations. He was estranged from his emotions, she said, and he could not tell the difference between a good feeling, such as a caress, and any old feeling, such as going *bzzz* through his nose for an hour, any more than he could love or hate. I used to like to watch her with him and think how we might have a child of our own someday, though one that didn't wave his arms so wildly.

One evening that fall when Mrs. Harrison and Corey and Kevin and I were sitting in the living room, Mr. Harrison came home in a bad mood. We asked him what was wrong, and I believe I can recall what he said with some accuracy. "It's the damn Lenny Feinermann case," he said. "We had something that's called a 'pretrial discovery' today, where the damn prosecution tells you the goddamned evidence they've got against your damn client. And the goddamn DA has got a goddamn *film clip* of Lenny hitting the officer right over the fucking head. I've seen it."

Corey looked at me. And I looked at the floor. And then we both looked at the floor. And I kept looking at the floor, and I said, "I hate to tell you this, but I know where that film came from."

So I told Mr. Harrison the story of the newsreel. And, lacking any other facts than those I've put down here, he and I and his daughter began to conjecture. We conjectured that the police had seen Bob and

Barry filming on the day of the demonstration. And that, on a hunch, they had gone to one of the four members of the newspaper staff and convinced or coerced that person into giving the film to the district attorney. Corey was out of the question. And so was I, as long as I was in the room. So it must have been either Bob or Barry who had turned informant. Oddly, Mr. Harrison was one more person who never asked why the film wasn't destroyed. And it's my belief now that he was no more immune than the rest of us to the excitation of intrigue. Instead we discussed how angry Bob had been about the attack and whether or not this was sufficient motive for him to have given the film to the prosecutor. Possibly, we thought, if the officer had died. But he had not and was back on duty. And even if he had, Bob was too kindly to turn anybody in to anybody else. To do so, anyway, would have deprived him of the only thing he had, which was the unanimous affection of every hairy, bead-decked creature under thirty in the area. It must have been Barry. Barry had rich parents, who, if they found out what he was doing with his allowance, might give him no allowance to do anything. That's a shameful motive to impute to a friend. But Barry was the only one of us open to pressure from the police.

It happened that, at that moment, Bob and Barry were together, en route to visit a friend of Bob's in Florida. They'd left that day in Barry's car and weren't expected back for a week. There would be nothing we could do or discover until then. So I stayed overnight in the guest room at the Harrison's and went back to the newspaper office in the morning. But when I arrived, Bob was there at his desk with his face in his hands, crying. It seems that Barry and he had gotten no farther than a hundred miles or so the evening before, and that when talking as they always did Barry had said he had a confession to make. He said it was something that he'd wanted to confess for a long time but that he hadn't been able to bring himself to do so—which was so unlike Barry that Bob said it made him start—and that this was the reason he'd wanted to go on the trip to Florida with Bob, because he felt closest to Bob and he wanted to be alone with just one of us so he could tell the whole of the thing that he wanted to tell, which was that he was a cop. An undercover cop, and he always had been. And that he'd been assigned to infiltrate radical left-wing groups and he'd thought he'd do that by becoming a staff member on the *Community Underground Press,* but then he'd come to love us all, Bob and Corey and me, and he was sorry now, and so on. Bob listened to him for a little while, too shocked, he said, not to, and then he told Barry to stop the car, just to stop the car and let him out. Barry asked him please not to leave, to hear his whole side of the story. But Bob just said to let him out. And Bob got out. And he'd been hitchhiking back all night. Bob couldn't believe it. Barry was his friend. If Barry had told him he was a cop first, Bob said, he still would have been Barry's friend. But to have been his friend and *then* be a cop . . .

I exploded. Barry was a spy. This time it *was* very important. We had to kill him. He had to be "offed," I believe I said. Bob began screaming no. Barry was *still* his friend. We got into a long loud argument about whether to kill him and I walked out.

After I walked out I realized a couple of things. I realized I had no place to go. I couldn't go back to the Harrisons'; only Mrs. Harrison would be there. Corey, Barry, and Bob were my only close friends. But I couldn't go back to the newspaper. And the Rosa Luxemburg Collective was out of the question just then. And I realized I couldn't kill Barry, either. Not because I could talk myself into thinking it wasn't important. I thought it was. I thought it was the most important thing ever in my life that I kill him. But I didn't have the courage. I maybe had the courage to pull the trigger and see the blood come out of his face and watch him fall down. But I definitely did not have the courage to hide from the police and be caught and be tried and be sent to prison. And then I also realized I didn't have a gun. Our only weapons belonged to Barry, which made perfect sense. So I wandered around feeling despicable and a little stupid and lonely and frightened. And beginning to feel chilly too.

Sometime that afternoon I came across a girl I knew slightly, Anna, a member of another one of the local radical groups. She was loading things into a borrowed panel truck. She'd just found a new apartment downtown. I helped her move there, and when we were done moving I moved in too, with the clothes I had on and about two dollars.

Bob wouldn't speak to Barry. I wouldn't speak to Bob. And Corey, after she found out about Anna, wouldn't speak to me. I got a job working construction. And then I moved to New York.

Bob put out a special edition of the *Community Underground Press* in which he explained that we, unknowingly, had had a member of the police force on our staff since our first day of publication. In an over-weening fit of truthfulness, however, he went on to say that he still felt affection for Barry and that in many ways Barry had been a true friend, while, of course, still being an informer, a spy, and a pig. The *Community Underground Press* expired shortly thereafter.

Red Lenny's case came to trial that winter, and Barry was put on the stand. He was not a rich kid. There was no allowance from home. The money he had was his salary. And his cameras belonged to the police department, the movie camera too. He did not have his film developed by a "friend from prep school who runs a film lab for his dad." That fellow, whom we'd met, was a police officer also. The police department developed all of Barry's photographs, giving him a set of prints and keeping a set for themselves. They must have had a nice col-lection of seminaked hippie girl pictures. Barry explained how, as a plainclothesman, he had been assigned to the surveillance of left-wing political groups and how he had accomplished this by becoming a staff member on an underground newspaper. To my humiliation when I later heard of it, he told the court that the staff members of this news-paper were not themselves considered dangerous. We were, he said, noisy but harmless—basically just high-spirited kids having fun and maybe trying to shock our parents. But being a staff member gave him access to groups who really *were* dangerous. And the Rosa Luxemburg Collective was certainly one of these.

Then Barry began to calmly muff his testimony. He claimed, under direct and then under cross-examination, to have been filming at some location far away from the incident. He said he'd been alone, and there was no one to corroborate the time or place. He confused the dates, and said it was hard to remember one demonstration from another. The prosecutor was angry. Barry identified the film as his own but said he couldn't be at all sure that the young man shown with the two-by-four was Leonard Feinermann. And neither could the jury, for Leonard, Red Lenny, was seated in front of them, shaven, shorn, and suited, with decorous parents at his back, and looking like the honors student that he'd been. So Lenny was acquitted and Barry was busted back to patrolman, and a couple of months later Barry quit the force.

Bob visited me in New York. And I visited Corey at her house. And the three of us became friends again, though we don't see each other often. One night Bob met Barry by accident in a bar. He told me he was cool to Barry, but he couldn't refuse to have a beer with the man after the way Barry'd acted at the Feinermann trial. Pretty soon they were drunk and friends again too.

A couple of years went by, and I came to know a New York lawyer who had been an assistant district attorney in '70 and '71 in the city where we had all lived. He'd known Barry as an undercover cop and told me several things. Our offices had been, as I said before, visited by the police on (wholly justifiable) drug raids. These cases had always been dropped before they came to trial. The same was true on the couple of occasions when one of us was arrested at a demonstration. We had figured it was just good luck, but my lawyer friend said that after each arrest Barry would rush to the prosecutor's office and plead that his "cover would be blown" if we ever came to trial. Such was the atmosphere of worry about Black Panthers, SDSers, and who-knows-what-all Barry was supposed to be watching from his vantage point on the newspaper staff, that his requests to have charges dropped were always granted. I told my friend about the weatherman with the wastepaper basket over his head, who really was a Weatherman, and actually wanted by the FBI, though just for a skipped grand-jury subpoena, I believe. I said Barry hadn't done much about that guy. My friend said it would have been a surprise if he had; for in two years of investigation Barry had not brought a single subversive into the hands of the law. Nor had he, after the first few months, provided the police with any information that was even vaguely useful. My friend told me something of the contents of our staff's police files. Mine, for instance, noted that my grandfather had been the chairman of the Matoon, Illinois, county Republican organization and a personal friend of President Taft. It was my great-grandfather, actually. I must have made a joke about it once. Barry did not even mean to incriminate Red Lenny. The police at headquarters had discovered the film of Lenny's assault the same way we had.

I never bothered to tell Bob about the things Barry had done to protect us. I figured Bob knew them already, and, knowing Bob, I figured he would prefer to think that he was the only person who believed them.

I saw Barry himself a little while ago, and I liked him as well as I ever had. He's a private detective now and specializes in insurance fraud. He lets the people who really need the money get away with it, though, he said.

Mr. Harrison went on to defend a number of other members of the Rosa Luxemburg Collective. One night in 1973 they tried to blow up a suburban branch bank with a homemade kerosene bomb, which destroyed a three-yard patch of lawn and an ornamental shrub. During the trial they came to his house one night and asked him to hide a gun for them. It wasn't an illegal gun, just a hunting rifle, and I don't believe they had done anything exciting with it. But they were sure they were about to be raided again and they didn't want to lose this gun the way they had all the others. Mr. Harrison broke the rifle down, wrapped it in oiled rags, and locked it in a closet, and he took the bolt mechanism and locked that in a file cabinet in his den. Somehow Kevin was able to make his way into the closet and to open the drawer in the file cabinet too, and he put the rifle back together. And one day when he was home from school sick and Mrs. Harrison was working in the rose garden in the backyard, he leaned out the kitchen window and shot her through the head.

Dynamite

I t was a perfect summer, the summer of 1967. Some friends of mine and I had a farm in southern Ohio. There was Michael Visconti, whom we always called Uncle Mike because of a certain avuncular way he had about him, especially when urging people to take more drugs. Uncle Mike is a professor of mathematics at Michigan State these days. And there was Terry Conners, who'd been hanging around the local college campus for years, a few credits short of a degree, running bars and owning pizza joints. He's building condominiums in Hawaii now. And there was Juanita and I. Last I heard, Juanita was living on a yacht in the Caribbean. But this was a long time ago and we were different people then; we had this farm, and we had a lot of hashish we were selling.

We used to get it from a fellow who would drive up from Mexico

in a 1948 Pontiac Streamliner Deluxe. Which wouldn't seem an incon-
spicuous way to travel with thirty pounds of drugs in the trunk, up
through Kentucky with his ponytail flying back to the package shelf.
Even in Ohio, in those days, you could get ten years in prison for simple possession. But, like I said, it was a long time ago, and we were different people. And one of the reasons we were so different was all the
hashish. It was thick, black-brown slabs of oily, opiated stuff that was
supposed to have the official seal of the royal hoo-ha of Nepal on it
somewhere, though I never noticed it. And it came wrapped in broiler
foil in a cardboard grocery box.

I'm sure that the hashish made our farm seem far grander in
extent and more lush and exotic of vegetation than ever it really was.
And the days rolled by slower and less predictably than they do today.
Maybe it was adolescence that did some of that, or maybe memory
does it, but certainly the hashish helped. It was particular fun to go
hunting or target shooting after we'd smoked some, because we never
knew what was going to happen. Terry claimed that his perception of
time would grow so acute and slow that he could see the bullet come
out of a rifle barrel and travel toward the target—well, travel toward
something anyway. And that he could see shotgun pellets spread, he'd
say, like a Roman candle, except not lit. That is, they didn't glow or
anything. He was lying, but it was a great farm.

It had a big, rambling, dirty farmhouse with dogs and a lamb and
a duck and some cats and a tame raccoon running around inside it.
And it had a dilapidated barn to make love and take drugs in, with a
big empty silo that you could climb up the side of, and peek over the
top of, and scare yourself silly with. And there were fields and woods
all around, a stream with little rills down to a half-dammed swimming
hole, hedgerows along the road and drive, and an old orchard with
unpruned limbs making bowers between the rows of trees. There was
a herd of sheep grazing in the back pasture. Someone must have come
in every now and then and watered them or sheared them or whatever it is you do to sheep. I know we didn't do it. But they were nice
to have around, very bucolic from a distance (up close they smelled and
looked dirty). And we had cars and trucks and motorcycles and guns,

and we'd sell the hashish or trade it for more guns or more motorcycles, and it was a perfect summer.

We'd go rabbit hunting with one of the dogs chasing rabbits back and forth in front of us while we blasted away. It's important to remember, when you're rabbit hunting, which is the rabbit and which is the dog. The rabbit is the one that isn't barking. In fact, they don't make any sound at all unless you hit them, but we never hit any, and it was still fun, until we hit one after all. When you do hit them they make a little tiny squeaking sound, or at least this one did, and it lay there and sniffled and wiggled in agony, all furry and cute and in horrible pain, and, being out of shotgun shells, we had to walk back to the house and get a .45 and blow its head off. Then, since it had died such a hard death, we felt obligated, in a way, to eat it.

But rabbits are supposed to carry a disease—rabbit fever, appropriately enough, which is very deadly if you have an open wound or a something else. We couldn't remember which. What you're supposed to do to make sure that they do have it or that they don't is to cut them open and look at their liver. You have to make sure it looks normal. What a normal-looking rabbit liver would be, though, none of us could tell. And once we'd cut the rabbit open we couldn't figure out what part of the stuff in there was the liver part anyway. But we were determined to eat it. It had taken so long to die that it couldn't have been all that sick; so we scooped out the guts and pulled off the skin and put it to soak overnight in a pot full of salt water, which someone had said that someone else said to do. Then we forgot it. I guess it was the hashish. The next time we looked in the pot, a week later, we wouldn't have wanted to look in it again. So all we wound up with was a lucky rabbit foot for Juanita. But, after a month, that grew horrible looking too, shrinking down so the bone end poked out, and turning black and losing its hair. I think one of the dogs got it. Sparrow hunting was much better. Throw out some bread crumbs and you can get a sparrow to come up so close that when you use a 12-gauge Magnum load, full choke, they just vaporize in a puff of feathers.

Terry and I found a bunch of old things up in the attic, some morris chairs and a cast-iron, pedal-operated sewing machine, some chamber pots, and an old washstand. And we set them up in the yard, in a sort of little sculpture garden, and then blew them apart by the hour from the upstairs windows using shotgun slugs and .30-.30 soft points to get the most impact and splattering of lead and shattering of wood and metal. We'd scatter some beer cans full of water in among the other stuff to explode with hollow-point .22s, also. It was as pleasant an afternoon as you can imagine, sitting in Juanita's bedroom window with a cold case of Budweiser and the hashish and twenty boxes of ammunition. Then we'd start up a car and chase the sheep around in their pasture and run motorcycles up and down the rows of corn in the front forty. We had rats in the house, and I sat up all one night downstairs, drinking whiskey and smoking hashish in an easy chair in the middle of the kitchen, waiting for them to peek out of their rat holes. Then I'd let loose with a .25 automatic. By dawn some of those rats poking their heads out of the walls were real and some of them were not. I don't think I hit any of the real ones. But I was enjoying myself. I was enjoying myself that whole summer.

Terry and I had a quarrel about something and decided we'd settle it with a duel. Among the various cars we had on the farm, there was a 1960 Chevrolet with nearly 150,000 miles on it and a 1961 Tempest that would barely run. We were up all night fixing the engines, popping the windshields out, and breaking all the knobs and handles and sharp protruding things off the doors and dashboards. Then we each painted our car with insults about the other and boasts and literary quotes and decorations. Then, in the morning, we put on motorcycle helmets and went down to the end of a mud lane that ran through the back pasture, turned the cars around, placed them side by side, and raced back to the barnyard, slapping sides and slamming into each other. The fenders of the cars, smooth and flexible, would come together with a kind of metallic lubrication, almost a splash, as we tried to shove each other off the path. When we reached the barn, we pulled apart and began circling around as fast as we could turn and slide— sending up showers of old manure and clipping the rickety chicken coops—each trying to position himself to take a run at the other.

Terry struck me on the passenger side, a T-bone collision. The window was rolled down and there was a beautiful geyser of glass up from inside the door. Then I did a bootleg turn midway in a head-on chicken run and punched in his radiator with one fin from my Chevrolet's rear deck lid. But we kept the cars going most of the day, calling a time-out whenever the fenders were bent in so that the tires couldn't turn. Uncle Mike and Juanita would then pry out the wheel wells with crowbars and we'd go back at it. We'd lunge and dodge and chase our friends out of the way, with Terry spraying steam until he blindsided me and I was plowed into a chicken coop that fell down around me; from there the car wouldn't budge and I could barely get out myself.

One of the dogs we had, Juanita's, was a Great Dane with an undocked tail the length of a human arm. It was a happy dog without many nerve endings and was continually wagging the tail, beating the end of it into a bloody sore against the furniture, kitchen cabinets, and walls. Everywhere it hit, the tail left a big red dot of blood—all the way around the living-room walls, at dog-ass height, and up the stairwell and around the rooms upstairs. The dots looked like perforations, and Uncle Mike, with his obsessive calculations, said that if you cut along this dotted line with a chain saw you could pull the house apart in a conical helix. I believe he would have tried it if he hadn't been so lazy from the hashish and if we'd had a chain saw.

We even had a little mystery and terror on the front lawn when we found the lamb (which was more or less a pet) with its stomach torn open and its insides gone. There were some fat paw tracks around, and Terry, who had more claim to woodcraft, since he was the one who had skinned the rabbit, was positive a mountain lion did it. I thought the farmers would laugh at us when Uncle Mike told this to everyone in the local roadhouse the next night. But they were sure it was true. It hadn't ever happened to any of them with any of their livestock, but you could see that they were envious it hadn't. I've had the story told back to me a number of times since, with the size of the paw prints and the number of dead lambs expanding every time.

One fellow volunteered that they might still have these mountain lions in Arkansas and that this one must have swam the Mississippi and come up through Tennessee and Kentucky and swam the Ohio River and that's how it got our lamb. There was even talk of a hunt with hound dogs and flashlights and another lamb staked out for bait and I don't know what all else. I bothered to look it up and there hadn't been a mountain lion in Ohio in well over a hundred years. I suppose it might have been a bobcat, but we had dogs running loose all over the place. And it was one of these dogs, Juanita's Great Dane, that killed the lamb. He wouldn't go near the carcass and didn't eat for two days. But it would have broken Juanita's heart to say so, and disappointed all the neighbors, too. Besides, this gave us an excuse to go armed outside at night and gave an excuse for all the men in the neighborhood to do so too and to scare their wives out of going into town for bingo. Anyway, life is dull enough in Ohio.

Although *we* didn't think so. There were supposed to be narcotics agents, up from Cincinnati, after us. We told each other we'd shoot it out with them if they came. We were lying again. But it was fun to think we would. And to talk about how we'd do it when we did. We had a rim-fire .30-caliber rifle and a lever-action .30-.30, a .308 Winchester Model 70, an old hexagonal-barrel single-shot .22, and a couple of semiautomatic .22 rifles as well, plus a Japanese 8-mm military rifle that we didn't have the ammunition for. And we had a 12-gauge Remington pump, a 12-gauge Ithaca single shot, an old Belgian double barrel made with Damascus-twist steel, a Sears bolt-action 20 gauge that jammed all the time, a sawed-off 16 gauge with a pistol grip that Uncle Mike had made and a High-Standard 20-gauge auto loader. Then we had the .45 service automatic, a snub-nose .38, a .25 Beretta, a .22 Astra Cub, a Luger, a .357 Colt Python, and a pair of old derringers. But, best of all, we had a case of dynamite.

This was Uncle Mike's favorite. He said the application of explosive force was as near to pure mathematics as you could come in the physical world; although how he proved this sticking it down groundhog holes I have no idea. He used the dynamite under rocks, which would come popping right out of the earth and roll over next to their craters. And he used it under stumps, which would not. He used it up in treetops to produce a sort of "instant autumn." He used it in a giant slingshot made of motorcycle inner tube to create a great starburst in the night sky. He used it in the stream, as he said, "to fish in the manner of the Filipino," though nothing but muddy water and parts of a few crawdaddies floated to the surface. And he used so much of it out in the pasture that by the end of July the sheep were skinny and looking haunted. He even tried hunting rabbits with it, setting out half a stick with a very long fuse and next to it a bit of lettuce or carrot. Then he'd wait, Zippo in hand, for a very long time—though it may have been the hashish that made it seem so—and no rabbit would come. Finally at even the rustling suggestion of a rabbit he'd set off the fuse. We never found a dead one, but Mike said they may have just disintegrated, like the sparrows.

One afternoon in early August we were sitting out on the front porch of the house, Uncle Mike and Terry and Juanita and I. We'd smoked a very great amount of hashish that day. In fact, we had started before breakfast and had become so disoriented that we'd been unable to fix any breakfast, or any lunch, and we were barely able to find some potato chips and Fritos and Cokes to make do with, because by dinnertime we were far too insentient to make any of that either. We were just sitting on the porch in a drift, barely able to talk, lost in our own languid fantasies and perceptual distortions, when Uncle Mike suggested a dynamite show. It would be a perfect attraction to view with our heightened senses, he said. Why, he'd wire up three whole sticks together and put them out at the far end of the lawn. The effect, he said, would be compared to a whole body orgasm, and there was none of us with energy for, or interest in, disputing him.

So Mike went down in the cellar, where we had the dynamite to keep it cool, and he was down there so long that we forgot he was down there at all. But he came back at last and then proceeded to fool and to fiddle with the dynamite sticks. I'm sure that his movements that day were deliberate and slower than the usual slow way that he moved, but the hashish rendered the pace of his activity glacial. It seemed an age at least while he lashed the sticks together and decided upon which was most central to the other two (itself a neat mathematical problem). Then, having selected one stick, he pushed the blasting cap into its end, and after that he had to find the brass cap crimpers that were lying around the house somewhere and crimp a fuse into the cap. When he was finally ready with the charge, he set off from the porch on what seemed to us a mission of enormous duration.

I could swear we watched him journey out onto the lawn for half an hour before he set the explosives down, carefully set fire to the fuse end, and started running back to the porch. I remember his running. Mike is not a slim man and is little given to running at all. But he seemed to be moving like a sprinter just then, yet a sprinter seen through a telescopic lens with such foreshortening that he made no progress at all, and no progress in slow motion, at that. Finally he set one foot of a plump high-pumping leg on the bottom porch step, and just as he did there was a god-awful eruption of dirt. I was beaten against the side of the house, and Juanita, who was sitting in the porch swing, went backward in it, broke through the railing, and was dumped into the forsythia. Mike was pitched through the front door screen into the living room, followed by a wave of lawn and soil, and every window on the front of the house was shattered and half the shingles were blown off the roof.

It seems that Uncle Mike had consumed so much hashish, and that his conception of spatial relationships was so grievously altered, that he had planted the dynamite five feet from the porch.

None of us could hear for a week. But no one was too seriously injured except Terry, who had part of a hash pipe blown up his nose, something they had trouble understanding at the county hospital emergency ward. He recovered, but that was the end of our perfect summer. We had to clear out before the landlord showed up.

We sold the rest of that dynamite to the ponytailed fellow who sold us the hashish, and I understand he took it out to a group of California political radicals who used it to explode a Pacific Gas and Electric high-tension transmission tower, an activity that was in vogue just then. I still have the newspaper clipping. No bodies were found at the scene, so I assume those radicals were drinking coffee.

Another Tale of Uncle Mike

For a while, in the spring of 1967, before we moved to the farm, Uncle Mike and Juanita and I shared a house in the nearby college town with a mystic fellow named Steve. Steve had very long fingernails and didn't often bathe. He was in love with the daughter of an Air Force colonel in Dayton. The colonel spoke of Steve only as "Dirty Eddie," kept his daughter in a local junior college, and had declared that if "Dirty Eddie" ever so much as set foot in Dayton, he'd kill him with his own bare hands. Taking the colonel at his word, Steve retired to the pursuit of his own particular brand of mysticism.

There were three bedrooms in the house. Two next to each other upstairs and one downstairs, which was Juanita's and mine. Steve had found an old stand-up radio which he had carried up to his room and placed in the middle of the floor. The radio was broken, but, plugged in, its large orange dial would light up and the speaker emitted a low buzz. Steve claimed that this radio was an "Om machine," and that the sound it made was the first syllable of the Buddhist chant *"Om mani padme hum."* He filled the room with folding chairs that he'd stolen somewhere, arranging them in semicircles around the radio, and spent most of his time in there with all the lights off, taking drugs and staring at the orange dial.

Few people ever joined Steve in his "Om Machine Theater," especially not Uncle Mike, who was a devout Catholic—something he showed every Sunday morning in his best suit and every Saturday night in a drunken rage. One such Saturday night, Mike came home more angry than usual and stamped upstairs. He was too drunk to notice that Steve was there. Even Juanita and I didn't realize Steve was home, so low or so familiar was that om sound. Mike shut himself into his room with the five or six locks he had mounted on his door, got out his guns, and began firing into the wall between his room and Steve's. He fired a hundred rounds or so before we heard the door locks come undone and the sound of Mike's footsteps headed for the bathroom. Then there was a pause and a loud scream from Mike. *"I killed him! I killed him! I killed him! . . ."*

Juanita and I ran upstairs. Mike, still screaming, was kneeling over Steve, who was face down on the floor in a tangle of chair legs. Juanita turned the light on and began feeling Steve's body for blood, trying to get him to talk. She rolled him over, but there didn't seem to be any wounds. "I'm dead," he said at last.

Mike, meanwhile, had gotten up and wandered into his own room, where I found him screaming, *"I killed him! I killed him!"* and staring at a wall full of bullet holes. I tried to tell him that Steve was still alive. But he wouldn't listen and stumbled back into Steve's room and started staring at the wall in there. There were no holes in that wall.

"I'm dead," said Steve.

"I killed him! I killed him!" yelled Mike.

"I'm dead," said Steve.

"I killed him!" yelled Mike.

"Look," I said. "There aren't even any holes in the wall."

"Of course there aren't," said Juanita. "That's his closet."

Which was true. Uncle Mike's closet was between the two rooms, and what he'd done was shoot up all his clothes. Which I demonstrated by putting on one of his sports coats and waving my fingers at him through the patch pockets. But it was some time before he left off screaming, *"I killed him!"*

Steve believed it, too. He didn't get up off the floor until the next afternoon. "I can't get up," he'd say, "I'm dead." And he remained convinced for quite some time afterward—often refusing to eat or wear warm clothing on the grounds of not being alive. Death also greatly emboldened him. So much so that he went to see his girlfriend at home and danced around her father, singing, "I'm dead. I'm dead. I'm dead. Eat shit." The colonel fled the house, and Steve and his girl were married a month later—a spiritual union only, however, since Steve had left the corporeal realm.

Everyone concerned eventually came to his and her senses. Steve fully admits to being alive these days. He lives in Miami, where he writes detective novels. And his girlfriend has a very wealthy second husband.

Ghosts of Responsibility

One fall when I was very young and very broke I returned to college and could find nowhere to live. For a while I rented a dirty little room, one of a dozen over a grocery store. There were rats in the walls and one windowless bathroom at the end of the corridor. Also, there was a cancerous old man, a sort of concierge, who lived in one of the rooms. He would not let my girlfriend come upstairs as long as he was awake, and he was always awake. But I couldn't afford anything else. Then one evening in a bar a young man named Gary Ballow told me about a place where he used to live. It might still be for rent, he said, if I'd want it.

Ballow did not, at that time, seem like a young man to me. He was about twenty-eight, and he was a writer. That is, he wrote every day. But one thing he wrote didn't often fit with any other thing he wrote. And his sentences, though splendid to hear, did not parse. He had graduated half a dozen years before but never left the little southern Ohio college town. He drank a great deal.

Until a couple of months before, Ballow had lived in a carriage house behind a deteriorating mansion on the edge of town. He told me to go see the ancient and peculiar Kentucky woman, Miss Beauregard, who owned the property. But I mustn't mention his name. He'd left owing half a year's rent and she'd sworn to shoot him.

The carriage house was comfortable, he said, and cheap, and, aside from Miss Beauregard, it had only one drawback: it was haunted. It was very haunted. And Ballow, who, as I said, drank a great deal, insisted on telling me the whole story of its haunting. He talked for two hours.

The carriage house had been converted to an apartment—a cottage, really—in the late 1950s and immediately began to accumulate ghosts. They were, said Ballow, the ghosts of responsibility. Each of these shades, he claimed, was a spectral representation of some duty not undertaken, some trust not executed, some human burden someone had failed to heft. And he said much more on the subject in a manner largely poetic. I remember none of it. But I do recall the stories of the four dead people who'd occupied the carriage house and who, he assured me, continued to reside in my future home.

The first was the first resident, a woman graduate student. I might hear her story from some professor sometime, Ballow said. If I did, I'd hear she died from some sudden biological lapse, headlong leukemia or galloping embolism or the like. This wasn't the case. He'd known her. She had failed to complete her dissertation on some aspect of phonic ratiocination in preschoolers. A completed thesis was necessary to her graduation with a doctoral degree. The graduation had been planned; parents, aunts, and cousins invited; presents selected; a dinner scheduled for catering. She came from a large Jewish family. They were poor and very proud of their bloodline's first Ph.D., so she committed suicide with a hundred Miltown pills.

The second and third ghosts were the result of a party in the spring of 1962. A friend of Ballow's, Woody Upton, was living in the carriage house then. Woody had been dating a local girl, a farm girl of no great intelligence but with a large handsome body. Perhaps dating isn't the right word. He fucked her sometimes. She was in love with him. He was not in love with her. She got pregnant. He refused to marry her. And she kept coming to see him, though he told her to stay away. By the time of the party she was nearly due. As pregnant a woman, said Ballow, as he had ever seen. It was a drunken party with loud music, and everyone danced the Alligator, which was a dance where you lay down in the beer on the floor and slithered on your stomach and then flopped on top of someone else, who wiggled on her back, and so on. The farm girl did it, too, though no one jumped on her. She was wiggling like everybody else and hollering like they were also, then she screamed and pulled up her skirt and took off her underwear, screaming all the while and breathing fast, said Ballow. No one knew what to do. They all stood up fascinated and still. A couple minutes later she delivered bloody stillborn twins on the floor, and a minute after that the electricity went out. Then everyone at the party began to scream. There was a terrifying commotion, a sound of moving feet and bodies. But when the lights came on everyone seemed to be just where they had been before. Except the babies. The dead babies were gone. The girl looked everywhere for them. Everyone looked for them. The farm girl kept screaming, but the bodies were gone.

I cannot provide the details, much as I would like to. Did the girl leap up fully vigorous from her accouchement and hunt behind the furniture? Or did she lie there prostrate and search the room with her eyes? What about the afterbirth? But Ballow was running downwind with his narrative and could not be made to reach or beat for interruptions. He said only that the babies joined the graduate student thereafter in the house.

The fourth ghost was a homosexual high school teacher named Rory. He died in 1963. At that time another friend of Ballow's, Bob Werhauser, was living in the carriage house with his wife and their newborn child. Rory and the Werhausers had been friends for some years. One night, when the baby was not a week old and his wife was just home from the hospital, Bob went off alone to a party. Ballow claimed to have been at this party also, as was Rory. Sometime after midnight Rory began to pinch and fondle women guests. This was taken to be a great joke. And sometime after that, Rory said to Werhauser, "You know what I'd really like to do? I'd like to fuck your wife."

"No you wouldn't," said Bob. "You're queer. Besides, she just had a baby. She's big as a ditch."

But Rory insisted and disappeared from the party.

A little later Werhauser got a phone call from his wife, saying, "Rory's over here at the carriage house. He says he's going to rape me, and he's trying to break the door down."

"That's insane," said Bob. "He's a homosexual."

She called back in five minutes with the same message and said she was very frightened. Bob told her she was nuts. She called again, and once more after that. Finally Werhauser told everyone to just let the phone ring. His wife was having delusions.

Rory succeeded in breaking the door down. Or, actually, it seems he didn't break it, because when Werhauser came home at four in the morning it was bolted from the inside and no one would answer. Rory and Werhauser's wife stayed in there for two weeks.

Again, I don't know the details. The Werhauser family reunion must have been interesting. But Ballow was too puffed up with philosophical speculation about Rory's sudden heterosexuality to give me the particulars. Anyway, Bob and his wife did get back together. And Rory went home, which was where he was found about a month later with the oven on and the pilot light out. An attractive boy, one of Rory's students, had stopped by for what Ballow said was some "special tutoring." When no one came to the door, the boy tried the latch and found Rory passed out on the bed.

It was several weeks before Mrs. Werhauser convinced the doctors to let her visit. She was shown to the hospital room and was there confronted by Rory covered in an oxygen tent, attached to an artificial kidney, with a glucose bottle running into his arm and feeding tubes up his nose. She shrieked and ran across the room, gathering

Rory to her chest, oxygen tent and all. The tubes and needles were pulled from his body, the dialysis machine was overturned, and Rory died an hour later.

I don't know what exact responsibility Rory's ghost was supposed to represent. And among the other things I never found out from Ballow were how he determined there were precisely four ghosts and how he discovered these four ghosts corresponded to the four deaths he described. Especially since they were perfunctory in their haunting. For the most part they just moaned or clanked a chain. They were ordinary ghosts, ordinary to the point of being hackneyed, he said. Sometimes he went so far as to speak to them about it, saying he expected something more original in the way of possession. But they never did better than bang cupboard doors and make footsteps when no one else was home. Their only point of novelty was that they lived in the heating system, a small stand-up oil burner in one corner of the living room. Into this they would retire, late at night, and sing Gregorian chants through the mica glass peephole.

But don't misunderstand him, said Ballow. (His speech was getting sloppy.) These ghosts were dangerous even so. They had the power to curse people who were shirking their obligations. Every irresponsible person who had lived in the carriage house—and there seemed to be no other kind—had been cursed and come to a bad end. Woody Upton, for instance, the father of the twins, had married a shrewish girl from New Jersey and led an awful life. And Bill Elliot, who had lived there between Upton and Bob Werhauser, had been involved in a hit-and-run accident and was afterward plagued by sebaceous boils. And Werhauser, who had failed to protect his wife from Rory, and vice versa, Werhauser had a job at *TV Guide* now, writing the preview listings. A worse fate than that Ballow could not imagine. Then there was Forrester, who had shared the carriage house with Ballow himself. I forget what Forrester's irresponsibility was; wasting a genius for something, I think. He was cursed too. I was perplexed when Gary said so, because Forrester was at the other end of the bar that minute and looked fine, in fact seemed to be having a swell time. But Ballow snorted at my objection. "Cursed," he said, "definitely cursed."

These ghosts, Ballow repeated, were dangerous to people who had responsibilities and refused to live up to them, dangerous to good people who had been slack about one thing or another. But *he* had never been bothered. He had escaped from them completely unscathed. Did I know why? I did not. It was because he, Ballow, was completely worthless and vice ridden. He was so totally reprehensible in his conduct that it was impossible to say that he had neglected any single responsibility. He was evil, you see, and the ghosts were powerless against him. They held sway only over good people gone wrong. He had outreached their grasp. He was worse than they ever were, and they could not so much as raise one of their two score spectral digits against him. Ha! He had them. Why, they all wound up rather friends, he said. And the only trouble they'd ever caused him was just when he was about to leave. He was sitting at the kitchen table writing letters telling various people his new address when inky black stuff dripped from the bare ceiling and blotted out his correspondence. And that was only because the ghosts were sad to see him go. He supposed it was a comfort to them to have someone in the house whom they had no mandate to torment. It was less work, he imagined. I'd have no trouble with the ghosts either, he was sure, and for just the opposite reason. I was a clean-cut, reliable young man. (I had paid for the last round.) Those ghosts would have no bone to pick with me.

I paid little attention to Ballow's assurances. And I paid no attention to his warnings (as, indeed, people in ghost stories must never do). I needed someplace to live, so I went to see Miss Beauregard in the mansion. She *was* peculiar and *very* old. Her house was littered with dirty and broken antiques, and the first thing Miss Beauregard told me was that she slept every night with a loaded .45 on her nightstand. Did I know a fellow called Gary Ballow? I lied that I didn't. Please tell her if I met the man, because, she said, she was going to kill him. She gave me a warm can of beer and a plate of cold chicken wings, which I was afraid not to eat.

Miss Beauregard owned a roadhouse, the Wagonwheel, eight or ten miles out of town. Her equally ancient brother, Sawtelle, ran a whorehouse behind the tavern in what had once been tourist cabins. Ballow's past roommate, Forrester, had worked for her once, tending bar. He told me later that Miss Beauregard and Sawtelle quarreled all the time. He quit after one of these arguments. Miss Beauregard was standing next to Forrester behind the bar when Sawtelle came in with a double-barreled shotgun. Forrester ducked, but Miss Beauregard pulled another shotgun from behind the counter and aimed it at her brother. They both fired, but so old and shaky were they that they missed each other with twelve-gauge shot at a dozen paces. A drunk sleeping outside the door was startled, however, and ran out in the road, where he was killed by the car of the same Bill Elliot who was living in the carriage house then.

One thing I had to understand about living out there, Miss Beauregard told me: the mansion was haunted. The fellow who had built it in the 1880s was a rich feed store owner. But his family took to spending his money faster than he could make it, and he took to the bottle. They ended broke and hiding from their creditors. They never lit a candle or answered the door; and finally when the sheriff came to evict them by force, he found the whole family dead inside. They'd killed themselves from shame. That was when Miss Beauregard had bought the house at auction. In 1910, she claimed. The original family was damned, and their spirits had to stay here on earth, she said, and try to make amends for the wasteful lives they'd led. These ghosts would burn lights in the windows at all hours of the night and make the front door open by itself to total strangers. I was to "pay these things no nevermind," said Miss Beauregard, and, besides, the carriage house was all right. That was a "modern place." It was mine for sixty-five dollars a month. I made a deposit and left with the keys.

My girlfriend, Juanita, and I lived in the carriage house for most of the winter of 1966–67. It was a handsome little brick building with a tile roof. Inside, there was one large room, with the supposedly haunted oil burner in a corner and wide-arched casement windows on either side. At the back was a small kitchen, with another arch of windows, that looked out on a field and the woods beyond. The bathroom was small and almost all shower, like the head on a sailboat. But the hot-water heater was much bigger than necessary, and we could stand in that shower for ninety minutes if we liked. In the living room there was a ladder that went up to a loft with a window in each gable. The place was clean and had been painted. We found a few pieces of used furniture for it—a table, a couple of chairs, and a mattress.

Juanita quit school that fall and worked as a model for life-drawing classes, so we had a little money. She was the most beautiful girl I have ever seen—small, tawny skinned, with sleek dark hair and wide brown eyes. She had long legs and a very small waist that gave her hips, though slight, a perfect roundness. Her breasts were large, placed high on her chest, with hard dark nipples. She cooked and kept house and treated me better than anyone ever has. We slept in a hug, arms and legs tangled together. I've never been able to sleep that way with anyone else. It's claustrophobic now, or an arm goes to sleep. We made love two or three times a day. Part of that was youth. But part of it was an attraction that cannot be explained at any age. I wanted to touch every part of her with my fingers, my cock, and my tongue. She rubbed me thick with soap lather once so I could try to push myself up between her buttocks, not knowing how much the soap would sting. But she just laughed when it hurt her. We stayed in the shower as much as we could, and in the bed when we weren't in the shower, and half naked all the time, even outside in the field. It was a very mild winter, freakishly warm for weeks at a time. Most mornings, when I got up to go to classes, there was an odor of timothy and alfalfa decaying in the fields, where it had been mown too late and damp for baling. It's a rare odor in the East, where I live now, that smell of rotting hay, and I'm glad it is, because I cannot smell it without overwhelming nostalgia, without crying, almost fifteen years later.

The carriage house was a perfect home to Juanita and me. We

talked about how it could be fixed up and told each other we never wanted to leave. That there was something spooky about the place only made it more intimate. And we heard no moans or chains or Gregorian chants. But after sundown it always did seem to be darker outside our door than anywhere nearby. And sometimes the rungs on the ladder to the loft would creak, one after another, as though something were going upstairs. And there was, on still nights, a persistent thumping at one corner of the roof, where there were no pipes or tree branches or even squirrels that I could discover. So maybe Ballow was right about the ghosts.

Unfortunately, Ballow was wrong about me. I was irresponsible. You fall in love with perhaps half a dozen people in your life, and a like number of people fall in love with you. But the affections are rarely mutual and almost never contemporary. It is the most irresponsible thing that can be done to let such a coincidence pass and not act upon it. Of course, I didn't know that. I thought that the world was infinitely supplied with romances and that I would be the willing recipient of each in its turn. I was very young. But ignorance of natural law is a weaker excuse even than ignorance of the criminal code.

I was in love with Juanita, but any man would have been. In fact, quite a few were. The remarkable thing was that she loved me. She asked me questions about myself (one sure way to tell). "Where were you on this day exactly ten years ago?" "What were you like when you were twelve?" She read my poetry. She even said she liked it. And she was the only person who has ever thought I was beautiful. I was sleeping one afternoon, naked on top of the bed, and woke to find her drawing me. On her sketch pad I was an Adonis, which I was not. She loved me. She wanted us to live together until we died. She wanted to have a baby. I gave her a puppy instead. She wanted to get married. But I was a poor kid and I could see the future. Me with a teacher's salary and her at home with the kids—a sea of small debts, rented homes, and used cars stretched out before us, a life like my parents' or hers. I'd get bald. She'd get fat. The kids would get in trouble. I was too cowardly to go through with it. And I was not yet nineteen. I'd never made love to anyone but Juanita. I wanted to fuck all the women in the world. So I did not do the decent thing and make her breasts and belly swell and buy a pair of matching goldlike rings. I didn't even treat her very well. I took her kindnesses for granted and yelled when there were no clean shirts. It's difficult to find someone who loves you, even more difficult not to abuse her for doing so.

So Juanita and I lived in the carriage house. And I was very happy, whether I knew it or not. The house creaked and pounded and made footfall noises, but the ghosts never harmed us, until March. We were asleep on our mattress in the loft when, about three in the morning, I awoke with a fit of coughing that turned into a retching gag. I got up from the bed and tripped over the unconscious puppy. The air in the room was thick and sickening with fumes from the oil burner. I shook the dog, but it wouldn't wake. Then I shook Juanita, but she was unconscious too. I got her under one arm and the puppy under the other and went down the ladder. I don't know how. I'm not a strong person, and Juanita, although small, certainly weighed a hundred pounds. With her in one hand and the dog in the other, that left no hand at all for the ladder rungs. But I did do it. Crying and choking, I got them out the door and slapped Juanita until she came to. We went naked through the streets to a friend's house. There were little blue crescents at the base of Juanita's nails. She was sick for several days, and the puppy nearly died. It was an unnerving experience. The more so since the oil burner hadn't been lit for three weeks.

I suppose we didn't entirely escape the curse. What happened between Juanita and me the next year was unpleasant, maybe tragic. Forrester didn't escape it either. He was drafted and killed at Hue. And Ballow's estimate of his own depravity was overblown, it seems, for he drank himself to death that summer.

A Perfect Couple

met Iris Carr in the fall of 1965. I was sitting down when I saw her, and at first glance she seemed to be all legs. Of course this was impossible, but there was more than the ordinary amount of leg to her and more than the ordinary amount of breast and shiny black hair, and, though she did not have more than the ordinary amount of face, the face she had was more than ordinarily striking. She seemed larger than life and, in fact, was considerably larger than the average female example of it. She was literally a great beauty.

She caused me to whistle—not a wolf whistle but the whistle that sometimes happens by accident with a sharp intake of breath. She heard me, too, and was gracious about it, smiled politely, sat down two seats away in the college lecture hall and arranged herself with that female inward folding of limbs. I saw her there every Monday, Wednesday, and

Friday at three in the afternoon. We spoke, and she was friendly in a composed and remote fashion. I became fascinated by her. But though I was just eighteen then and my sexual fantasies were constant and catholic, Iris did not enter them—not even when I tried to concentrate on her remarkable form. She was just too fundamental and overwhelming, almost frightening in her femininity. I could no more stimulate myself with thoughts of a lubricious Iris Carr than a pious Athenean could have jacked off over the goddess Diana.

But she was amazing to look at. And she had a husband to match. Trevor Carr was rugged and handsome—too handsome. He was aware of being too handsome, and this made him too rugged. He was putting them both through college by modeling for menswear advertisements. He stood six feet four at least and exhibited more postures and attitudes of masculinity than are necessary except in times of national emergency. His speech and manner toward Iris were emphatic, dominant, and possessive. She responded with equanimity. People said they were a perfect couple. Perhaps they were. They were a little too vivid, like all perfect things, and like all perfect things they were destined for destruction. (And it is invariably satisfying to note that all perfect things are destined for destruction. Unfortunately, all imperfect things are destined for destruction also.)

But Iris was lonely. She said so to me. She called it being bored. "I'm so bored," she said. "My husband doesn't like to go out." She was too beautiful to have women friends, and I gathered that Trevor was too jealous to let her be friends with a man. So when Iris and Trevor were seen, they were seen together. Trevor even began to audit those of Iris's classes where he wasn't already enrolled. After that, she still smiled at me, but she didn't say much.

Iris was from Oregon. Trevor was from New York. They had both come to the school in Ohio two years before. They met during the first week of their freshman year, dated steadily for six months, and were married. They rented a house on the edge of campus. On holidays and breaks, Trevor flew east to be photographed and Iris flew west to see her family.

Anyone who watched Iris—and I watched Iris as much as decency and Geology 101 allowed—could see she was restless. And anyone who watched Trevor—and if you watched Iris, you could not help watching Trevor—could see that he was restless also. He didn't seem to be interested in other women, and he was too busy keeping Iris away from men to make friends with any of them. I believe he was as lonely as she.

In the spring of 1966 Iris did something to solve at least her own isolation by making friends with Gary Ballow. Ballow was an ex-student, in his late twenties, and a soi-disant writer, though really more of a budding alcoholic, living on an allowance he received from his family with the stipulation that he never set foot in Grosse Pointe, Michigan, again. But, more important, he was a homosexual. Therefore he could associate with Iris to Trevor's heart's content. Iris began to divide her time between Trevor and Gary. She'd spend her evenings at Gary's apartment while Trevor fiddled with his gun collection. Ballow was a smart man and a lover of beauty and perfection in everything except his personal habits. He told people that Iris was a girl who could be "shaped into the mythic dimensions of womanhood." It is something I've never understood about homosexuals, their interest in the mythic dimensions of womanhood, who have so little use for real women. But, anyway, because of Gary's acquaintance or through his tutelage or something, Iris changed. She became more lively, talkative, more typically womanish. I guess one would say she gained self-confidence. And, what is even rarer in a beautiful woman, she gained some degree of wit. I remember her telling Trevor one night in the J-Bar, where we all spent our evenings, "Why don't you go *flirt* with someone, Trevor—it would pep things up and do wonders for everyone's opinion of you." Trevor did not laugh, but he went off to play the pinball machine, leaving me and two other young men alone with Iris for the first time I could recall. But it was curious to me that Iris's liveliness made her no less remote. She was one of those very unusual people who become more mysterious by being chatty and familiar than they do through silence and austerity of manner. But what was more curious was that Trevor did not dislike Gary. I had expected that Trevor, even if he approved of his wife's association with Ballow, would be uneasy with the man himself. But this wasn't so. Trevor would fulminate in general about "fags" and "cocksuckers," but he seemed to genuinely like this example of the kind. And Gary was polite enough or careful enough not to make fun of Trevor's exaggerated masculinity. Gary told Trevor that Trevor was not his type. He said he liked cute and sissy little blond fellows. This was a lie, but Trevor believed it, and he was safe to do so. Ballow wasn't interested in Trevor. No one but Iris ever was, not even as a friend. Once Trevor had been relieved of shielding Iris from all things heterosexual and thus joined in the normal male pursuits of the town, he proved to be a companion of no merit. He couldn't hold his liquor and didn't have a thought in his head. This combined poorly with his heavy drinking and penchant for endless talk. It also amused him to start fights and amused him more to let others finish them. He wasn't even a good hunting or fishing pal. He insisted on dry-fly thrashings at the runoff from the local reservoir—water that was populated only by bullhead and carp. He hunted pheasants as though these animals were a danger to the natives' livestock. And during deer season he was a considerable danger to the natives' livestock himself. But Trevor seemed happy. And Iris seemed happy. And Gary seemed happy, too. Iris's poise was elevated by double attentiveness. Gary's style was decorated by two attractive people. And Trevor's aggression was emphasized by twin examples of apparent passivity. They made their own miniature social set, and their names ran together as a compound noun, and by the next year they all talked alike. If one met them separately, they would each say the same thing. Iris would say it in a womanly manner. Trevor would say it in a manly manner. And Ballow would say it as it had been said in the first place.

That fall, in 1966, a young man named Jack Becker returned from Vietnam and enrolled at the college. He'd been a Green Beret sergeant and this had not been a pleasant experience. He was a funny-looking guy, full of nervous energy, and tremendously glad to be back in the United States. He was in college, he said, because it was the closest thing to doing nothing that he could find and that his GI benefits would pay for. He was in a nearly constant state of euphoria, more than a little of it chemically induced. He didn't give a damn about anything now but having fun, he said, and he was certainly open to any suggested activity remotely construable as that. He insisted on drinking at every hour of the day, and could not resist any drug no matter how loathsome its effects were known to be—he'd juxtapose it to the leeches and clap of Indochina and pronounce the narcotic delectable of sensation by comparison. He bought a huge Harley-Davidson motorcycle and drove it worse and faster than anyone I've ever seen and right into people's houses out of pure good fellowship and eagerness of greeting. And for sex he'd do anything also, sometimes flopping backward over a table at the J-Bar, pulling out his reproductive organs, and yelling, "Take me! Anyone!" adding with some wistfulness, "But gently."

Jack was an appealing character. He had actually been somewhere. Most of us had only been to college. He had had real and violent, dangerous adult experiences involving not just death (which seems familiar to the romantic adolescent mind) but responsibility (which does not). And not only had he been out in the world, but he had come back from it acting more like us than we did. This was affirming. Also, opposition to the war in Indochina was then beginning to eclipse civil rights as the chief orthodoxy of the nonconformists. Iris said the draft was "an invitation from people we have not met to go to a place of which we've never heard in order to shoot people whom we do not know. And, what's worse," she said, "they are expected to shoot back." Whatever, it was an issue that touched home. Becker's firsthand opinion of the thing confirmed our most dreadful hopes. Everyone liked him.

Everyone liked Becker, and Becker liked everyone, but he liked Iris best. *"That is a white woman,"* he said, the first time he saw her. It was the middle of the day. Iris didn't say anything. They walked out of the bar together and didn't come back for three hours. It was clear, in a general way, where they went. Specifically, they went to my house, where my girlfriend and I were taking a nap. We got up and gave them the bed. It was an urgent case. Then we sat on the lawn and listened to them. Jack made a great deal of noise, and, surprisingly, so did Iris. But the sounds that Iris made were the only dignified lovemaking noises I have ever heard. They were chilling.

Iris and Jack's affair was passionate to the point of psychotic compulsion and fully public because Jack had no fixed home and bedded down wherever he could and so did he and Iris. They were continually being walked in on and caught in the bedrooms, bathrooms, living rooms, and any other rooms of acquaintances and half strangers (Iris was always said to look quite composed on these occasions). They were at my house almost daily and I know that was only one of a dozen places they regularly went. Jack must have been a man of great biological capabilities. And more than a little daring—they were reported by one person or another as having achieved the act of congress in the most remarkable places: in a tree, for instance, or in the beer cooler at the J-Bar, or on a piano in the music building, or from the back through a gap in Iris's skirt while packed in a crowd at a football game, or in the foot well of a sympathetic graduate instructor's desk while the instructor conferred with a student on a midterm paper. They screwed everywhere but on crowded street corners in broad daylight, and some people said they did it there. One person even claimed to have seen them rolling down the highway on Jack's motorcycle with Iris nude from the waist down holding the handlebars and Jack sliding into her from the jump seat. But I don't think this last thing was true. Iris was not the kind of girl who would have known how to shift gears on a motorcycle.

Iris and Jack's affair was so obvious that even a husband must have noticed it. And Trevor was still a very jealous man. But this jealousy did not extend to Jack any more than it did to Gary Ballow. Jack was Trevor's hero. Trevor was always pestering him for details about military ordnance, rates of fire, and types of explosives, about tactical details and strategies, and always asking him to tell war stories. There was only one war story Becker had any interest in telling, and he was tired of telling that. He'd hated the Vietnamese, he said. The ones on our side weren't on our side and the ones who weren't on our side were a nasty bunch. He had been out on patrol once in an area more hostile than most when something moved in the brush. The point man of his squad and another soldier emptied four or five clips into the shrubbery. A rifle and the body of an eight- or nine-year-old girl fell out onto the path. Perhaps she was carrying the rifle somewhere for someone, or perhaps she really meant to plunk a GI, though there was more gun than girl. Anyway, when Becker got to the front of his squad, the two soldiers were standing beside the body, arguing. Jack said he assumed they were accusing each other of killing the child. He said he couldn't now imagine why he'd thought that, but that was what had occurred to him at the time. They were not accusing each other. They were quarreling about who had made the kill and who would get to search the body for papers. There were no papers, said Becker. She was just a little girl. She didn't even have pockets to put papers in. It was a pathetic sight. She'd been a pretty little girl, too. And if she'd really meant to kill them, then it was a very pathetic sight indeed, sickening and horrid. The soldiers kept arguing and Jack said he felt, all of a sudden, caught in the middle of something without beginning or end. He said he felt awful.

"Boy, war *must* be awful," said Trevor one night when he'd had Jack tell the story for the half-dozenth time. "What kind of gun did she have?" Several times I noticed Trevor using mannerisms or patterns of speech that were definitely Jack's. The only trouble Trevor gave Iris and Jack was by tagging along. This resulted in some extraordinary scenes. Jack once fucked her while they were supposed to be playing pinball in a dark corner of the J-Bar, Iris bent over the machine with her slacks down, trying to keep the bells and buzzers going and an eye on her husband at the bar. Another time, I heard, Jack had Iris in the same way, or at least effected penetration, while they both leaned out the window and talked to Trevor as he mowed the lawn.

Gary Ballow wasn't jealous of Jack's affair with Iris either. He fell in love with Jack himself. Becker didn't mind. By Christmas he and Gary were sleeping together also. Becker was as fond of Ballow as he was impassioned with Iris. I thought this the first time I saw Jack read a book. And I was sure of it when I heard him say something about Artemis and Leto and "the Great Mother of the Gods." That was not how Becker had talked when I first met him. It was a less obstreperous affair than his relationship with Iris, but, again, it was obvious what was going on. People even mentioned it to Trevor, though Trevor denied that he'd heard any such thing. And Ballow and Iris became more intimate than before, always whispering together. Someone later told me Gary and Iris tried to have intercourse but Gary couldn't do it. Now they both fucked Becker. But I did not hear that the three of them got in bed together. It was as though some peculiar delicacy or balance was being maintained. It was a juggling act I didn't understand.

Trevor, Jack, and Gary would also go around together sometimes, making as strange as possible a boys' night out—three people so diverse in character that it was hard to imagine them on the same planet let alone in the same booth at the J-Bar, and if Iris joined them, their peculiar personalities would turn more peculiar. Trevor would bellow louder, crack the tops off beer bottles, and drink from the jagged neck. Gary would turn viciously effeminate. And Jack's omnivorous good humor would reach to a pitch of hysteria. All the while, Iris grew ever more beautiful and remote and imaginary to those of us who weren't involved.

This situation endured for a remarkable length of time—that is, for about three months. Then it exploded. I don't know exactly what happened, but I had a theory and I heard a rumor and the rumor I heard was close enough to the theory I had for the both of them to stand together in the place of fact.

Trevor had made a pass at Gary. Maybe he sought to complete the circle. Maybe he was impressed by the facility with which emotional molecules can be rearranged. Maybe he thought the polarities of human relationships were so easily reversed. Or maybe he was just queer. It was Trevor, of course, not Gary, who reacted with shock to what Trevor did. Iris was giving a party that night, with mostly Becker's friends there. Trevor ran down into the basement and locked himself in and began shooting through the floorboards at the guests with a submachine gun. Fortunately it was only a .22-caliber replica of an old-fashioned Thompson—one of those things that in those days could be bought through the mail and which Trevor had converted to fully automatic fire. The slugs didn't have enough force to penetrate the hardwood parquet squares. Here and there a little leaden nose would poke up through some splinters. That was all. But the guests panicked and ran out of the house. And when they did, Trevor fired out the basement windows after them. But these windows were sunk into deep wells along the foundation and Trevor could not shoot out of them except almost straight up and was only able to shatter a streetlight. Iris began to yell at him in language that cannot be reproduced. Now, there is no longer any such thing as language too strong to be printed, though Iris's was very strong. It was the even, ladylike tone in which she delivered her invective that defies replication. She told Trevor what she thought of him and she told him what everyone thought of him and what Jack thought of him and what she and Jack had been doing and what Jack and Ballow had been doing, and I think she was about to start in on what he had been about to do with Gary when Becker went crazy, which he did with a heart-stopping howl, a sort of terrible scream, and then animal hollering. He went through the hedges and over the neighboring backyard fences as though pursued by something awful, or in pursuit of it, I couldn't tell which. Then Trevor came out of the cellar bulkhead unarmed and said, "Is there something the matter with Jack?" Jack clambered a mile across town through garden plots and clotheslines to my house. He took my shotgun from the corner of the living room and the whole night long performed a frenzied zigzag of advances or retreats through the town's shrubbery. About fifty people called the police, who assumed, and were not told otherwise, that it was Jack who had shot up Iris and Trevor's basement. They called out every member of the force, and the university's security guards and the volunteer fire department besides, and cordoned off everything they could think to cordon off and threw up barricades whenever it occurred to them and launched a general dragnet of alleys and shrubbery. But on any warm spring night in a college town there are so many youngsters running wild through backyards and making loud noises that the search came to nothing and the police found only a few half-dressed dates and some adolescents poisoned by beer. I guess

Becker was acting out his combat experiences. Or maybe he was acting out the combat experiences of others. Perhaps he was even acting out combat experiences dating well back into the previous century, because when I finally retrieved my old Belgian side-by-side—my only possession of any value—it was stuffed with leaves and dirt that had been rammed down the barrels with a beanpole or a stick, as though it were a muzzle loader. Becker quieted down about dawn and went back to Ballow's apartment and hid under a bed. Iris seemed to hold Ballow responsible for her husband's behavior or Jack's or her own, or for something. Anyway, she went over there at nine that morning and hauled Becker out from under the bed and took him away. I don't know what she said to Ballow, but it must have affected him, because when she and Jack left he tried to commit suicide by throwing himself out his apartment window. He ran straight at the closed casement and burst through the glass. This cut him badly, but it did not kill him, because he rented the first floor of a duplex and fell about two feet into a flower bed. So he went back inside and threw himself through another window and repeated this action until every window on his floor of the house had been smashed. Finally he threw himself through the storm door and lay unconscious in splashes of blood on the front porch. I think it was Trevor who took him to the hospital.

Jack didn't stay with Iris very long. Later that afternoon he got away and reenlisted at the post office. Then he disappeared. I suppose he went back to Vietnam. No one ever heard of him again. Trevor checked into a motel on the edge of town that night and shot himself through the roof of the mouth. Ballow recovered from his cuts, but by August he had drunk himself to death. Something awful should have happened to Iris also, to round out the story, but she finished school that spring and moved to Boston, where she married a wealthy older man. They live on Beacon Hill to this day and summer at Lambert's Cove.

An Atheist in the Foxhole

I got an unexpected phone call last October from a friend of mine, Calvert Fell. Calvert is a native of Maryland, a banker and a sportsman. It was not like him to be more than a skillful shot away from the Eastern Shore during duck season. But he said his son and the son's wife had bought land in Vermont an hour's drive from my place. "Come over," said Calvert. "I'm being bored to death."

This son is about my age, but I had never met him. I think he'd gone to school somewhere in the West and been in the Peace Corps for several years.

Calvert was not being bored to death, of course, but he was being bored into a very bad mood. And that's worse as far as Calvert is concerned since, he says, there is nothing dramatic about facing a bad mood with dignity. The son, named Charles, called Chuckie, and the wife, Ana (two short *a*'s), were lacto-ovo vegetarians, did not allow smoking in their house, and brewed their own beer, which tasted like nothing so much as bread dough dissolved in mud.

I had hoped Calvert and I could find some beaver ponds to jump-shoot. But the National Rifle Association decal on the windshield of my Jeep sent Chuckie into a soliloquy on firearm registration. And after that I didn't have the nerve to get the guns out. Calvert and I spent a gray afternoon around a kitchen table half-stripped of perfectly good paint discussing green woodstoves with the junior Fells. Chuckie and Ana said green wood was an excellent fuel. The chilly room argued otherwise. At last the baby (born six weeks before the wedding, named Dovē, sex not determined) needed something. I could swear the parents said "aerobic dance exercise," but that can't be true, or can it? Anyway Calvert and I were free for an hour to wander the grounds or whatever one calls 175 acres of former Christmas tree farm and abandoned gravel quarry.

We peeked into the unfinished chicken coop. Leghorn hens nested in the sawdust and hand tools. "God knows what they're going to serve for dinner," said Calvert. I invited him to come back with me and have a steak. "No, no," he said, "I couldn't do that. Charles, that is, Chuck and I are just beginning to see eye to eye again."

"I didn't know you'd had a falling-out with your son."

"Oh, nothing like that. We just didn't see eye to eye for ten or fifteen years." Calvert kicked at a large box trap on the chicken coop floor. It was baited with soy protein. "Take this thing, for instance," he said. "This is how he's going to catch a fox—because he 'doesn't like to take a life.' Even assuming there is a fox dumb enough to crawl into this, what's going to happen? He'll take the fox out. The fox will come back and get in the trap. He'll take the fox out. The fox will come back. He'll take the fox out . . ."

I admitted it was too humane for me.

"Before," said Calvert, "he and I wouldn't have seen eye to eye about a thing like this."

"You mean you agree with him?"

"Absolutely. He believes he's being moral. I believe he's being stupid. We're in perfect agreement." Calvert sat down on the box trap. "But a few years ago we would have had a huge fight."

"Really? Over a fox?"

"Oh, yes," said Calvert. "You know how it is with my generation. We can be very stout-headed. Why, I know about a man who got in a fight with his son over a fox—a much worse fight than that. He was Master of Hounds at the Carroll County Hunt Club."

I got a bottle of Scotch from the Jeep. Fox hunting is something I have no notion of, and a long story about it can be worse than a syndicated bridge column. "I hear the members drink a lot," I said, hoping to change the subject.

"Haven't been there for years," said Calvert and he made a dismissive wave with my whiskey bottle to indicate he had begun a tale. "Anyway, this man was a really avid hunter. And his son was an awful hippie sort of fellow."

More or less involuntarily, I glanced toward the house.

"Oh much worse than that. A great hairy sort of mystical hippie always talking about Hindu people and how President what's-his-name was going to be reincarnated as a goat. Which I personally don't doubt. But be that as it may, he was positively the worst son I ever saw a man have. He and his father were always arguing. They argued about politics. They argued about drugs. They argued about the right to ownership of private property. And finally they got in an enormous, really monstrous, argument about religion."

"I thought it was about a fox."

Calvert took a large drink. "Furry little animals, religion—all comes to the same thing. If you know what I mean."

I didn't.

"Where was I? Well, it was right there at the Hunt Club. I can't think why they let the boy in, except his father was so rich. And that was just what he was yelling at his father about. Said his father was 'too rich to know God.' I'm afraid the son had a point. The old man was completely unreligious. I don't think he'd ever had a metaphysical thought in his life. And, no doubt about it, wealth makes materialism easier to bear. But that doesn't excuse the boy's manners—telling his

93

father he was too rich in front of half the money in Maryland. Then he began to shout that this was why his father and his father's friends had killed all those people in Nagasaki and were killing them again just then in Vietnam. (Though I assure you not a single person the father knew had had a role in government since Willkie was defeated.)

"The boy just would not shut up. He said he'd studied real religion and all the mystical truths of the East and so on. He claimed he understood the sanctity and eternal existence of the soul in all its forms or something like that. And then he turned on everyone in the room and shrieked, 'Fox hunting! Fox hunting is just what I'd expect out of a lot of murderers like you! Why the fox is a million times more in tune with the universe than you are, a more developed being on any scale!'

"By this time the father had had enough. He picked the son up by the scruff of the neck and marched him out into the parking lot, meaning to bang his head against the side of the station car. But as soon as they were alone the son lowered his voice and said, 'You may be strong, but you don't have the power of enlightenment.' Well, this was said in such a confident and uncharacteristically dangerous-sounding way that the father let go. Whereupon the son did and said some kind of oddball Oriental thing and turned the Master of Hounds into a fox himself right there practically in the suburbs of Baltimore."

I took the bottle back from Calvert.

"Well, that's how the father tells it," he said and took the bottle back from me. "Of course he ended up being hunted, not a week later, too, and by his own hounds and his own former friends. You can imagine how he felt."

"Must have been interesting."

"Exactly!" said Calvert. "He loved it! You know how built up Maryland is getting? It didn't take long for this new fox to get his pack and the crowd of hunters into some very unfamiliar territory indeed. He ran them right through a shopping center. Mrs. Elmer Buxley and young Burton Combs were both unhorsed in a Sears Muffler Center. Elliot Templeton rode through the window of Hertzenfeld's Jewelry

Store and was shot dead by Mr. Hertzenfeld, who was later let off by the courts when it was discovered that he'd been forced by his wife to take an entire Cub Scout pack to see *The Wild Bunch* the night before.

"Half a dozen of the hounds ran into the Golden Dragon Inn and never emerged. Two others jumped on a woman in a fox stole and were killed by her schnauzer. Mrs. Arnholt Fricks had a very fine Irish hunter that took a magnificent jump at a Chevy Suburban it mistook for a five-bar gate. They got tangled in the luggage rack and were last seen headed for Silver Spring with a load of marigold flats.

"The fox, that is the Master of Hounds, hid in the men's cologne department of Wanamaker's, completely disguised by test atomizers of Brut and Canoe. And the rest of the pack was eventually run over on I-95.

"Of course the hippie son felt terrible about all this carnage. He dropped the mystical nonsense immediately and took up a more prosaic form of hippieness—something in the organic gardening line, I think."

Calvert handed me the Scotch bottle and picked up a hen from on top of a Skil saw. He stroked its feathers absently. "What happened to the fox?" I said.

"Oh, the spell wore off eventually," said Calvert, and he bent over and took a huge bloody bite out of the live chicken's back.

Days of Wage

National Lampoon

1972–1981

The National Lampoon *was founded in 1970 by Doug Kenney, Henry Beard, and Rob Hoffman. I started to write for the magazine as a free-lancer when I first came to New York and was hired full-time in 1973, starting out in low puns, working my way up through rude japes, wisecracks, and witty ripostes until I finally became editor in chief. The National Lampoon was my writing education, and it gave me the one academic idea I've ever had. If I wind up a drunk hack with nothing left to say and nowhere to say it (well, when I do), I intend to follow in the weaving footsteps of many a better scribbler and get a job teaching creative writing at college. Then I will assign the kids nothing but parodies. First, this will spare me from reading endless sensitive, self-obsessed, first-person mewling (vide previous section of present volume). And, second, it will teach the whelps to write. At the National Lampoon we parodied every type and style of prose. To do this it was necessary for us to understand the construction and workings of the objects of ridicule. My job was that of an aspiring watchmaker disassembling a fine timepiece. There I was with a thing of value and beauty, pulling it apart, ruining it for everyone, scattering small, useless springs and gears of irony and derision all over the literary workbench, and . . . Perhaps I should go back to the National Lampoon and study metaphor.*

A Few Thoughts on Humor and Humorists

Foreword to a 1980 *National Lampoon* anthology

The most important thing in life is to have a sense of humor. A sense of humor is more important than food, because if you have a sense of humor, you can laugh even though you're starving, while if you laugh too hard on a full stomach, you'll throw up.

It's often said that "laughter is the best medicine." This actually isn't true. Penicillin is the best medicine, followed by tetracycline and the sulfa drugs. But, judging by what a joke the Carter administration's State Department turned out to be, laughter *is* the best foreign policy. In fact, laughter serves many purposes. Laughter is the way we cope with conflicting emotions. For example, your mother is dying of cancer. You're sorry she's dying, but she's been in pain, so you're also relieved by the prospect of her imminent demise. Why not kid her about it? Put on a little skit—wear her bedpan on your head and use

the oxygen tent noises to pretend you're Darth Vader. Laughter allevi-
ates fear, too. Your mother really won't mind dying now, especially if
the bedpan was full and she saw you stick your head in it.

Humor can be an effective substitute for aggression, the way it was
for Roberto Duran in the second Sugar Ray Leonard match. Sugar Ray
may have won the fight, but it was Duran everybody laughed at. And
humor can also be used as a defense. Humor was used as a defense in
the trial of Richard Speck. Speck's attorneys claimed their client should
be freed because one of the investigating officers, upon entering the
building where all the dead nurses were found, was heard to say, "There's
something funny going on here."

Still, what is amusing to one person may seem simply squashed
flat and run over in the road to another. And what is considered unat-
tractive and sad by some may be peeled up and sailed through the window of the girl's gym by others. What do we really mean by the word
humor? Consider the following list of common colloquial phrases
involving mirth:

When people say:	They actually mean:
"That's funny."	*"That's not funny."*
"Don't make me laugh."	*"That's not funny."*
"That's not funny."	*"That's funny."*
"She has a wonderful sense of humor."	*"Don't make me laugh."*

Yet there are many things that *do* make people laugh, and sometimes people laugh for no apparent reason. For instance, let's examine
a room full of teenage girls at a slumber party. They are all giggling.
Let's examine them very carefully. (We'll say we're doctors, or something.) What are these girls giggling about? They're probably discussing
sex. Perhaps their humor is a means of coping with fear, like the time
you spilled a bedpan all over your dying mother. But there's no reason
for young girls to be afraid of sex. We'll be gentle. Of course, unless
they've been naughty already, it's still going to hurt a little bit. So maybe
they're using humor as a defense mechanism like Richard Speck did.

But Richard Speck was convicted. And we will be too if that was Mom and Dad who just pulled in the driveway.

Even if the causes of laughter cannot be exactly defined, there are still several recognizable types of humorous activity. There is *parody,* when you make fun of people who are smarter than you; *satire,* when you make fun of people who are richer than you; and *burlesque,* when you make fun of both while taking off your clothes. But the key to all types of humor probably lies in the folk saying "I didn't know whether to laugh or cry," or possibly in the folk saying "I didn't know whether to shit or go blind." The latter would seem to be an easy choice, but the truly funny person may have trouble making up his mind. For a real humorist is a special sort of person, a man apart, different from the rest of us. He brings to everyone around him the wonderful and unexpected gift of laughter. Think of him this way: If all the world were a church and all the people in the world were silent prayers going up to heaven, the humorist would be a fart from the pulpit.

Unpaid Bills

by Truman Garbage

There have been more tears shed
over unpaid bills than over any others.
—The Author's Accountant

Editor's Note: For some years now, Mr. Garbage has been devoting his
time exclusively to the writing of a major novel, *Unpaid Bills.* Several
excerpts from this work-in-progress have already appeared in other
publications: most notably, "Le Boeuf et Brew, 1965," which told the
tale of a wealthy society matron whose breath was murder, and "Red
Desert," the story of a woman who deliberately left her blind husband in a Michelangelo Antonioni movie. More recently, we have
been treated to the appearance in print of "Horrible Icky People,"
"Part of the Middle and Some of the End of My Big New Book,"
and "Sky King's Niece, Penny." Now, the honor of publishing
Mr. Garbage's latest segment of *Unpaid Bills* has fallen to the
National Lampoon. Therefore, without further comment, even though

it doesn't seem to be quite finished and really could use a lot of work, we are pleased to present . . .

La Rent Est Due

"Coco Chanel used to fart in bed and pull the sheets up over her nose." It was Mrs. Important Last Name, "Impy" to her friends, who was doing the talking—a big, breezy, peppy broad built exactly like a man in every detail, and raised on a ranch in Cleveland. We were sitting in the good booth next to the steam table in Le Café au Lait. Outside, it was a day filled with [adverb adjective adverb adverb adjective], but inside the hallowed precincts of Le Café, all was [use *tout le monde, art deco,* and *snobbisme*—especially *snobbisme*]. Le Café is owned by Monsieur au Lait, the same fabled restaurateur who for years ran La Côte of Brisket—that landmark of *très chic* where ordinary rich people or garden variety celebrities were merely shown to a comfortable table and served a delicious meal, but where the truly, truly select were made to squat outdoors on the sidewalk and eat offal. Le Café is a more casual restaurant—a simple seat close to the men's room is enough to show the esteem in which you're held by its proprietor, and Impy and I could see every inch of the urinals (not that many men pee standing up in Le Café).

Lee Radziwill came in the door, and was shown to a table with Andrew Mellon, Dick Van Dyke, Garry and Pierre Trudeau, and Baron Rothschild-Lafite. Le Café is a quiet bastion of wealth, a watering hole for the world's great fortunes, a culinary retreat at midday for the well-heeled and the well-fixed. And Impy could afford it. This was her milieu. She had married a doctor.

Brandon De Wilde was seated next to us with Alice Roosevelt Longworth and Countess Maria Ties. Monty Python came in with Houghton Mifflin and Tatum O'Neal. Charo was having cocktails with Anheuser Busch, the young brewery heir. And Merrill Lynch, Pierce Fenner, Jean Shrimpton, and Ralston Purina arrived with a very prominent woman who's the Queen of England. Carol Channing had been there yesterday.

Impy and I were having brunch together—a sort of combination breakfast and lunch—but when Monsieur au Lait glided to our table with menu in hand, Impy regally waved him away, ordering instead bottle after bottle of [call Byron over at *Esquire* and get the name of that really expensive kind of Cold Duck].

My name is P. J. Clarke, and I'm of two minds—whether to skillfully weave my personal history into the warp and woof of a subtle plot structure that evolves through the play and counterplay of mimetic imagery to reveal my narrative point of view as an integral part of this literary work, or whether to just dump my life story into your lap out of sheer lack of writing ability.

I've been peddling my ass since before I could walk. When I was six months old, I was already performing sex acts for money, or even for a change of diapers. I wouldn't shit in my potty unless somebody gave me a quarter. I said, "If you want the kinky stuff, you're going to have to pay." Later, when I was growing up, I wouldn't jack off unless I found money under the couch cushions. I'd suck the legs of a chair just to sit down. There was nothing I wouldn't do, and where I grew up, everybody was queer, too. All the kids in the neighborhood were queer. The nuns at school were queer. A lot of the trees and plants in our yard were queer. My dad was queer—the only way he could get Mom pregnant was to blow himself and spit at her ass. I even had queer toys. I let my teddy bear fuck me. But he had to give me his little button eyes first. You bet he did.

Then, when I was four, I ran away from home and this real rich man was passing by in his jet airplane and gave me a lift. He had me stick beans in his ears with my peter. He was really in love with me, and gave me bundles of money and took me all over the world. We went yachting in Aspen and skied the Riviera, and he taught me all the really important things to know if you're going to be friends with high society types, like that you're supposed to keep the napkins and wash them and use them over again, and don't wear a blue suit without socks. Since then, I've been everywhere, even Europe, and always hung around with really, really rich people who just adore me because I'm so good-looking and have lots of manners even though right now I'm living in the YMCA and am a male whore. Or was, until I got this job as the self-conscious motor-mouthed narrator in Truman's new novel just in case anybody sues. That's why it's really important to remember that I'm very good-looking. That way, you won't get me mixed up with Truman. I'm really good-looking and people pay to fuck me, so this can't possibly be Truman's thinly disguised real life story, because can you imagine anybody paying to fuck Truman? *That* would be perverted.

Actually, Truman wasn't so bad-looking when he was young, but he sold his soul in a Polish Dorian Gray deal. He made an agreement with the devil so that the photograph on the back of his first novel's dust jacket will always remain exactly the same, and all the horrible disgusting stuff happens to him.

Over the empty Cold Duck bottles, Impy begins a fascinating story of scandal and intrigue, all completely true, involving Lauren Bacall, the Tate–La Bianca killings, and three presidents of the United States. None of the names have been changed, either. It begins in the August 1968 *Esquire* and continues in February and June 1969, then in *Argosy* (May 1970), *McCall's* (December 1971), *Commonweal* (March 1973), *The Kansas City Star* Sunday magazine section (September 15, 1975), and ends as a poem in last week's *New Yorker.* Though you probably won't be able to make heads or tails out of it without referring to the October 1968 *Redbook* "Short Short Story Complete on These Two Pages."

In the meantime, I listen to the conversations buzzing around me. I could just overhear Wallis Simpson, huddled with Margaux Hemingway and Ford Maddox Ford, whispering the story of Judge Crater. "Changed his name to Karter," she intoned, "and had a chain of car washes in Buffalo and Rochester—'Karter's Kar Kleen,' I think they're called. Son by his second marriage still runs them. Never found out who his old man really was."

Two tables away, Stavros Niarchos was tête-à-tête with Mrs. Robert Taft. "It was never really a government spy mission," she was saying, "she was just supposed to keep her eyes open. But she *was* captured. Naturally, they treated her very respectfully. 'Missy Ealhalt this . . .' and 'Missy Ealhalt that. . . .' She was really rather enjoying herself, I'd say. Died of intestinal blockage in 1944, in Kyoto."

Closer to our left, Bianca Jagger and the president of General Motors discussed assassinations. "Actually," sighed Bianca, "the second gunman was one floor down in the Book Depository and three windows to the left—Sergio Conners, a half-Mexican, half-Irish guy. The same fellow who shot Marty King."

"Oh, yeah. I remember him," said the president.

"Well, he lives right over in Queens, 35-06 Woodside Avenue, Apartment 9 or 10L, I can never remember which."

Farther away but still audible were Esther Williams and Nadia Comaneci chatting with Nelson Rockefeller (whose close friends call him "Deep Throat"). Esther was telling them about the real Howard Hughes will: "Sizable trust funds for the family, of course, but the bulk of the estate's left to the Air and Space Museum at the Smithsonian. It's all perfectly signed and witnessed and notarized, and it's in the Ogden, Utah, Public Library, tucked inside the flyleaf of *World Enough and Time* by Robert Penn Warren. But it's been ages since anybody checked out one of Bobby's books."

"You know that story, 'The Lady or the Tiger?' The one by Frank Stockton?" I was listening again to Wally Simpson. "Well, he gets the lady. The man in the iron mask was just some petty noble who killed his wig maker. He wore that mask all the time because he had a harelip. And the last five bars of Schubert's 'Unfinished Symphony' go like this:

It was just the usual small talk of the very rich, who are indeed different from you and me—they have tails. Little short ones with smooth silky hairs, right at the base of the spine. If you ever want to know whether somebody is very rich or not, just pull down their pants. If they're very rich, they'll have a tail. No kidding.

Impy orders more Cold Duck. I ponder life: Dean Martin doesn't drink nearly as much as he pretends to. But William Faulkner used to drink a lot. So did F. Scott Fitzgerald. Cole Porter was queer. None of the other Beatles like John's wife, Yoko. Gertrude Stein and Alice B. Toklas were lesbians. Don Rickles insults everybody all the time, but in private, he's really a kindhearted guy. Somerset Maugham was queer. President Eisenhower had an affair with his female chauffeur during World War II. Elton John is queer. Tyrone Power was actually very short. David Bowie is queer, and I think Paul Lynde is, but I'm not sure. Anyway, *Hollywood Squares* is all rehearsed ahead of time. Janis Joplin used to take a lot of pills. And Princess Margaret wants a divorce. James Baldwin is queer.

I know these things because of all the really famous and important people that I hang out with all the time, and the only reason that I'm living at the Y and being a male prostitute is because something *really, really* terrible happened to me, but I don't know what it was because Truman left the plot outline on a bus. But I'll tell you something I *do* know. I know that this isn't parody. I mean, what you're reading right now. Because parody implies some respect, however grudging, for what's being parodied. Parody pays its subject a backhanded compliment. This is not parody. This is Truman being dragged through the gutter and peed on by dogs. That's what they're doing to Truman. They're dousing him in kerosene, and setting him alight in a ditch. Metaphorically speaking, of course. But what do I care? I'm just the fag narrator. And anyway, you should see the movie deal. Whew!

Here's Truman's laundry list:

6 shirts (no starch)
1 bathrobe
12 bed sheets (presoak!)
5 prs. Bermuda shorts
8 prs. Jockey shorts size 52 ultrabrief
1 truss
2 dish towels
4 hankies

This book is the real stuff, all right. The real inside dirt. A lot of people have committed suicide since the first excerpt was published: an out-of-work electrician in Dayton, a teenage mother of four in Memphis, and a woman with incurable cancer in Maine. Just to name three. It's a *roman à clef,* you see. Truman's calling the bus company right now about the plot. Incidentally, there's no truth whatsoever in that rumor that lots of the writing is being done by a fifteen-year-old boy he picked up in the Greyhound station. Christ, I'm practically twenty.

Back in Le Café, all the famous people who ever lived on earth have just spilled the beans about everything you ever heard of. Monsieur au Lait has told a waiter to pick them up. Truman's tired now. He wants me to go help him make wee-wee. Is this 2,500 words yet? That's what we promised the *Lampoon.* Close enough for government work, huh?

continued on the moon

The Problem with Communism

Editorial from the 1979 "Politics" Issue

What's there to say about Communism, anyway? I mean, besides that it's bad and don't do any of it. We all know it's bad. It's bad because it's based on unsound socioeconomic premises, has no respect for individual liberty, produces a totalitarian autocracy in every example of its practical application as a system of government and plenty worse, besides. But that's not why it's *really* bad. Who cares about all that egghead guff? The real reason that Communism is bad is because it isn't any fun. It's no kicks, no giggles, no laughs—a nine-inning goose egg in the hoot-and-holler league. And there's a simple reason why that's so. Communism is no fun because of Communists.

Why, your Communist is the type of guy or gal who only cares about great big rights and wrongs—the really tremendous and large ones the size of whole countries and stuff. And there's nothing worse in the world than somebody who cares about rights and wrongs that big.

Now, everybody cares about regular rights and wrongs, rights and wrongs that are about our size. Your wife, for instance—just what has she been doing during the day? Do you think that's "wrong"? Would it be "right" to give her a pop in the yap? Everybody cares about rights and wrongs like that. That's only human. That's what keeps us from being like animals and only having rights and wrongs that you have to pee around the boundaries of to get established. Human beings should never have to pee on anything to establish their rights. That's written straight into the U.S. Constitution, I think, or should be. Incidentally, what your wife's doing *is* wrong and it's all right to hit her in most states so long as it doesn't leave a mark. But these other rights and wrongs, the really big kind, are a different matter. When people start getting thoughtful about these it just louses them up. That's because if you have a gigantic "right," well, it's just too big to ever really get to see much of. And if you have a huge "wrong," it's just too enormous to ever get it fixed. Whereas little rights and wrongs, the kind normal people like us have, aren't that fancy. I mean, sooner or later the old sow runs off with a Bible salesman or, at worst, you go to jail for a while. But the people who care about the great big rights and wrongs never get them to go away, and this turns these people sad and gloomy.

Not that being sad and gloomy is what makes such people so awful, because some sad and gloomy people—you know, the kind who drink for hours and then suddenly jump up and rip the bar stools out of the floor—are interesting and more or less okay, sometimes. But it's different with the sad and gloomy people who care about big rights and wrongs who are sad and gloomy and also really drips in spades.

They're whiners and criers, and nothing is ever right so far as they're concerned—somebody's always being persecuted against or exploited on or suffering with something somewhere, and we should all be out doing something about it instead of just having fun, like drinking gin or getting a little leg in the back of your Ford. This is what the Communist-type person says. And look at their countries, such as

Russia: no good bands, no dance halls, no racy movies, no spicy magazines, no horse tracks, no burlesque shows—they don't even have
modern art (and there is nothing on earth more boring than modern
art, but even *that's* too exciting for them). This comes from having a
country full of Communist-type people—the kind of people who
worry about great big rights and wrongs. I'm here to tell you that turns
them into dips and limpwicks and weenies. I don't know how it works,
exactly, but it does. Maybe thinking about all that big important stuff
makes them sit the way they all do, you know, with their legs crossed
at the knees and pressed together too hard so that the lower part of
their body doesn't get as much blood as it needs so that they don't
develop all their sex hormones, which are the hormones that make you
want to have a good time, and therefore, they don't want to drink a lot
and eat good food and get loved up like we do, but just want to worry
instead. Whatever it is, it makes for the kind of person who, when he
was a kid, used to do next Tuesday's homework on last Friday night, if
you know what I mean. Lots of times he used to be a minister's son,
which isn't a Communist, exactly, but usually was a Presbyterian, which
is not *as* bad but still stinks. Well, what you did to the minister's kid was
tie him to a fence post with his pants off and dip his pecker in fresh
cream and turn a half-weaned calf loose on him. Which is exactly what
we ought to do to all the Communists in the world, except with atom
bombs.

How Fluoridated Water
Turns Kids into Communists

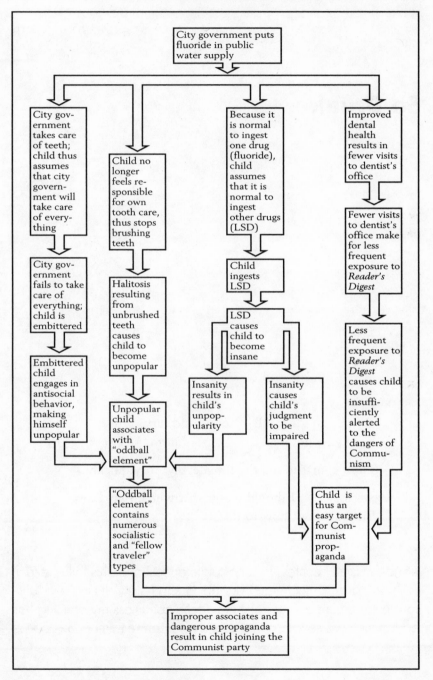

So Drunk

MACBETH: . . . a tale
　Told by an idiot, full of sound and fury,
　Signifying nothing.　　　　　　*Enter a Messenger*

　Thou com'st to use thy tongue; thy story quickly.

MESSENGER: . . . I should report that which I say I saw,
　But know not how to do it.
　　　　　　　　　　　　—Act V, scene v

AUTHOR'S NOTE: I confess to a nostalgic affection for this failed experiment in narrative technique. It's not a short story. It's not even fiction. But, I assure you, it's also not fact—not unless my drinking has led to much worse loss of memory than I can remember. I suppose you could call it a tall tale or, to use the proper academic term, baloney. Anyway, "So Drunk" has the distinction of being the only piece I wrote for the *National Lampoon* that the *National Lampoon* wouldn't print. We had no fear of publishing sexist, racist, perverted, fascistic, or communist articles, but when Julian Weber, president of the company that owned *National Lampoon*, saw this . . .

"P.J.," said Julian, "the only people left on earth willing to advertise in this damn magazine are liquor companies."

I was going to vigorously defend my work on highly principled grounds of First Amendment rights and artistic freedom. Then I reread it. "If we have to choose," I said, "between liquor companies and the Constitution . . ."

Said Julian, "Let's have a drink."

There are times I wonder how you survive. There are times you can abandon any attention to consequences, any inhibitions, any pretense to self-control and just slide for weeks and still emerge unscathed. I don't know how this works, and after you reach a certain age or position in life it doesn't. It's like Saint Peter on the water, or a cartoon character who has overrun a cliff—the instant you have a self-conscious thought, you fall. But until then you slip away in an entropic blur of grace, immune to retribution for the havoc you generate. I often think the universe exists in this condition perpetually.

Not that my friend Ivan would know. He is, just the opposite, always caught for every crime and made to pay on every debt, and he never takes a chance but loses all he stakes. Still, it's with poor Ivan that this adventure begins and ends. He stands in unhappy contrast to my general good fortune in misbehavior, though to what instructive purpose I don't know.

Ivan's bad luck was proverbial. In the summer of 1969 he and I were living in the basement of an old house in Baltimore. We'd divided the cellar with used shower curtains. I'd swept out my half and had in there an army cot, my knapsack, a table, and one chair. Ivan's half had the untouched dirt of two hundred years, with a rotting mattress on the floor and a great litter of tools and metal parts and sculptures, for Ivan was an artist. Every month his half of the basement, and only his half, would flood. Three or four inches of foul Baltimore groundwater would seep in, and recede, leaving a stink, after which I would burn incense on my table and he would curse and sleep in the landing of the basement stairs. During one dry period Ivan took his motorcycle apart and brought it down into his room and rebuilt the engine and painted the frame, only to find that, reassembled, it was too large to get back out again. We had to take a wrecking bar to the stairway and hoist the thing up with a block and tackle. The landlord was crazy with anger, and we came and went through the foundation windows or by climbing a rope to the first floor until we were evicted one week later.

Ivan then decided to move to a crumbling slum on the Baltimore waterfront, where he found a three-story wooden building from which an Armenian or a Lebanese or a gypsy or some such sold rug scraps and brass things. This foreigner had his shop on the first floor and he and his family lived behind it, leaving the top two stories vacant. These were a wreck and were rented by Ivan for seventy-five dollars a month. He enlisted me and those few of his other friends who would risk being anywhere near Ivan while he operated a power tool to help him fix it, promising us all free rooms when we were done. This would still, he said, leave him space for a studio in what had been an attic before the roof collapsed. So we worked on this place, tearing out plumbing and putting plumbing in and jury-rigging electrical wiring and hauling out loads of cracked-plaster mess and broken lath and dumping it in the harbor in the middle of the night. I say we, but it was Ivan who did almost all the work. The rest of us, me and Joe the Poet and a couple of others, would hammer and haul for a while and then retire across the street to Nick's Hotel, which was a flophouse with a bar downstairs where a draft beer was fifteen cents. Every now and then, one of the winos who lived above would die and what Nick called the "pie wagon" from Johns Hopkins hospital would pull alongside the curb, not bothering with lights or siren, and orderlies would carry the dead man out on a stretcher while we bellied up to the bar to make room for them to pass.

Ivan labored for months, and we were almost ready to move in when a fellow walked out of Nick's one night, crossed South Broadway, went into the rug-scrap store, and shot its owner in the face with a .45. When Ivan arrived the next day there was an entirely new family of foreigners in there, and they screamed at him and chased him out, the fat women pulling their skirts up over their heads and exposing vast patches of genital hair, which seemed to be some awful insult among these people. Indeed, Ivan said, it was nothing a heterosexual male should ever see. So all his work was as, as they say, nothing.

Next, Ivan was giving a crabby girl he'd screwed once or twice a ride to the 7-Eleven on his motorcycle. He was going around a curve when he hit, he swears, a patch of ice—something that does not much exist south of the Mason-Dixon line in September—and went head-long into a truck. The girl was crippled, or said she was. Anyway, she limped when she thought people were watching, so Ivan, out of pity, married her. Pity is not a sound basis for marriage, Ivan said he dis-covered later. And worse, he said, he discovered a crippled wife is not grounds for divorce in Maryland even if she nags.

After four or five months Ivan began hiding from his wife. He was hiding at my house when we began the longest drunk I've ever been on. Joe the Poet was hiding at my house, too. I don't know whom Joe was hiding from. It may have been the finance people who were trying to repossess his television, but I don't think so, because he'd already dropped it out his second-story window. Or maybe it was his landlady, through the glass tops of whose cucumber frames the TV had fallen. But I don't think it was her either, since Joe had so terrorized the old woman that she collected her rent by thrusting a garden rake out her chain-locked door and making him spindle a check on its tines. Maybe he was just hiding. I remember he said, "I won't be found here." And that was especially true if nobody was looking. I was hiding from, or rather was in retreat from, a love affair that I couldn't have made worse if I'd married the girl. Which was just what I wanted to do. Her name was Vicky Lewis, and she had agreed to it. Then she disappeared, leaving no hint of why or whereabouts. In stories more romantic than this, such women vanish due to dark secrets in their past. In ordinary life they do so because they're nuts. Which made me nuts, and we were all hiding at my house.

Now, if you drink a lot, and I do, it's hard to date the exact nascence of a bender. When is it that ordinary heavy drinking leaves off and a true bust, a tear, a bat, a jag begins? There's drinking in the morning—that's one sign, of course. Unless it's beer; there's nothing more delicious with sausages and eggs than beer. And a medicinal shot or two doesn't count. And if it's getting on to eleven o'clock—and in those days I was never awake before—it's nearly lunchtime, and you can hardly say you're launched on a hoolihan with a drink or three before the midday meal. Then there's the shakes and a bleary thirst, but those signify alcoholism, which is but the sickly repetitious cousin of a real rampaging toot. No, I think, at least with me, I'm on a bender when I start carrying a drink, a real drink with ice cubes in a cocktail glass, with me wherever I go: to the grocery store, for instance, or to the bank, or into the shower, which is a better place than you might think, if you pour your Scotch strong and use plenty of ice. A little warm water never hurt a good blend like Chivas or Dewar's, but a single malt should only be had on the toilet or at the sink.

Not that we could afford Scotch in those days. We were drinking Maryland rye and screw-top wine and cheap gin with reconstituted lemon juice squirted in to kill the oily smell. After several days of this we were on a binge by any definition. We certainly were by the time Joe threw his marijuana at a hippie. It made him sensitive to smoke the stuff, he said, and he couldn't bear the thought of that. Then he went off to fuck a fat girl to get diet pills so we could stay awake and drink some more.

This must have been about February 1970 when we were drinking so and staying up all night. One morning the weather turned sunny and extremely warm, fifty-five or sixty degrees. We got on our motorcycles and rode into western Maryland, where Ivan's cousin, who was also a sculptor, kept a studio in a converted barn. This cousin was on a sabbatical to Brazil for some reason, and we broke into her house and drank all her liquor and ate up the canned goods. I think we ruined some of her artwork, too, though we didn't mean to. Her sculptures were airy, light, gauzy, stupid-looking things made of thread, yarn, and filament strung every which way, and Joe walked right through one of them. Some other of her pieces were rope and cord and woolen stuff tangled into wall hangings; we took these down later and slept on them. She had a woman's liquor cabinet, with a dozen bottles of one-tenth-empty dairy-product aperitifs and mocha-marzipan-cocoa-butter-flavored cordials and other silly things to drink after dinner. These didn't sit well with the handful of pills we'd brought along, and Ivan threw up in what he thought was a bidet in the middle of the room, except it proved to be a work by a woman potter friend of the lady, or that's what the paper plaque attached to the base said, according to Joe, who had found Ivan's cousin's flashlight and was using it to go through her lingerie drawer. The place had a lot of rustic decorative touches and we couldn't find a light switch.

Joe wanted to, as he put it, "roar through the woods." So we roared through the woods, or we tried to. But maybe roaring through the woods takes practice, or a special talent. Ivan tripped over a string of barbed wire and vomited into his own face. Joe and I ran a little ways and yelled a couple of times—and then we were out of breath, so Joe went inside and had more to drink. After that I wandered through, rather than roared through, the woods. And I wandered into a long, narrow, stony clearing where I half passed out, sure that I could hear the heartbeat of Vicky Lewis pounding louder and louder, making the earth itself shake beneath me. Until I realized I was lying on a railroad track.

I found my way back, eventually, to the house or the barn or whatever it was, and crawled between the wall hangings and poured Mars-bar-flavored alcohol all over my face until I slept. But Ivan came to an hour later and woke up Joe and me, saying we had to help him chain his motorcycle to a tree. Ivan had a lousy motorcycle, a two-cylinder Jawa with siamese heads, a pig of a bike. The only person for a hundred miles around who'd steal a motorcycle like that was Ivan. But it had to be chained up, and he put the chain through the wheel and around a tree trunk and around his ankle, too. Then he dropped the padlock key. And though we searched until morning we never found it. So we left Ivan chained to the tree and put everything useful we could find within his reach—toilet paper, matches, cigarettes, crème de menthe. Then Joe and I rode back to Baltimore to find a pair of cable cutters or a hacksaw or something. But we were hung over, so we stopped at Nick's Hotel first, and after we'd had eight or ten beers we were falling asleep, so we took some more Dexedrine and then had a couple of shots to take the edge off that, and by then we'd forgotten Ivan.

I decided I had to kill Vicky Lewis. Joe said he thought that was a good idea and maybe he'd kill the girl he was in love with, too. Or maybe he'd just borrow her car. I couldn't go shoot somebody on a motorcycle, he said. A motorcycle makes too much noise. So we rode to his girlfriend's house and parked our motorcycles in a flower bed and took her car. Then we went to my house and got my pistol and began to drive. We'd been driving for about an hour when Joe said, "Are we there?"

"Are we where?" I said.

"Where Vicky is."

"I don't know where Vicky is," I said. "If I knew that, I wouldn't be this drunk."

Joe wanted to know how I was going to kill her if I didn't know where she was. So I changed my mind and decided I would forget about Vicky, the girl who I loved in Baltimore, and go back to Kathy, the girl who loved *me* in Akron.

It took us a long time to get to the airport because, since we hadn't been going anywhere, we had no idea where we'd gotten to. So we turned around and went the other way, which was a mistake, because I think we were at the airport when we decided to go there. But I'm not sure. Anyway, I accidentally bought a ticket to Toledo, Ohio, where I was raised, instead of Akron, Ohio, where Kathy lived, but I didn't realize it until I'd gotten where I was going and found out I wasn't there.

During all this time I remember nothing about money. I must have had some. But I can't remember where I got it. I was always broke in those days. I used to sell drugs sometimes, but I doubt I ever made more than forty or fifty dollars at a time. I can't remember any other source of cash. I don't know. Joe and I took the last of the diet pills in the airport bar. Then I went to get on the plane, walked through the metal detector and was jumped by a dozen policemen, plainclothesmen, sky marshals, and whatnot. I was dirty and addled-looking and much in need of a haircut, and I had checked no luggage and carried none, and I must have fit perfectly some preconception of a hijacker. Also, the metal detector had screeched like a fucked cat. I had the plug wrench for my motorcycle shoved down in one jean pocket plus a big ring of keys and a Zippo. But what I did not have in my pocket was the gun.

As I don't know where the money came from, I don't know where the gun went. I had it on my hip when I got in the car to go kill Vicky. And Joe said I didn't take it out, and he didn't find it in the car. I didn't find it again until that spring, when it turned up in the pocket of my only sports coat while I was packing to move. Eventually, I did try to kill Vicky with it, but that time by accident, and that's another story anyway.

So they didn't arrest me. In fact, they apologized. And I had as much to drink as I could on the plane and flew to what I thought was Akron and walked and hitchhiked toward what I thought was Kathy's apartment and wound up in front of my mother's house. She wasn't home, but her car was there, so I took it.

My mother had a clapped-out old Buick, a 1963 Invicta Estate Wagon. But it had the 401-cubic-inch engine that Buick used to put in its big cars—three-hundred-odd horsepower—and even with ninety thousand miles on the car it would go a hundred miles an hour.

The left wiper blade broke in a freezing rain near Sandusky and began to flail and hammer against the windshield. I tried to fix it without stopping, but the whole thing came off in my hand. I had to drive with my face out the window and buy a bottle of brandy to keep warm. I slowed down to eighty, but that wasn't slow enough for the bald old tires. On the turnpike outside Elyria I tried to pass a car and went sideways out of control into the left lane. I steered with the skid as well as I could, but when I poked my head out the window to see what was going on I saw a big slow truck in the passing lane. I tried to drift back to the right, but the driver I had passed had, as a passed driver always will, speeded up and was square alongside me. After that there was a whirl of vehicle sides and truck behind.

There's certainly an explanation for the money I spent on this drunk, probably something I've forgotten, and the same must be true for the gun that got into a sports coat I hadn't worn since a traffic court appearance in 1968. But there is no way to explain how I survived in the Buick. All I know is that the next time I could bring myself to open my eyes I was in the clear, whole and untouched. Albeit I was backwards, facing the car and the truck I must have somehow slipped between. Alberto Ascari or Juan Fangio or some such famous race driver is supposed to have gone off the course on a road-race circuit once and driven between the gateposts of a house and up onto the lawn, and when the distance between the gateposts was measured it was found to be less than the width of the car. He must have been drunk too. The Buick continued to rotate, and when the front end was within fifteen or twenty degrees of forward I took my hands off the wheel, stamped on the accelerator, and the car straightened out, still doing eighty.

Kathy from Akron did love me once, I think. But I hadn't visited or called or replied to her letters in more than two years. I didn't even know that she still lived in the same place. But she did, and she was surprised, and not pleasantly, to find me filthy, wet, wild-eyed, and inebriated at her door.

It was a peculiar evening. Her boyfriend was away somewhere, so I took a shower and some of his clothes. But it needed a lot of talking, more talking than even I can do, to get her into bed.

I woke the next day with an erection and a headache, and I looked around for Kathy, but she wasn't there. There was no note. She didn't come back. I waited all day and drank and ate most of what was in the house. When she hadn't returned by two in the morning I tried to leave, but the car wouldn't start. So I went back and drank and ate the rest of what was in the house and took all of her boyfriend's drugs and stayed up all night and, I admit, did some damage to the place, breaking a piece of furniture or two and one glass and then another, up to about a dozen, and putting my fist through a pressboard wall.

When it was light I tried the car again. It hadn't started before, I think, because I'd had the trunk key in the ignition.

I got some beer and drove to Columbus and found my friend Cullen Fitzpatrick coming out the door of a big run-down house he shared with twenty people. He was carrying an enormous backpack and a sleeping bag and a folded-up pup tent and a pair of snowshoes and was wearing a new down parka. He was hitchhiking to the airport, he said. He'd given away everything else he owned and he was going to Colorado forever. We went inside and began to drink. We drank there for a while and then took all the camping equipment to Buck's Stumble Inn.

The next day, or the day after, or maybe the day after that, Cullen told me again that he'd given away everything that he owned and was going to Colorado forever. But I said why didn't he come back to Toledo with me, because Toledo is farther west than Columbus and therefore must be nearer Colorado, even though it's more north, because it's less east, so doubtless the plane fare would be smaller, and besides I'd stolen my mother's car.

We fell into a dopey lethargy in Toledo. Fitzpatrick is given to periods of inertia anyway. He once lived with an ugly fat girl for six months because she had a Barcalounger reclining chair, and she'd serve him meals in the Barcalounger, and the TV was in front of the Barcalounger, and she'd kneel down and give him head in the Barcalounger, and then he'd tilt the chair back and pass out at night. She'd look the other way while he pissed in empty beer cans and tossed them out the window. Every now and again he'd have to get up to shit, he said, and that was all. So we sat in my mother's living room, drinking the two cases of beer she brought home from work every day until she got so angry at the bad impression we were making on her boyfriend that she told me just to *take* the car, for Christ's sake, and get out of there.

Cullen wanted to go to the airport, but I said, No, come on, let's go down to Cincinnati. That's much farther south than Toledo and therefore that much closer to Colorado.

So we went to Cincinnati, but here I run out of adventures. No really sustained drunk consists of all Homeric moments, unless the drunkard is telling even more lies than I am. We stayed drunk and took as many drugs as we could find and stomach. But nothing much happened, nothing like what happened to a friend of mine, Mahoney, who was riding around with a friend of his in the other fellow's Austin-Healey. The young man who was driving was very drunk and melancholy and was telling Mahoney of his decision to commit suicide. Mahoney said, oh, no, you'll feel better in a day or so, or maybe just after another drink. Mahoney gave him another drink from the bottle they were carrying, but the fellow said he had his mind made up. Everybody feels that way sometimes, Mahoney said, you'll never do it. "The hell I won't," said his companion, and he drove straight off a curve and into a tree, and the steering column went through his chest. Which is the way that all good stories of drunks should end, with a great catastrophe, a horrible death, or at least a sad ironic turn. But neither this part of the story nor the story as a whole has that kind of ending, or much of an ending at all.

True life, even loudly exaggerated, has deficiencies in organization and plot line and a muddiness of symbolic content. It's hard to draw even the most common wisdom from the messy events of daily existence until they've been told over and polished and improved upon a few hundred times. Such as the story I heard in the French West Indies about a drug-smuggling pilot who was in Saint Barthélemy on a drunk and, between cocaine and Chivas and more cocaine and rum, hadn't slept in four or five days. There's a road out of Gustavia, the main town on the island, that goes up a steep hill to the top of a bluff then turns to the right along a ridgeline. When you come up this hill and reach the turn you can see, some fifty feet below, the island's landing strip, which runs out from the bottom of the bluff to the sea. This is particularly impressive on a moonlit night, with the marker lights stretching down each side of the strip and the painted center stripe aglow. The smuggler pilot was driving up this road from Gustavia on just such a night, and when he reached the top of the hill and looked down he forgot he was driving a car and thought he was landing a plane. He adjusted the vent knob, which he took to be the throttle, yelled, "Gear down! Flaps down!" and went right off the top of the bluff, over a stone wall, and upside down into a hedgerow. I understand he still flies a plane but will not drive a car. Mahoney will still drive a car, but he won't ride in one when someone else is driving. He says he'll tip a cab driver fifty dollars to slide over and let him take the wheel, and he says he'll never again argue the question of suicide. In fact, he says, he won't even discuss abortion.

But nothing of this sort happened to Cullen and me in Cincinnati. Though we were smoking hashish on the roof of a house one afternoon when somebody who was with us said that the treetops, which came up around the eaves, were certainly soft and fluffy looking—"cuddly and cushiony," he called them, and we agreed more or less—and then he ran off and flung himself into one of them and was badly scratched and broke a thumb when he hit the ground.

That night, I think it was, I met a girl in a bar who was going to Pittsburgh. I convinced Fitzpatrick that there was really no difference between Toledo and Cincinnati, both being about the same distance east of Colorado. And I convinced the girl that Toledo was north, so it must be on the way to Pittsburgh. The three of us drank until the bars closed, and for a while after that, then drove two hundred miles back to my mother's house, arriving at ten in the morning. We were awakened at four in the afternoon by my mother, who was screaming and throwing us out.

When I'd taken my mother's car to Akron, she'd reported it stolen. But when I brought it back, she hadn't reported it returned. The highway patrol couldn't find the car while I was driving all over the state, but they found it easily enough while my mother was driving to work. She'd left her driver's license and identification and so on in another purse and had had to spend the day convincing police she wasn't a car thief.

We hitchhiked to the airport, dragging Fitzpatrick's equipment, and when we were there, and with the help of a bottle of J. W. Dant, I convinced him that Pittsburgh, too, was on the way to Colorado. We didn't get that far. We were thrown off the airplane in Cleveland. While we were in the airport bar, the girl, who was named Candy or Katie or Cora, disappeared. I don't know where she went. Cullen got the bartender to bet him that he would not drink a "flaming hooker." A flaming hooker is a shot glass full of Bacardi that is set alight and then drunk, to the amazement of bystanders. We'd turned the lights off in the bar to dramatize this. The trick is to do it fast, before the flame heats the rim of the glass, and to do it in one motion, so that the fire is smothered in your mouth. But the bartender had substituted a three-ounce juice tumbler for the shot glass, so there was more liquor than Cullen could get down in one gulp. He was a spectacle with his mustache alight. The result was a sort of toasted Amish look, with a fringe of smelly beard char left around his face.

We got on another plane, and this time neither of us paid any attention to where it was headed, which was Washington, DC. From there we made it the forty miles or so to my place in Baltimore in only three days.

By then Ivan was out of the hospital, where he'd been treated for exposure and alcohol poisoning. He and Joe were getting ready to leave for a college in southern Maryland, where Joe had been invited to give a poetry reading at a writers' workshop populated, I understand, by middle-aged women with a bent for historical fiction who planned to write under pseudonyms of three names. Personally, I don't remember anything about the audience except a shocked hush. Joe had decided it would be more fun if he took friends along to read with him, even though none of these friends was a poet. Actually, that's not true. He did turn up one other poet, a strange young man named Nevin who had devoted four years to composing a fifty-thousand-line dramatic versification of Maeterlinck's *Life of the Bee*. Nevin's interpretation of this book was in no wise hampered by having read it. And his ignorance of his source was surpassed only by his ignorance of its subject. He insisted on giving his reading dressed in a bee costume, which he made by tying an imitation-tiger-skin lampshade to his rear end, wrapping his arms in packing tissue, and holding the broken-off end of a bamboo fish pole between his teeth to represent the stinger. The man had absolutely no idea how a bee was constructed.

His reading was not very popular. Neither was Joe's, though it was shorter and, if slurred, much easier to understand, since he held nothing in his mouth but the neck of a whiskey bottle, and that but momentarily.

Fitzpatrick said he didn't know any poems but knew a good story about a poet, one of the original beat poets, who got stoned one night and decided he was hungry for chili and made a big stew pot of it. The poet seasoned the chili with jalapeño peppers. He tasted it and thought it was good, but not hot enough, so he put in some more jalapeño peppers. That was better, but it still wasn't hot enough, so he put in more jalapeño peppers yet. Finally he put a whole quart jar of jalapeño peppers into the chili and sat down and ate the entire potful. He wound up at six in the morning, Fitzpatrick said, on his hands and knees in the bathtub, running his butt hole under the cold-water tap.

I don't remember what I did at the reading, but earlier we'd been given a dinner by the college president and Ivan amazed everyone by eating a whole chicken without using his hands.

We were asked, then told, to get off campus. Hints were made to us concerning the state police. And the college people should have called them, because it was definitely not safe for us to be on the highway.

We were taking mescaline, which doesn't mix with whiskey. It makes you argumentative without the capacity to follow the argument, and combative, which it is difficult to be when you're in combat with things that aren't there. And even more difficult when you're in combat with things that *are*. Cullen got on the wrong side of a giant redneck in a roadhouse on Route 301, and we had a fight with everyone in the place.

We escaped without many injuries, really, except for Ivan, who took a bar stool on the forehead. And we had to make a sort of sacrifice of Nevin in his bee costume. Nobody ever saw him again. But the mescaline began to give us stomach cramps and Joe sideswiped a couple of cars, and by the time we got back to Baltimore we were in bad shape. Joe's girlfriend, especially, since it was her car. When we got out, she jumped back behind the wheel and started chasing Joe down the street in it. That was the last I saw of Joe for a while, galloping down the middle of the road with this crazy girl trying to run him over, and him without enough sense to jump up on the sidewalk or behind a tree.

Then, Ivan and Cullen and I began to really drink. We'd been drinking before, yes, but it was nothing to this. We'd been on a cheerful, circumstantial, convivial sort of drunk, or I had, anyway, for nearly three weeks, but now we went at it as an assigned task, as a measure of will, as a test of the body physical. We drank and puked and drank and passed out and kicked each other awake and drank some more and still kept drinking. I don't know why. Maybe we thought to reach some zenith, some efflorescence, some supreme perfection of uttermost drunk, and so be done with pleasure for the rest of our lives. It's hard to say.

We got very drunk. But we did not succeed in becoming the drunkest people ever. Fitzpatrick's father had a story about those folks which he used to tell before he died of drink himself. It seems that one evening a group of senators and representatives were drinking in a Washington bar. They were getting drunk. First they got pretty drunk. Then they got very drunk. After that, they got drunker than anyone had ever seen senators and representatives get, which is very drunk indeed. And all the while, their colleagues were coming into the tavern and getting as drunk as that themselves. Finally the entire United States Congress, with the possible exception of a lady senator from Maine or so, was drunk as a coot, skunk, monkey, hoot owl, red Indian, or anything else that you can be as drunk as. About two o'clock in the morning the Speaker of the House stood up on a table and said, "Gentlemen, we are sloshed. We are fried, oiled, canned, and in the bag cross-eyed. We are awash in tonsil paint, afloat upon a sea of coffin varnish. We are swimming in stagger soup. We are lit, tight, stinking, bombed, and tanked with three sheets to the wind. In point of fact we are drunk. And in point of more fact we are drunker than anyone has ever been. And in point of more fact than that we are drunker than anyone is ever going to get, because we've got a quorum right here, so let's go over and open Congress." Which they did, stumbling up to the Capitol building and unlocking the door. Then they called themselves into session and passed a law saying no one could ever get drunker than they were then, and that's where Prohibition came from, according to Fitzpatrick's father.

And I did not even personally succeed in becoming the drunk-est I have ever been. The drunkest I've ever been was when Fitzpatrick and Uncle Mike Visconti and I were all in college. One night we were having a party and ran out of whiskey at three in the morning. Uncle Mike and I went out in the country and woke up a moonshiner we knew. He brought us out some pop bottles filled with clear liquor that had little pieces of things floating in it like river water has. We took it back to the party and everybody drank it and it gave us a woozy, crazy, different sort of drunk—very nice until people began throwing up. But a certain amount of throwing up is expected at a good party, required even, if the hosts are to know that the full thrust of their hospitality has been felt. It didn't seem to me that anything was very wrong until I saw my girlfriend Juanita, normally a fastidious girl, retching into a sink full of dirty dishes. I had a few more drinks and I was sick, too, sick as I've ever been. I felt my insides pulled out on a rope of filth. It was a convulsive, projectile vomiting that brought no relief. I remember puk-ing into a wastepaper basket, through a window, out the back door, into a plant, and onto the davenport. Finally, exhausted, I crawled upstairs to the bathroom.

I woke up with a burning sensation in my gullet and a horrible headache. It was a struggle to open my eyes, and when I did open them there was nothing there, just a blank expanse of whiteness. I blinked and rolled my eyes in their sockets and blinked again. Nothing. Nothing at all. Nothing but a featureless white glare. I was blind. *"Blind,"* I thought. *"I drank moonshine whiskey and it made me blind. I'm blind. Blind! Wood-alcohol blind! I can't see a thing! I'm blind! Blind! Blind! . . ."* And I was half an hour like that until Juanita came in and found me just where I'd passed out, with my head upside down in the toilet bowl.

So we didn't get as drunk as you can get, but we got as drunk as we could. And coming after so much drinking before, the effect was bound to be bad. There was nasty business with three high school girls. I wish I could remember some of it, but I can't. I don't remember anything. I'm not really sure the high school girls were ever there. We were so drunk that . . . So drunk that what? I have no idea. That's the problem, finally, with getting so drunk. The next thing that I truly recall was Fitzpatrick and I in the filthy bathroom at Nick's Hotel, and we each had hold of one of Ivan's arms. Ivan had passed out while taking a crap and had fallen back with such force that he'd gotten his head stuck between the wall and the standpipe behind the toilet. We pulled on his arms, each of us bracing a foot on the porcelain bowl, and his skull came loose with a pop. Ivan's eyes opened and he pulled his pants up and said, "Boy, this is an awful job." What job? said Fitzpatrick. "Being longshoremen," said Ivan. When we came out of the bathroom and back into the bar the place was filled with longshoremen, and we were apparently longshoremen, too. We didn't remember being hired. And we didn't remember unloading any boats. But there we were. And all the other longshoremen seemed to know us. Ivan got up the next morning and went to work, and to the best of my knowledge he's a longshoreman in Baltimore to this day.

Cullen and I did not go to work. Cullen packed up his tents and sleeping bags and rucksacks and so on and hitchhiked back to Columbus. He never has been to Colorado, not even to visit. I eventually recovered and got a regular job. But not before I went on the wagon. And I'm going to go on the wagon again just as soon as I finish typing this.

Why I'm Not Afraid of the Dark
Editorial from the 1981 "Kids" Issue

When I was a child, I was, as most children are, afraid of the dark. I insisted on a night-light in my room *and* a lamp left on in the hall. I did not like to go to the basement after sundown or into the attic at any time of day. The stairway to this attic, in fact, opened into my bedroom, and I could not comfortably get in bed until I had checked the door lock at least three times. I hated to look into a dark window from a lighted room, and if I was left home alone, I would pull the shades and drapes. Outdoors the dark was somewhat less fearsome, at least when I was accompanied or there were plenty of streetlights around. But to be outside by myself on, say, a windy night without moon or artificial illumination was horrifying. So much is not unusual. I understand it is considered normal and even healthy for a child to feel this way. But when I grew older the fear did not diminish.

On the threshold of puberty I was more frightened of a dark room than I had been when I was five. As my mind developed and my imagination improved, nameless dread gave way to vivid phantasmagoria, and general mental unease was replaced by specific terror. I was no longer afraid of just the dark; now there were *things* in that dark. Summer camp was agony. Staring out the cabin windows, I slept so little watching the wolf ghouls and bear ogres formed by the breeze in the treetops that I had to be sent to the infirmary and there slept not at all on a bunk above a boy who had been bitten by a spider and claimed his leg was rotting. I could smell it all night long. I once spent my Christmas vacation with an aunt and uncle and had to share the bed with a younger cousin who had the disquieting trait, as some people do, of sleeping with his eyes open. I would have killed him if I hadn't been sure he was one of the undead already. I developed a custom during those two weeks of getting up and going to the bathroom six or seven times after I'd gone to bed—in order to be back in the light with the adults. It was a habit that took years to break. And when I was fully thirteen years old I could not fall to sleep in a Florida motel room because the owner had decorated the place with a luminescent picture of Jesus on the Mount of Olives and the phosphorous paint formed horrible patterns in the dusk. The thing was awful on the wall, worse under the bed, and still unacceptable facedown in a dresser drawer. It finally wound up outside behind the ice machine, and if the owner of the Gulf View Courts in Pensacola would like it back, it's probably still there now.

The fear, of course, was unpleasant, but the embarrassment at having it was worse. I was, I thought, for all practical purposes an adult. I would be in high school the next year. Soon, I hoped, I would be taking girls to bed, and presumably that would be in the dark. I wished for—more than anything except perhaps those girls—freedom from this panic.

As it happened, quite apart from my fear of darkness, I was having an uncomfortable childhood. My father had died when I was nine, and my mother, a kindly but not very sensible woman, had remarried to a drunken oaf. He was a pestering, bullying sort of man whose favorite subject of derision was my fondness for books. But when I did try my hand at sports and fishing and so forth, he teased me for my ineptitude. He described me as a "hothouse flower" when I stayed inside, and claimed I was running wild like a juvenile delinquent when I went outdoors. I was accused of spinelessness when I did not respond to his goading and of impertinence when I did, told I was dumb when I was quiet, and to shut up when I spoke. My mother tried to intercede, but this only made things worse and made me feel like a coward and a mama's boy besides. As for the remainder of my family, I had only a pair of nattering younger sisters, and I did not like them any better than I liked the rest of the household. Weeknights at home were the most difficult. Our house was cheap and small, and it was impossible to get away from the others. My bedroom was above the living room, where they all sat and watched television from sundown until bedtime. I could hear every word they spoke, many of these words being about me and what a problem I had become. Then my mother would come upstairs every half hour or so to ask, "What are you doing?" And if I tried to go down to the basement—which, as I mentioned, I didn't like—my stepfather would yell, every time a commercial came on, for me to leave his tools alone. This was very painful. Not many of those tools were really his. Most of them had been my father's. And if I tried to sit in the kitchen, which at least kept them from talking about me in the next room, then I would be criticized for moping. Therefore, most evenings, wet or dry, cold or warm, I would sneak out of the house and walk around. The single explosion of abuse that I'd receive when I returned was preferable to the constant multiple irritations I received if I stayed. And though I was scared of the darkness outside, I was not as scared of the darkness as I was exhausted with my family. Most of the time I was not even really that scared. We lived in a city neighborhood. It had lawns and trees and so on, but there were busy streets nearby and I would meander along the well-lit storefronts, avoiding alleys, parks, and other dark places, supporting my timidity fairly well, and hoping and mooning and worrying the way adolescents do. I tried to calculate my return with precision, so that I would be late enough for the stepfather to have drunk himself to sleep but not late enough for my mother to have called all the neighbors, or worse.

There was one night, however, when I would not have gone out if things hadn't been much worse than usual at home. My sisters became engaged in some prolonged and stupid screaming match with each other and I had slapped the louder one to shut her up. This set off a general row in the house so that by the time I bolted for the door my sisters were shrieking like banshees and my mother was crying aloud and my stepfather was bellowing threats and the dog was barking and the television was blaring in the background of it all—a scene I still envision whenever I hear the phrase "hell on earth." It was moonless and very windy and there was an overcast that blotted out the stars but was too high to reflect the city lights. It was early spring, I think, and still cold, and the wavy forms of the naked tree branches were especially macabre. I stuck close to the store windows and huddled in well-lighted doorways several times for warmth. I was doing just that when a police car stopped. What was I doing prowling around in the middle of the night? said the officer. I wasn't prowling, I said, I was just walking home and got cold and stopped for a second in the doorway to get out of the wind. He pointed out that it was not my doorway to stop in and that, anyway, stopping in doorways was suspicious activity at that time of night. He asked me where I lived and I told him, since I could not think of a lie. He said I'd be *plenty* warm, he thought, at least on one part of my body, if I were to arrive there in a police car instead of immediately under my own power. So I strode off in the direction of my house, attempting to look purposeful, and turned into a darkened playground where I was out of sight and a police car couldn't follow me. There were no lights at all on the playground, and besides the spectral things I always felt around me in the gloom, I was worried there might be quite corporeal bums or drunks or, worse, older teenage boys there too. I was frightened but I was stuck. I couldn't go back to the main streets or else the police, I was sure, would get me. And I couldn't go home. I couldn't bear to do that. So I stayed where I was, trembling and miserable, and after a while I began to think. I did not really believe that there were monsters in the shadows, and I didn't see any drunks or teenagers, but this did nothing to allay my terror. I must have read somewhere that it was useless to rail against panic, that the source and causes of fear should be examined and meditated on, to see if the fear will respond to reason. And I was not completely ignorant of primitive psychological theory. I asked myself why I was afraid of the dark. Nothing very bad had ever happened to me in a dark place, that I could remember. No, the worst things in my life had transpired in broad daylight or well-lit rooms. It, the darkness, must "symbolize" something to me, I thought. I had only recently heard about symbolism, and I thought it was a swell concept. Perhaps, I thought, darkness symbolized the death of my father. But I could remember being afraid of the dark before he'd died. And, in truth, I had not been that close to the man. It was his absence in the present, not his loss in the past, that was sorely felt. I didn't think his death was it. I decided darkness must symbolize something more general for me. Evil, I decided. That's why I imagined monsters in the dark. Monsters are evil because they do evil things, which is what makes them monstrous. But I recognized that as circular reasoning. No, I had to consider what evil really was. Evil was harm and destruction. Murdering people, that was evil, or burning their houses down. These were the sorts of things evil forces might do, the kind of forces that darkness symbolized for me. Such forces might rage into a home like my own and murder one of my sisters or both of my sisters or even my mother and tear the house to pieces, breaking it into little bits and then blowing the ruins to smithereens with nitroglycerin and setting fire to what was left, and then take my stepfather and break both his arms and slice off his feet and poke his eyes out with red-hot staves, disembowel him, skin him alive. And then they'd attack the rest of the neighborhood and the police force and the school and burn and bomb and steal and break everything in that part of Ohio, from the filthy oil refineries on the east side of town all the way to the moldy, boring cottage we rented every summer at the lake. And who knew what such evil forces might do after that? I didn't. But I sat on the swing set considering suggestions for a very long time. And I have never been afraid of the dark since.

Drives to Nowhere

Automotive Journalism

The great advantage to humor as a trade is that ignorance has a positive value. I don't understand the balanced budget amendment. Isn't it like trying to stop smoking by hiding cigarettes from yourself? I don't understand term limits. Do we want a dog who knows where all the bones are buried, or do we want a dog who'll dig up the whole yard? I don't understand abortion arguments. Why is it bad to kill a little baby but okay to kill a teensy-weensy one? And I don't understand why the same newspaper commentators who bemoan the terrible education given to poor people are always so eager to have those poor people get out and vote.

Most of my professional life has been spent expressing my ignorance of politics and current events. But there are other subjects I don't know about. Cars being chief among them. My grandfather and my Uncle Arch owned a Buick dealership. My father was sales manager. Uncle Joe ran the used car lot. All the O'Rourkes worked there, myself included. My first vivid memory is of a car— a 1949 electric blue Buick Century convertible with red leather upholstery. I love cars. But I love cars the way I love women. I don't know how to fix them. I wouldn't presume to design one. And, when they are beautiful and fast, they make me stupid enough to say such things as "I love cars the way I love women."

My career as an automotive journalist I owe to David E. Davis, Jr. When he took over the editorship of Car and Driver in 1977, Davis realized that many of the magazine's readers, while enthusiastic about motor vehicles, were almost as unknowlegeable as I. He wanted an editorial link to the dumbbells. I wrote for Car and Driver until 1985, when Davis left to found Automobile magazine and I followed. During these eighteen years I have driven the best cars, traveled through the most beautiful scenery, stayed at the tip-top hotels, and tasted the highest cuisine (and finest libations) of a dozen countries, all on expense account. This goes to prove something I've long believed, that journalism can make the world a better place—for me.

The Welsh National Combined Mud Wrestling and Spelling Bee Championship

Mucking About in the Fforest Fawr, Llanddewi Brefi, Pontrhydfendigaid, and Other Orthographically Difficult Places

***Car and Driver*, 1984**

AUTHOR'S NOTE: In late 1983 a party of sixteen *Car and Driver* staff members, friends, and dependents drove nine off-road vehicles across the pavement-free middle of Wales. Ostensibly, our mission was to test a cross section of American four-wheel-drive products against their British, German, and Japanese counterparts. In fact, what we were doing was illustrating the central idea of all automotive journalism: getting money to do what one would spend money to do if one hadn't found a way to be paid for doing it.

A Ford Bronco II, a Chevrolet S-10 Blazer, a GMC S-15 Jimmy, a Jeep Cherokee, a Land Rover, two Range Rovers, a Mercedes-Benz Geländewagen, and a Mitsubishi Montero were used on the trip. Since these are now a dozen model years old, I have excised the technical chatter about them. Wales, on the other hand, has not had a major redesign since Owen Glendower got whupped at Harlech Castle in 1409.

You might think off-road driving in the British Isles would be a matter of: "Very good, sir. We'll have Mrs. Twickham take down her front trellis, and you can motor about in her rose garden, then turn sharp at the rookery, and go right through the privet hedge and into the vicar's kitchen yard." But it's not like that at all. Even though Britain has a population density about double that of Macy's toy floor at Christmastime, there are still vast tracts of empty moor, fen, bog, wold, and other kinds of wilderness that the Brits have funny names for.

The really tough part, however, is getting out of London. The Limeys just can't shake their national dyslexia about which side of the road is for tailgating and which is for head-on collisions. And I can't remember to list to port. But I have, I think, finally come up with the proper mnemonic device; what you have to do is think of yourself as a well-dressed Socialist: "Keep left, look right. Keep left, look right." See? This makes driving in England a snap as long as you don't have to pass, change lanes, go through roundabouts, or shift gears.

The English also have a road-numbering system based on the Duke of Wellington's cribbage scores. Thus it was in a dither of confusion, occasional naked fear, and also rain and jet lag that we made our way fifty miles west up the Thames to the village of Streatley. There, with hoots of relief from the Yanks, we got off the paved road and into some nice safe precipices, cliffs, and escarpments.

A remarkable geological feature called the Ridgeway begins at Streatley. The Ridgeway is a narrow fold of chalk highlands that stretches west for forty miles along the crest of the Berkshire Downs and into northern Wiltshire. The country falls away in perfect symmetry on either side, and the view of England is too wonderful to be fact. If you were the kind of child who created imaginary worlds on your bedspread, this is what you saw from your knees.

The Ridgeway has been in use as a thoroughfare since 3000 B.C., and it is still in better shape than most streets in New York. Even so, wet grass, slippery chalk soil, and gale-force winds blowing up off the Salisbury Plain made the going tricky. I had no more than sighed with relief to be out of traffic when I became what's known as "cross-rutted," meaning I got the front wheels into a set of ruts that were headed toward Lisbon and the back wheels into a set pointed at Reykjavík. As a result, I spun. I barely dropped anchor in time to avoid committing an act of civil disobedience, protesting the General Inclosure Act of 1801. That is, I nearly hit a fence.

At midday we stopped in Wantage, birthplace of Alfred the Great (A.D. 849), which like most English villages is possessed of a millennium's accumulated cuteness. We needed lunch, and we also needed enough petrol for our Afrika Korps–sized expedition. If you're planning an off-road jaunt in England, or anywhere else, you might try it with fewer people and vehicles. We went through the Midlands and Wales at about the same rate of speed as Geoff Chaucer's Canterbury package tour. It was fun, though, carrying our own house party with us, and the Wantage pubs appreciated the 2,000-percent increase in custom.

Back on the Ridgeway, we did some serious rooting about in the truffle pit of history. Here, between Wantage and Swindon, is the immense White Horse, a 365-foot-long, 130-foot-wide equine figure carved into the chalk hillside. Alfred the Great supposedly dug the thing himself, as a memorial to the drubbing he gave the pagan Danes at nearby Ashdown. More likely it's twice as old as that and was the totemic emblem of some gang of Celtic biker types. Anyway, it gives its name to the fine valley below, the Vale of White Horse, and also to the White Horse Tavern on Hudson Street in New York, where Dylan Thomas drank himself to death in 1953. A fine description of the area (the vale area, not Hudson Street) was left by Thomas Hughes in *Tom Brown's Schooldays*. (And the Scotch was left by us in the Land Rover. Whoops. It gets awfully cold and windy out in the middle of history.) Actually, the White Horse is not best viewed from the Ridgeway heights. From up there it looks like something you might get yourself into on a golf course and need a chalk wedge to get out of again. There is a nice hill alongside, however, where Saint George slew the dragon. (Unanswered questions: Was it dragon season? Is it sporting to slay them when they aren't on the wing? Was Saint George careful to extinguish all dragon-breath fires and pick up the spent lance tips and empty mead cans in his dragon blind?) No grass will grow on the place where the dragon's blood was spilled. This is because people walk around on it all the time, looking for the place where grass won't grow.

Back closer to where the whiskey and the cars were is an ancient hill fort called Uffington Castle. Nothing is left of it now except the turf mounds where the ramparts stood. Eerie to think of my blue-painted ancestors squatting here among the watch fires and plotting the same kinds of things my cousins are plotting tonight in some Belfast pub.

A bit farther along the Ridgeway is Wayland's Smithy, a New Stone Age "long barrow" of prodigious size. Presumably it was a burial chamber, but it may have been used for prehistoric games of nude stoop tag. There is, after all, much we don't know about the peoples of ancient Britain.

A Saxon legend of later date makes the barrow home to Wayland Smith, a blacksmith. If your horse threw a shoe while you were riding along the Ridgeway, you were supposed to leave a silver coin on a stone, whistle three times, and turn your back; Wayland would then shoe your horse and take the money. However, this does not work with a pound note and a Land Rover. But who wants a horseshoe pounded into his Land Rover's tire anyway?

By now we were full to the gills with history, and practically empty of Scotch, so it was time to push on to the night's lodgings. These were in Cowbridge, seventy miles away across the Severn and down the Welsh coast past Cardiff.

We'd planned to get on the M4 at Swindon and speed across the Severn Bridge in time to get really stupid and loud before dinner, but the high winds we'd been fighting all day caused the bridge to be closed. We had to make a massive detour up the Severn estuary, forty miles to Gloucester, then seventy miles back down to Cowbridge.

It was nearly eleven by the time we got there, so we had to settle for getting loud and stupid during dinner instead of before. The people at the Bear Hotel were lovely, though. That is, they didn't evict us at gunpoint. *Caveat gobbler,* however, about U.K. food, especially if you're tired and have had a few and are in the giggling sort of mood where you order what sounds funny on the menu. I ordered "whitebait," which turned out to be a plateful of deep-fat-fried guppies. The nearest McDonald's was 153 miles away, in London.

The sun (and the whitebait) came up the next day, and we pushed west to Port Talbot, where Richard Burton went to high school. Port Talbot bears a striking resemblance to Muncie, Indiana. We then avoided Swansea, where Dylan Thomas failed to drink himself to death because he didn't get home from New York in time, and motored inland along the River Neath to Aberdulais, where, according to local history, nothing much has ever happened.

In Aberdulais we left the pavement and turned onto the Sarn Helen, the principal Roman road linking north and south Wales. The name comes from Helen, wife of Magnus Maximus, who was Roman emperor for about five minutes in A.D. 383. Either that, or the name comes from *Y Lleng,* Welsh for "the legion," or from *elin,* which means "angle," or from anything else you can think of. Although the Sarn Helen is much newer than the Ridgeway, it's in much worse shape. The Ridgeway has good natural drainage, and it remained in active use until the early 1800s; but maintenance on the Sarn Helen stopped in A.D. 410, when the emperor Flavius Honorius took time out from being chased around Italy by Alaric the Visigoth to write a letter to the Britons telling them to take care of their own damn roads.

The Romans made a better road than anyone ever has since. For a primary road like the Sarn Helen they dug parallel ditches more than eighty feet apart and excavated the soil between them. Then they laid in a sand-and-quarry-stone foundation bound on either side by tightly fitted curbs of dressed and wedged stone blocks. On top of this foundation they built an embankment four or five feet high and fifty feet wide, constructed of layers of rammed chalk and flint and finished with a screened-gravel crown two feet thick.

Even so, 1,573 years of neglect have taken their toll. The road has worn down and topsoil has accumulated along it, and the Sarn Helen has turned from an embankment into a ditch. There are washouts and mudholes and boulders in the ditch, too. But the Sarn Helen *is* still there. I doubt we'll be able to say the same about I-95 in the year 3556.

Our first problem, however, was the work of man and not nature. Some farmer had dropped a big oak across the right-of-way—one of those very tangly and many-branched oaks. Apparently, it was felled on purpose to keep such trendies as ourselves from lurking about and luring sheep and daughters to chic London nightspots. Fortunately, among our horde of traveling companions was Roger Crathorne, demonstrations manager for Land Rover, Ltd. Roger is one of the most accomplished off-road drivers ever. Also fortunately, Rovers have winches. Roger used the winch on his Range Rover and the winch on the Land Rover to create something that looked like what I flunked in high-school trig. Then he deftly set the oak back among its roadside mates, while the rest of us stood around and gaped and drank Bloody Scotches. (A Bloody Scotch is what you drink when you want a Bloody Mary but don't have any vodka. It's just like a regular Bloody Mary, but with Scotch instead of vodka, and without tomato juice, Worcestershire sauce, celery sticks, or any of the rest of that stuff. You drink it right out of the bottle.)

Once past the tree blockade, we drove uphill through gullies so narrow that the bigger vehicles were digging mud with their door handles until we achieved a crest from which rustic beauty positively vomited forth—mist upon the heather, scudding clouds above, tree trunks artfully gnarling, all the usual stuff. A ruined stone house commanded the hill. There were arrow slits built into its walls. This farmstead stood fortified against . . . Saxons? Normans? Roundheads? Pesky neighbors with unruly kids? Probably lots of things. For centuries these hills ran wild with—well, with wild hill runners.

We traveled along heights fenced four hundred years ago by practitioners of the lost art of building dry stone walls, then entered the great pine woods known as the Fforest Fawr, and took a wrong ffork somewhere and got lost in an open-pit coal mine. This was neither interesting nor scenic. But we picked up the Sarn Helen again in a little town called Onllwyn.

Now the going turned dirty. There was nothing in the scenery to warn us, but the Sarn Helen became as bad a road as I've ever been down in anything except a metaphor. We were in rolling, pleasant upland. Parts of Beverly Hills look more ferocious. But the track across this peaceful greenery was vicious slop, broken only by chapel-width boulders and ruts where you could lose Kareem Abdul-Jabbar. The roadbed bucked and dipped like an amateur prostitute, and the bank angle tipped to the limits of a protractor's descriptive abilities. All this was spiced with greasy, knife-sharp ledges of shale, oleaginous grass clumps, Olympic-sized mud puddles, and just plain great big holes.

Half an hour in, soldiers began appearing. They sloughed toward us along the road, muddy and exhausted-looking. One of the Brits among us claimed they were candidates for some special commando force. He said they're put out at the end of the Sarn Helen with one extra pair of dry underpants and a piece of zwieback or suchlike, and, if they find their way back alive, they're in.

At the end of the Sarn Helen we forded the quick headwaters of a river and found ourselves looking down into what may be the most beautiful valley on earth. It is a wide and gentle-sided dell done up in all the most exquisite shades of green—emerald, hunter, loden, apple, jade, and olive—with tiny farms curling up each slope as though some wonderland were cupped in vast angelic hands.

But enough aesthetic palaver. If we had wanted beauty, we'd have been riding women, not cars and trucks . . . *Ouch! Stop! Ouch! Ouch!!* (It's important, when writing macho-type automotive journalism, to do it where your girlfriend can't see over your shoulder.)

From the beautiful valley we followed secondary roads northwest to Llandovery, getting caught in a herd of sheep along the way. The sheep were being drovered in the time-honored dog-nipped fashion, except that modern Welsh sheep have big iridescent-orange patches spray-painted on their sides for identification. This would certainly spoil the looks of any Staffordshire pastoral china figurines depicting Daphnis and Chloe his shepherdess love. The sheep looked as if they had been hanging out in the New York subway system.

Llandovery, an old center for Welsh drovers (sheep cowboys), had great charm in a sober Methodist way. All the more sober since we missed pub hours.

From Llandovery we went north up the River Tywi into the Cambrian Mountains. From their peaks we could see Cardigan Bay, twenty-five miles in the distance. The Cambrian Mountains were the hideout of Twm Sion Catti, the Welsh Robin Hood. The difference between the Welsh Robin Hood and the English Robin Hood is that Twm stole from everybody. Also, he had a sense of humor instead of a Maid Marian. According to my guidebook to south Wales, Twm once went into an ironmonger's shop and asked to buy a cooking pot. The storekeeper showed him one.

"No," said Twm. "That has a hole in it."

"I don't see a hole," said the storekeeper.

Twm took the pot and jammed it down over the storekeeper's ears. "If there's no hole," said he, "how'd I get your head in it?" Then Twm cleaned out the store.

A teeny but perfectly maintained byway led through the mountains past the Llyn Brianne Reservoir to a small chapel called the Soar y Mynydd. We paused while David E. Davis had his picture taken in the pulpit and I pondered why some Celts got John Wesley and dirty old coal mines while other Celts got whiskey recipes and popes with swell hats. If you ask me, the Welsh couldn't spell well enough to find the boat to Dublin.

Outside the chapel was a steep hill, its bottom third a smooth, wet, and naked rock face. The proper driving technique here was to take a fast run at it and stand on the gas and pray. We side-slipped and slithered. It was like trying to stuff a snake up a drainpipe. But we all made it to the top. I with my eyes closed.

Then it was national debt–size ruts and bogs as soft as a politician's conscience as we descended to Llanddewi Brefi, site of the sixth-century synod where Saint David refuted the Pelagian heresy. By this act he saved all of Western Europe from a religion that sounds like a skin disease.

In Tregaron that night, at the Talbot Inn, a wedding breakfast was being held in the bar. It had been going on for ten hours. Welshmen like Mr. Davis put great stock in Welsh singing, but to my Irish ears it sounds like men jumping off chairs into a bathtub full of frogs. As soon as dinner was over, Philip Llewellin, who was serving as our chief of reconnaissance and native gillie on this trip, decided to prove to the wedding party that, although he is only half Welsh, that half is from the throat to the liver. Of course the rest of us had to help. Our tab outran the wedding's within an hour, and by midnight we were as drunk as any leek-wearing Taffy you could find in a day's ride by sheepback. Pubs in the U.K., it's true, close their doors at 11:30, but what does it matter as long as you're on the inside of them when they do? The landlord waxed fond with our spending abilities and slapped down two bottles of whiskey, gratis, on our table. (The landlord's wife slipped in and prudently took one bottle back.) This whiskey was, I swear to you, named "Old Sheep Dip" right on the label, which proves once again that Protestants will drink anything. (Methodists serve grape juice at communion, you know.)

We finally put a stop to Philip's singing, so he began to tell stories. Llewellin is a marvel at this. "The rise and fall of empires, the passing of ages and eons, 'tis but the wink of the eye, a cloud across the sun, a breeze playing in the summer wheat . . ." He was quoting Shelley's "Ozymandias" when I left him at 3:00 A.M.

As I tucked myself into bed, the wedding party was beginning a giant brawl in the street below. I dozed off to the merry sounds of police whistles and breaking crockery. (How do you tell the bride at a

Welsh wedding ceremony? It's important, because she's the one you're not supposed to punch in the face.) In the morning Llewellin looked as though he'd been on the losing side, but he couldn't remember whether he'd gotten into the fight or just finished the bottle of Old Sheep Dip.

We refueled in Pontrhydfendigaid (pronounced "huh?") and took a gravel road back east into the huge stretch of grazing lands known as the Great Welsh Desert. Not many people live here, and I'm not so sure about those who do. Every time I got out of a car to relieve myself, the sheep would start backing toward me, looking over their shoulders expectantly.

About noon we left a rough gravel drovers' road and attempted to strike out across the great moor on the divide of the Cambrian Mountains. Llewellin, in the Cherokee, was in the lead at the top of a hill when, *squish,* Cherokee and Philip all but disappeared. Now, how can the top of the hill, where we were, be wetter than the bottom of the hill, whence we came? It is the miracle of the peat bog. (Peat, by the way, is found only in Celtic countries because God realized the Celts were the only people on earth who drank so much that they would try to burn mud.) Our hill had once been a basin where constant flooding encouraged the growth of ferns and their ilk. Dead fern bodies accumulated in a waterlogged mass that finally even other ferns couldn't grow in. Sphagnum moss took over. This can grow in the vilest muck. Layer after layer of sphagnum was laid down until the bog began to rise above the level of the surrounding land. By all rights this mound should have begun to drain and turn itself into a nice dry hummock or knoll or something, but instead the collected sphagnum acted as a giant sponge and swelled prodigiously with rainwater so that after 7,000 or 8,000 years we had a convex swamp thirty feet high at its peak. We also had a stuck Llewellin. Crathorne charged to the rescue with his Range Rover and went down too. Then I put the Blazer in, because three is a lucky number. We spent an hour and a half winching one another out.

The only way across such mire is to use an actual boat anchor on the end of your winch line and pull yourself across, but it would have been irresponsible and dangerous for us to have tried something like that, plus we might have missed lunch. So we gave up four-wheeling. We took a drive around the Elan Valley reservoirs instead and paused to view the great Edwardian edifice of the Claerwen Dam. It looks like Hadrian's Wall never did but should have. The reservoirs are a sore point with the Welsh, however. Their water goes to Birmingham, England, where water rates are much lower than they are in Wales. Also, the reservoirs cover a cottage where Shelley lived in 1812, and the Welsh don't hold with throwing cold water into the windows of poets' houses.

And that was it for us. Sunday afternoon was waning, and we were all due back in London that night. From the Elan Valley we continued east via normal roads. On our way to the English frontier we stopped at Rhayader for a delicious lunch. There we were set upon by punk rockers and thrashed nearly to death.

Actually, that last sentence is a lie. I just put it in to keep readers from being jealous. I mean, we're out wallowing in fun all the time, while you have to stay home and buy magazines. So I thought if I told you we all got beat up, you wouldn't get mad at us and go buy *Motor Trend* or anything.

Besides, I'm an honorary Welshman now. And as Gerald the twelfth-century archdeacon of Brecon said in *Descriptio Cambriae* ("The Description of Wales"): "A formal oath never binds them. They have no respect for their plighted word, and the truth means nothing to them. . . . To a people so cunning and crafty this seems no great burden, for they take it all very lightly."

Boom Squeal Boom Squeal
Yip Yip Yip
A Day Spent in a Bugatti EB110

Automobile, 1993

The Bugatti EB110 has 552 horsepower. The imagination lurches and fishtails. There at the command of my scuffed Bass Weejuns— 552 horses. What would 552 *real* horses do? Besides make a mess on this scenic road in the Apennine foothills? And would I make a worse one? But the clutch was facile, the accelerator smooth and positive, the car entirely comforting. I headed up a short, rising straightaway toward a tight right-hand bend. This was an automobile of power but power with sangfroid, gentlemanly power. There was a fine, light, diplomatic touch to the EB110. It was a well-bred *gran turismo.*

Until the tachometer reached 4,000.

The quadruple turbochargers kicked in. My brain flattened against the back of my skull cavity. The blood was driven out of my knuckles, knees, and nose. All my bodily orifices shut with a snap except for my eyes, which I'll probably never be able to close again.

I went around that hairpin before I could think. This didn't matter. I was in a realm beyond thought. I was transformed. A force, an inspiration flowed from the Bugatti's overbored 3.5-liter fuel-injected V-12 engine, through the throttle linkage, up my leg, and into this dull middle-aged corpus. My waist nipped in. My jowls grew taunt. The lines in my bifocals disappeared. I had the acuity of a twenty-year-old, no, a ten-year-old tall enough to see over the dashboard. I had more skill, better coordination, and quicker reflexes than I'd ever possessed—than *anyone* had ever possessed. And the Weejuns became made-to-measure hand-sewn antelope-skin driving shoes from Lobb's.

Five hundred fifty-two horsepower in a 3,572-pound car—almost the same power-to-weight ratio as a Messerschmitt 109 but the Bugatti is able to stay on the ground. Triple differential all-wheel drive distributes the largesse of torque. Twenty-seven percent goes to the front end's galactically large Michelin Pilot SX MXX3s with their eighteen-inch BBS forged composite wheels set like metallurgical jewels in rubber signet rings. Seventy-three percent goes to the even bigger possum mashers at the back. What ensues is not handling but a Nietzschean dream of will. There is no sense or hint or inclination of any movement other than forward. I was going seventy miles an hour in second gear coming out of the first turn and, hell, I shifted *up* for the next switchback.

Five hundred fifty-two horsepower in my control like steak on a dinner plate, a wheel that came to hand better than a custom-fitted Purdey shotgun and a leather seat that was a hug from behind by a naked Guess? jeans model. I suppose the EB110 is very, very wrong, a terrible waste of the earth's precious resources and a vehicle that's been described in blatantly sexist terms besides. We're entering another of Western culture's episodic fits of puritanism, and this is no time for the kind of loose money and big fun entailed in buying a $347,000 non-public transportation system without room for the car pool or even a spare copy of *Earth in the Balance*. Maybe I can excuse the Bugatti in

1990s terms by saying it makes me feel "empowered." But I suspect what the virtue twerps of Clinton World mean by *empowerment* is having a hissy fit at the local school board for not distributing enough preschool-size condoms to Head Start students.

Our president—that fat kid who played saxophone in the school band and told on us when we were smoking in the boys' room—him and his wife, the Iron Dingbat, don't even drive a car. They ride around in the back of long, black tax tractors fogging the windows with damp exhalations about reinventing government. What do the likes of the Clintons know about real empowerment? What do they ken of aluminum engine blocks, five-valve cylinder heads, and twin banks of dual overhead camshafts? A fig for your politics of meaning, Pudgy and Ruffles. I have touched and held a thing so exquisite in its delivery of puissance that it can cause a professional journalist to recite John Milton in a car magazine:

> *And joy shall overtake us as a flood,*
> *When everything that is sincerely good*
> *And perfectly divine,*
> *With Truth, and Peace, and Love shall ever shine . . .*
> *Then all this earthly grossness quit,*
> *Attir'd with Stars, we shall for ever sit,*
>   *Triumphing over Death, and Chance, and thee O Time.*

A time of zero to one hundred kilometers per hour in 3.46 seconds to be exact. The EB110 was so empowering it made me a citizen of Reagan's America again, richer, happier, never married, and—YOW, GREAT BIG TANKER TRUCK ON LITTLE ITALIAN BACK ROAD—slightly hyper. Fortunately the Bugatti has huge brake discs with four-piston calipers on each or I would've this earthly grossness quit too soon big time.

Anyway, there I sat after my first drive, attir'd with Stars—or, at least, with a bunch of them floating in front of my pupils—and triumphing over Death, Chance, et cetera. Some people have wondered whether the new Bugatti company is serious about building automobiles. No less an authority on seriousness (not to mention puritanism) than John Milton says, "And how."

David E. Davis, Jr., and I were the first members of the American automotive press to be allowed to take the EB110 on real roads. We flew to Bologna and settled in at the magnificent Grand Hotel Baglioni, with room ceilings as high as a Grateful Dead fan and service faster than Andre Agassi's and much better mannered. Here we were met by the charming Dr. Stefano Pasini who is both the public relations director of Bugatti and a prominent ophthalmologist (a good thing considering how corneas go squash when the Bugatti's turbochargers light off). Dr. Pasini—a man with such an Erasmian sweep of automotive knowledge that he is able to name what Elvis drove in the King's car-racing movies—entertained us lavishly. In case anyone is wondering whether our journalistic objectivity was being unduly influenced by Bugatti's hospitality, of course it was. That's Dr. Pasini's job. And let me tell you, for a city named after a brown bag lunch, Bologna has some remarkable restaurants. Not that it made any difference. We could have been given an, as it were, bologna sandwich and a test drive in an *autostrada* rest stop and we would have gone all faint and blushing over the EB110.

Properly rested and sobered up, we drove from Bologna, past the outskirts of Modena, to Campogalliano, where Bugatti's astonishing factory is located. The buildings were designed by Giampaolo Benedini, who also designed the EB110 itself and who is a vice chairman of Bugatti Automobili S.p.A. The main offices are made up of a huge tinted-glass cylinder, a huge tinted-glass cube, and a couple of other huge tinted-glass shapes that I don't know the names for because Sally Bungart had missed a button on her blouse the day they taught those in solid geometry class. Directly behind the offices is an engineering facility covered in enameled steel siding colored deep Bugatti blue. This structure is gently rounded at the roof so that it resembles either very handsome industrial architecture or the world's largest and most frightening Jell-O dessert. After dessert comes the factory proper, a kind of louvered affair like a venetian blind tossed out at the Brobdingnag dump.

Not that there is anything dumpy about any of this. The whole compound is designed to the furthest extent, plated, etched, turned, and milled in platonic industrial style. The rugs, the walls, the reception desk, even the ashtrays are all at Euro-aestheticism's cutting edge. And plop down on the sofa and you'll find cutting edge to be no empty phrase. The bathroom is so *alto-tecnico* that there are no light switches. The building senses when you're in there and the lights come on automatically. Of course this *is* Italy, and the lights come on automatically late. So you discover you're taking a leak in the sink. Or maybe not since the fixtures are so modern it's hard to tell the sink from the urinal from the soap dish from the hand dryer.

But—being fair to Giampaolo Benedini—I may not like his bathroom but he's done a hell of a job on the automobile. The problem of supercar styling is aerodynamics. They all look like jet-propelled cheese wedges. Benedini has worked on the basic shape, moving the wheels to the ends of the bodywork, plumping out the Kamm back, integrating the roofline in a smooth dorsal curve, bobbing the blunt little nose, putting sensual lines in a functional medium. The result is compact, beautiful, even cute. Benedini has created personality in a supercar without resorting to the Fokker triplane brutalism of the Countach or gimmicks like those Testarossa side strakes that make me think of an old Briggs & Stratton lawn mower engine or the crew-cut attachment on a barber's electric razor.

The factory part of Bugatti is rather small. But it's very busy and very clean and so well organized that it exerts a strong visceral appeal to that aspect of the male psyche which has too much coffee on a rainy Sunday and goes to the basement and sorts all the finishing nails into labeled mayonnaise jars.

Only forty-seven Bugattis had been delivered as of the beginning of September. Total production for 1993 is targeted at ninety-eight. Three cars a week were being made when we were there. They hoped to be making one car per business day soon.

Even at $347,000 a pop it's hard to see how this is going to make money for Romano Artioli, who bought the dormant Bugatti marque in 1988. But I gather that other companies—Michelin, Elf, BBS, Nagamichi, Aerospatiale, Belco Avia, IHI—have signed on, using the EB110 and the forthcoming EB112 saloon as test beds and rolling advertisements. Bugatti's engineering staff will undertake consulting and research and development work for other corporations. And Artioli's wife, Renata, has begun a design firm that will market clothing, accessories, jewelry, and luxury goods under the Bugatti name. (I hope she stops short of a men's cologne. Though the various scents of garages, showrooms, and racetracks have pleasing associations for me, I've yet to hear a woman say, "Mmmmmmm, you smell like a car.")

Dr. Pasini explained all this but I was distracted by the Bugatti headquarters conference table, the most complicated piece of furniture I've ever seen, made out of a sheet of glass as thick as Donna Shalala supported by enough alloy tubing to build a birdcage Maserati. Also, the Bugatti test track is right there on the company grounds, and I don't mean over in the corner of the lot behind a bunch of crash barriers. The track goes from the back door of the factory around behind the engineering department, takes a hard left at the management parking lot, comes within pit stop distance of the conference room window, hangs a Louie at the front side of the Jell-O mold, and becomes a high-speed straight directly in front of the assembly-line employees' entrance. Everything Dr. Pasini said to us was punctuated by baritone exhaust notes, shrieking tire treads, and a peculiar sound the Bugatti makes when its turbocharger waste gates close down—a noise David E. likened to small dogs being run over by Radio Flyer wagons. BOOM SQUEAL BOOM SQUEAL YIP YIP YIP. When was the last time anyone sat down to talk about the car business with a GM executive in earshot of an actual car?

We had to get into one of these Land Lears. Dr. Pasini sent us off with Giuseppe Montorsi, a test driver of great ability and courage who proved to be a passenger of even greater courage, plus self-restraint.

We drove up into the hills toward Mt. Cimone on the road to Pisa until Montorsi found us a squiggle of secondary pavement that went through a couple of villages whose signposts passed in a blur of Romance language vowels. The small road emptied into a long down-hill sweep of two-lane highway, which we would turn off for a bad fly cast of a hill climb back to the small town streets. This was testing in real-life conditions with kids and cats and Fiat Unos and tiny old ladies in black scattering out of the way and that great big tanker truck which didn't.

The more I drove the EB110 the more hopelessly enamored I became, and I'd been a regular Tristan to this vehicular Isolde since my first tug at its neat little self-centering, race-gated six-speed gearshift. The Bugatti's transmission is housed within its engine block, below the right cylinder bank and parallel with the crankshaft. But, unlike most cars whose gearboxes are not quite where you'd expect them to be, there's no feeling of slack or play in the 110's shifting. The stick is as positive and the throw is as short as on any old muscle car with a Hurst. And the 110's chassis is as rigid as Detroit Iron although this is achieved with Aerospatiale's carbon-fiber technology instead of a ton and a half of welded steel frame. There was no feeling of structural flex inside the car, and there was "road feel" only in the purest sense of that term. I could feel the road all right and plenty of it, but I couldn't feel any-thing in or on the road—none of the bumps, dips, paving cracks, pot-holes, and cobblestones with which rural Italy is liberally provided. And, if I crushed some nuns or baby carriages, I didn't notice that either. The 110 is the only hugely powerful car I've driven that has what an Oldsmobile salesman would call "ride." This is the result of a double-wishbone pull-rod suspension system possibly as complex as the Bugatti conference table. David E. and photographer Martyn Goddard were standing by the side of the road between the two villages as I came missiling through a photo-op bend. David E. said he could see the Bugatti's wheels and axles in frantic, bubbling, liquid motion against the pavement surface while above it all the Bugatti itself was steady as the liner *France*. Personally I'd say the liner *France* has a lot more body roll.

David E. did quite a bit of standing beside the road. Despite his superiority in rank, age, and merit, I shamelessly hogged the auto. I practically had to be pulled out of the car by my hair. And, considering the 110's sill height and the snug dimensions of the Poltrona Frau glove leather upholstery, being pulled out by the hair is almost the only way to exit the Bugatti gracefully.

Herewith a few other small criticisms. The folks able and willing to purchase a GT for a third of a million dollars are likely to be men of substance and probably not too young. I'm not too young myself and am getting to be a man of substance, in girth if not in wallet. Fortunately I'm a short man of substance, and the 110 fit me very well. But, for a more physically imposing fellow—David E. Davis, Jr.—it was a squeeze. And memo to all designers, automotive and otherwise: will you please quit reinventing the door? There are certain things—sex, beer, radios you could tune with a knob—that mankind got right on the first try, and they don't need improving. The 110's doors open with an upward/forward throws-like-a-girl motion. And they are closed by reaching way out of your seat and making like you're going to do a one-armed chin-up then not getting the thing to fully latch, whereupon you can't find the door handle to open it again. Also, for an automobile that has more glass canopy area than I. M. Pei's new entrance to the Louvre, there's not enough air-conditioning. And the Subaru SVX–style window within a window is not big enough, especially if, like me, you're trying to jettison your cigar ash at a hundred miles per hour.

But these are my only complaints, and they are of a "Sharon Stone has ugly toes" caliber. (I do not, alas, *know* whether Sharon Stone has ugly toes, though I certainly have seen the whole rest of her on the movie screen.) Speaking of feet, here's another rarity in a very high performance car—the 110's pedals are all in the right place and not mashed together like the tiny buttons on a Japanese car stereo or pushed so far over to one side that you might as well let the passenger operate them. Nor does the 110 have any noticeable motor vibration, which is unusual in any mid-engined car and amazing in one where the mill sits behind a glass partition closer to your head than Grecian Formula 16.

Except for those puppy-squeal waste-gate noises and whatever tire skid sounds you can summon the courage to make, the car is very quiet inside. I'd even prefer a stronger exhaust note. But such things are not allowed by all-knowing (and hearing) governments these days. And, on the subject of government, keeping an eye out for uniformed, ticket-dispensing representatives of same will be a big job in a car that can go 213 mph. Fortunately, the Bugatti has excellent visibility in every direction but the back. And nobody's going to be coming at you from there.

I took a few more loops around our ad hoc testing ground. There is no exaggerating what the proper use of four-wheel drive does for road holding in a massively powerful car. And no describing it either. "On rails" hardly serves as a metaphor since that Amtrak mess near Mobile. The Bugatti 110 simply goes in the direction you tell it to go before you've finished telling it and stops going in that direction exactly when it ought to. Neither its front nor its rear has any opinions of its own or crackpot notions about where the car should be headed.

I took the 110 down onto the highway and let it out—80 in second, 100 in third, 140 in fourth (and, this side of the Bonneville Salt Flats, just forget about the rest of those gears). All these speeds were as quickly achieved as a remote-control channel change and without grazing the 8,200 red line. I didn't deign to consider oncoming traffic. Anything that hadn't reached me yet would never do so before I was back in my lane. And thus, empowered as all get-out, I swatted past any number of puritanical trucks and democratic buses and cars lumbering at Clintonic jog pace. In a Bugatti EB110 you can triumph over Death, Chance, Time, and even Hillary. I know John Milton got blind and sanctimonious later on but, before he did, he must have done some fast driving. Possibly in a post chaise drawn by 552 horses.

A Borderline Experience

Touring the
Impoverished Mexican Frontier in a
Lincoln Town Car with a Flashy Blonde

Automobile, 1987

The U.S./Mexican border region isn't one of earth's garden spots. Especially not now, when low oil prices, corruption, and enormous foreign debt have created the worst* economic crisis in Mexico's history (and that's going some). But the truly devoted tourist likes to avoid the crowds, and the only crowds on the Mexican border are swimming across it.

Automobile said they'd get me a car and a photographer if this was really where I wanted to go. I went to pick up the car at the Ford offices in Dallas. I was expecting a Bronco or a four-wheel-drive

---

*Whoops, spoke too soon.

160

pickup. Ford handed me the keys to a Designer Series Lincoln Town Car, metallic silver with silver leather interior, silver vinyl landau top, power moon roof, and a big sign reading "Cartier" on the trunk lid. Driving this through the barrios of Juárez would, I thought, be like sending the Pasadena Rose Parade through Watts in the middle of an outdoor Run-DMC concert. Then the photographer arrived. It was Maria Krajcirovic, the beautiful Czechoslovakian girl whose hand-colored photos make the editors in the front of this magazine look a lot better than they do. But Maria is a bit *too* beautiful—blond, tall, and emphatically shaped. Between Maria and the Lincoln, I was sure I'd attract less attention in Mexico if I brought the Pope.

Czechoslovakia is a serious and orderly country. And Maria had emigrated from there to Ann Arbor, Michigan, one of America's most serious and orderly towns. It was news to her that people keep goats in their kitchens, throw soiled Pampers out car windows, and use the ditch beside the road for the family Maytag. As soon as we'd crossed the Rio Grande, Maria began calling the border "The Tropic of Dirt."

We crossed at Eagle Pass, into the Mexican town of Piedras Negras, about 145 miles southwest of San Antonio and somewhere near the bleak locale of Larry McMurtry's *Lonesome Dove*. I piloted the Lincoln through Piedras Negras's warren of tiny side streets feeling like the captain of the QE II on a cruise through the canals of Venice. No rocks and bottles were thrown by the populace, however. I'd figured this car would get us sentenced to life in prison for first-degree Gringoism. Not so. We received nothing but approving looks and profuse compliments. The Mexicans thought the Town Car was *muy bueno,* an *automóvil superior* or, as one Pemex gas station attendant put it, *el car boss.* This says a lot about the unenvious good nature of the Mexican people. I'm not sure what it says about the Ford styling department.

To tell the truth, I was glad to get into Mexico. All the minimall clutter and highway strip development disappeared in Piedras Negras. The market was still downtown in an ancient adobe building. Music blurted from loudspeakers in the market stalls. Outside, mufflers dragged behind cars and people were all over the place laughing and yelling. Mexico is a mess, but it's a lively mess. And, best of all, there are no Taco Bells. Mexico is the only place in North America where you can escape the horrible Mexican restaurant plague. They have great *hamburguesas* in Mexico, excellent *perros calientes* (hot dogs), delicious *quesadillas* (toasted cheese sandwiches), and wonderful *huevos revueltos* (scrambled eggs). But if you want a double dog food taco in a rock-hard corn tortilla, you have to go back to the States.

But I used to be a hippie, so you shouldn't trust me about Mexico. Anything that reeks of natural materials and native tradition is better than anything plastic as far as I'm concerned. Of course, I might think differently if I had to choose between an artificial heart valve made of polystyrene and one made of adobe, as Maria was quick to point out.

Maria was also quick to point out the stuffed frogs. "Oh, God, oh, God, what's *that?!*" she screamed when she got her first look at three shellacked amphibians standing upright with miniature mariachi band instruments in their webbed forelegs. Stuffed frogs posed in various clever ways were for sale in all the border towns. But for sale to *whom?* Even the most addled tourist isn't going to bring home a frog swinging a golf club as a souvenir. Souvenirs are supposed to evoke memories. Who'd want to remember a thing like that? Stuffed frogs are one of the aesthetic mysteries of Mexico. I only bought a couple of the really good ones working out with Nautilus equipment.

There were a lot of other aesthetic mysteries in the Piedras Negras market. Who wants a sombrero the size of a hot tub? Or a forty-five-pound onyx bunny? Or a three-foot sculpture of Don Quixote made out of welded coat hangers? Maybe nobody, because vendors were throwing themselves at us as we walked through the aisles.

"Señor, a painting of Sean Penn on velvet for the lady?"

"Señorita, Aztec pottery—almost genuine!"

"The largest selection of cement burros for your yard!"

"Many fine wallets embossed with the Virgin Mary!"

Maria said this importuning was a sign of economic desperation. But I don't know. You have to remember the national sport of Mexico is getting a large farm animal into a sports arena and teasing it. I think the Mexicans just know how to get the most fun out of their tourists. And I think New York's Fifth Avenue would be a lot more festive if the salesmen at Tiffany's ran out the door and chased you down the street yelling, "My dear man, simply observe the understated elegance of this sterling silver baby porringer available with the baby's own future country club name engraved upon it."

We headed northwest out of Piedras Negras along the Rio on Mexico Route 2. Here my second big worry about the Lincoln disappeared. It's hard to describe Mexican pavement conditions without using swear words. I figured the Town Car would get its Cartier signature self shaken to rubble in a twinkling.

The Lincoln has a mush-bucket suspension in the great Buick Roadmaster, Packard Caribbean tradition. But this is a mush bucket that works. The wheels just slurped and gobbled all the heaves, holes, and whoop-de-dos. I've driven a lot of miles through Mexico in everything from off-road racers to Saab turbos and this is the first time I've been comfortable. It was also ninety-five degrees outside with Hiroshima-class sunshine and the Town Car's air conditioner was still able to give us frostbite with the moon roof open. Furthermore, I'd filled the poor vehicle with horrible Pemex gasoline, which has less octane than fruit cocktail, and the engine just purred along, not a knock, ping, or burp to be heard.

The scenery, unfortunately, was not as pleasant as the ride. Scattered along the highway were little rancheros made from cement blocks, wattle, corrugated tin, and whatnot—chickens and children all over the place and yards festooned with old car bodies, oil drums, and bald tires. The North is to Mexico what the West is to the United States, the place people pick up and go to to make a new start. Except, in Mexico, they're not looking to get a bit part on *Dynasty*. They're hoping for two acres of scrubland, one cow, and a twenty-year-old truck.

Maria was shocked at the living conditions. She looked like Eleanor Roosevelt must have the first time somebody showed her a coal mine. I didn't have the heart to tell Maria these people were doing pretty well.

Route 2 stops at the Del Rio border crossing. Beyond this are the trackless Serranías del Burro, the Donkey Highlands, which form the Mexican side of the Big Bend country. To continue west we had to go back to the United States.

The U.S. Customs agents took a long look at the dirt-smeared Lincoln. Its vast backseat was filled to the windows with camping gear, bags of canned goods, suitcases full of Banana Republic clothes, tubes of sunblock, coolers, thermoses, and fifteen gallons of bottled water. You can't be overprepared south of the border.

"How long have you been in Mexico?" asked an agent.

"Six hours."

They went through the car and everything in it and on it and under it. I wanted to ask them if this is how narcotics usually come into the country—with good-looking blondes in something that probably belongs to Liberace. (If so, you'd think they'd be able to stop a lot more of the drug traffic than they do.) But I restrained myself. The agents were already grumpy enough trying to figure out whether shellacked frogs are on the endangered species prohibited import list. (They aren't.)

Customs let us go after an hour and we drove west across the spectacular Pecos River canyon and into the broad, grassy basins of Val Verde County. The land was astonishingly empty, and you'd better come see it quick because I'm sure some new Phoenix or Houston is slated to go up here any minute.

The Lincoln was swell on its home turf. We just pointed it at the setting sun and let it go. I have a few minor complaints. The speedometer only reads to eighty-five miles an hour while the five-liter V-8 will easily shove the car to a hundred and maybe well beyond. (Road manners were so good and wind noise so minimal that it was hard to estimate top speed.) There was a tiny shimmy up around ninety-five, but I think this was a result of what Mexico had done to the wheel alignment. The cruise control also stops at eighty-five, and this is not fair to those of us with a lead-filled but lazy accelerator foot. On the plus side, the Town Car's trip computer is way too complicated. This didn't happen to be an advantage for Maria and me. But, if you're traveling with a pesky teen, all the function buttons will keep him silent and enthralled for hours.

We stopped at a restaurant in the total middle of nowhere, and the food was so good that I bought the chef a drink. I wanted to find out what kind of person knew this much about cooking and this little about getting to New York or Paris. He was an ex-Marine, about twenty-eight. I'll call him Dave. Midway through his third Jack Daniel's Dave began telling me how he smuggled drugs.

"I go down to Boquillas Canyon in the Big Bend Park and go across the Rio with a backpack. I've got a connection down there, in this little dirtball Mexican town, with the *La Familia,* which is, like, the Mexican Mafia. Then I walk out, traveling at night. It takes a couple of days."

"U.S. Customs doesn't mind this?" I asked.

"They don't expect anybody to take a backpack and walk out. But it gets a little hairy sometimes. I was working with some other guys once and I got caught in an ambush and three of them got shot."

Maria was looking at the ceiling by now, but I'm a credulous type. "Customs agents ambushed you?" I asked.

"No way. I think it was the guy who sold us the stuff. You know, so he could get it back and sell it to somebody else. He makes more money that way."

Maria and I continued west to Marathon, where we found a great little hotel called the Gage. We arrived just in time to see a Texas plains lightning storm, rated R for violence, from the Gage veranda. I don't know what all these first-rate travel amenities are doing out here. I can't imagine the lightning storms attract *that* many tourists. Maybe people buying drugs like to stay and have a nice meal and a snooze.

In the morning we drove south toward Big Bend National Park. I pushed the Lincoln back to top speed. The car never loses its road feel. Of course, it doesn't have a lot of road feel to begin with. But what it has, it keeps. Usually driving an American luxo car at exotica speeds is like the last half minute of landing an airplane with the gear up.

(Often with the same results.) But the Town Car hangs in there and could almost be said to track if you don't count the four inches of on-center play in the power steering.

Big Bend is more desolate than awesome or rugged. It's interesting, if you've been very bad and want to see what the afterlife will be like. Otherwise, not. We saw some signs to the Boquillas Canyon Dave, the soi-disant drug smuggler, had mentioned. We followed them and arrived at a small parking lot by the Rio Grande. An old Mexican was sitting on a stump. For three dollars he said he'd take us across. He led us along a half-mile path through the cottonwood and canebrake to a rowboat pulled up on the bank. There were no gates or customs agents or formalities in sight.

On the Mexican side of the river we hired two burros and rode up to the canyon rim, where we found a nasty and impoverished-looking town. The sole café was nothing but a shaded patio with a cook-stove in a shed beside it. On one corner of the patio sat a dark, barrel-chested man of about fifty in a shiny American wheelchair. His legs were covered with a blanket though the temperature was almost a hundred degrees. He wore a large Rolex watch and a freshly pressed shirt and a new straw hat with sharp creases.

We had lunch at the café, or, rather, I did. Maria took a look in the cookshack and demurred. As we were leaving I said *"Buenos días,"* to the man in the wheelchair. "Good afternoon," he answered affably enough. But he had a smile like a lizard's and all his teeth were gold.

"I don't know," said Maria on the way back down to the river, "maybe Dave wasn't lying after all." As far as I could tell we could have brought the treasure of the Sierra Madre, or the Sierra Madres themselves, back to the United States and no one would have been the wiser.

Look alive, you customs people. If Americans spend all their money on crack and so forth, they won't have any left to spend on swell cars, and then where will this magazine be?

We went west out of the park on Texas 170. The Rio Grande canyons are lovely here but there were park ranger speed traps all over the place so we were going too slow to really appreciate the beauty.

Spectacular scenery should always be driven through at a hundred miles an hour. That way it has poignancy. It's a fleeting glimpse of paradise. But, if you dawdle or stop to gaze, you'll realize scenery is pretty static stuff. There's no plotline to speak of and Debra Winger is not going to bound through it nude anytime soon. You'll get restless and bored.

To be bored with beauty is a terrible thing for the soul so I was anxious to get back to Mexico, where I could drive the Town Car like a maniac. There are no rules on Mexican highways, at least none that a ten-dollar tip to the Federales won't get you excused from. And there are practically no Federales on the highways anyhow. They are napping in the towns.

We blasted out of Presidio on Mexico Route 16 south into the IUD coil switchbacks of the Sierra de la Magdalena. The pavement, such as it was, was a lane and a half wide with no guardrails and abysmal drops on every side. Enormous trucks doing five miles an hour blocked the blind curves going uphill. Enormous buses doing eighty blocked them coming down. Stray cows and goats wandered in between.

Maria may have been a sissy about lunch, but she was no coward in the passenger seat. She opened the Town Car's moon roof and, bracing herself with one foot on the trip computer, stood up out of the car and began clicking photos. The Mexican truck drivers were appreciative to the point of distraction. I refused to look in the rearview mirror for fear of seeing what kind of accident she'd caused. "The light is exquisite," yelled Maria.

We reached the broad plateau leading to Chihuahua City at sunset. Maria was hanging out of the moon roof again when suddenly her face swelled like a melon.

"I cwan't bwief," said Maria, dropping into the car. Her eyes looked like coin slots between the great red puffs of her forehead and cheeks. She was shaking all over.

"Insect bites! Are you allergic to insect bites?!" I said. "Pollen?! Truck fumes?!" I was panicked. If they'd given me all that trouble at customs about stuffed frogs, what would they say about a dead blond photographer?

"Nwo!" said Maria. "Mwexago! Um awergic twa Mwexago!"

"You're allergic to Mexico." I mentally cataloged the first-aid kit I'd brought along: whiskey, extra cigarettes, a large Buck knife in case I had to cut my leg off because of snakebite. "Would some whiskey and cigarettes help?"

"NWO!"

I drove at top speed for Chihuahua and just on the edge of town I saw a sign, *"Médico,"* on a ramshackle little house.

I knocked and was invited in by a smiling fellow in a doctor jacket who looked to be about nineteen. His living room was littered with clothes and newspapers just like my own, which was not reassuring. There was a desk in one corner with a prescription pad and some tongue depressors lying on it.

"Médica emergencia!" I said and added *"por favor,"* remembering that Spanish is a language where courtesy is very important. *"Mi amiga es muy . . .* um . . . sick."

"Tiene un enfermedad?" asked the doctor, picking up a tongue depressor and advancing on me.

"No, no, mi amiga!" I said, running to get Maria out of the car, which was surrounded by a crowd of urchins admiring its styling excesses.

"Es alergia," said the doctor when he saw Maria looking like a pumpkin.

"Sí, sí, alergia," I said.

The doctor got a stethoscope and one of those pointy ear and nose flashlights out of an end table drawer and examined Maria's giant head. *"Alergia,"* he confirmed and took a big hypodermic needle from the bookshelf. The doctor patted his behind and pointed to Maria.

"NO!!!" said Maria, who'd pulled a phrase book out of her purse and was frantically paging through it looking for the Spanish word for no, which is *no.*

"What is, I mean, *qué es* that?" I said, pointing to the needle.

"Es vitaminas y antihistamínicas y cortisonas y anfetaminas y otras vitaminas y etcétera."

I wouldn't have minded a shot of this myself, but Maria was adamant. "Just some capsules! some *cápsulas!"* she said, tearing through the phrase book, *"los capsulidads! el pills!!"* Maria was getting her voice back remarkably well.

The doctor shrugged. What could he do if the patient didn't want to be cured? With the help of the *Berlitz Passport to Spanish,* he made of list of things Maria shouldn't eat: eggs, fruit, vegetables, dairy products, meat, fish, poultry, alcoholic beverages, soft drinks, water, bread, salt, and candy. Then he wrote out several elaborate prescriptions and charged us $3.50.

By the time we got back in the car Maria was completely well. At least she said, "I'm fine now and don't stop at any more doctors," though she still looked a little basketballish around the face for the next couple days.

I immediately got lost in Chihuahua, which is not the sleepy ranch town I'd pictured but a city of 300,000 people and two working streetlamps. Asking directions was hard since not only didn't I speak the language but I also had no idea where we were going. It hadn't occurred to us to make hotel reservations.

I asked various passersby, *"Dónde es el hotel grande?"* This met with the inevitable Mexican answer to any question about which way to go: *"Sí, sí, bueno."*

"Es el hotel aquí?" I'd ask and point up the street.

"Sí."

"Es no hotel aquí?" I'd ask and point the same direction.

"Sí."

A Mexican will never admit he can't understand any more than an American will admit he can't be understood. Mexicans are, however, very agreeable about this.

We did find a hotel eventually, because eventually everything happens in Mexico. The trick is to drink enough so you don't mind if it doesn't. By the time we'd found the very pleasant and reasonably priced Sicómoro on Boulevard Ortiz Mena, I'd been doing that for hours.

Don't bother to take that address down. Chihuahua is the Gary, Indiana, of Mexico with the same charming combination of heavy industry and unemployment.

We had *desayuno,* a.k.a. breakfast, and drove north on Route 45 toward Juárez. It was raining and the road took us through rolling green hills that could have been in Switzerland except for the roadside shrines full of Virgin Mary statues wearing clothing and jewelry. Sixty miles north of Chihuahua the rain disappeared and the land turned to flat scrub with the Sierra Madre Occidental peaks rising to our left, real purple mountain majesties stuff, though minus the fruited plain.

In Juárez we stumbled onto a remarkable antidote to stuffed frogs and cement burros. In the middle of town there's a government store selling Mexican folk arts and crafts. It's called FONART—short for *Fondo Nacional para el Fomento de las Artesanias.* Here was the brilliant part of Mexico's mystery aesthetics. The place was filled with handsome rugs and blankets, beautiful pottery, papier-mâché work, wood carvings, and basketry. All cheap, with the peso going for 780 to the dollar, and all leavened with just the right grotesque sensibility. For instance, there were Oaxacan Indian ceramic sculptures of demons and dead people, but they weren't just hanging around being demonic and dead. The pottery demons were driving pottery buses or riding pottery motorcycles. Skeletons were having jam sessions, feasts, and fiestas. These sculptures were anywhere from a foot to three feet across, painted in amazing colors and fired to a brilliant glaze. Maria bought herself a huge demon mermaid playing a piano made of human skulls. I thought she was beginning to change her mind about the country.

Anyway, Juárez was nice. We stayed at the El Presidente hotel, which is quite luxurious if you don't mind some of the luxury coming off in your hand when you try to turn on the shower.

The next day we went west on the resumption of Mexico Route 2, through the desert and up into those purple mountains. At the Continental Divide, on the border between Chihuahua and Sonora states, there is the most amazing view I've ever seen from an automobile. You push uphill through the mountain passes for an hour and suddenly an enormous V-shaped notch opens before you and there, a thousand feet below, is the immense north Sonoran plain stretching green and cottonwood dotted away to three horizons. Much as I hate stopping and gazing, I had to stop and gaze at this. And I noticed that even the truck drivers and the crazed bus pilots stopped there, too.

We drove through those grasslands and up to the border and spent the night in Douglas, Arizona, at the Gadsden Hotel. The Gadsden is a splendid remnant of Douglas's days as a silver mine boomtown. Huge Corinthian columns of travertine support the lobby ceiling. One wall is pierced by a series of windows in Tiffany stained glass, depicting the local landscape. It was the only desert mural Tiffany ever did. The broad marble staircase has a chip out of one step where Pancho Villa is said to have ridden his horse upstairs.

But, again, I was glad to get back to the freedom and disorder of Mexico, where I could really let the Town Car holler. We would ultimately cover 2,200 miles over some of the worst major highways north of the Darien Gap, and the Lincoln never developed a single rattle or had the slightest mechanical malfunction. Fuel mileage worked out just a little shy of eighteen miles to the gallon—not bad at full throttle on Pemex and with the AC going all the time. Only one quart of oil was needed. I defy anything, army tank or tricycle, to go through Mexico with less trouble.

We continued west on Route 2, back into the mountains, and about four in the afternoon we came upon a fiesta in the town of Magdalena. It was some saint's day, we never figured out which. You could buy plaster images of his dead body in a glass box, and hundreds of people were lined up to go to confession. Once cleansed they spread out under an acre of awnings, where there were a dozen beer taps and two dozen mariachi bands all playing different tunes at teenage radio volume. People were coming into town from every direction, walking and driving and crammed in the back of stake bed trucks. Seventy or eighty Indians were sleeping in the bushes behind the church. All sorts of gaudy things were for sale. Barbecue pits had been built in the plaza. Chickens sizzled on grills, and beef chunks smoked on skewers. And on the banks of the Rio Alisos a traveling carnival had set up shop.

Maria and I were standing near the Tilt-O-Whirl ride. "I love Mexico!" I said, *"Yo amo Mey-he-ko!"* (I'd had a few beers.) "There's something about this place," I raved on, "a bighearted heedlessness, a spirit of feckless life, an air of wild slapdash. There are no insurance salesmen, no retirement benefits packages, no DOT or Department of

Consumer Affairs. It's one of the last mad, wide-open places in the world. Anything can happen here!"

Maria was looking intently at the Tilt-O-Whirl mechanism. There was an unoiled mangle of gears at its center with rusty pulley wheels radiating a dirty nest of slack V-belts. "If you like Mexico so much," she said, "I dare you to get on that carnival ride."

The Ultimate Politically
Incorrect Car

Automobile, 1992

AUTHOR'S NOTE: The following was part of an article in which *Automobile's* writers picked their favorite excessively fast, unsafe, fuel-wasting motor vehicles with not enough trunk space to carry things to the recycling center.

If you're looking for something to upset the multiculturizing tofu nibblers, something to scare the holistic eco-pests back into Biosphere 2, something that will tell the "Think Globally/Act Locally" crowd to "Eat My Shorts Totally," I commend to you AM General Corporation's High Mobility Multipurpose Wheeled Vehicle, the Hummer.

The Hummer is a regular Pat Buchanan on wheels. In the first place, it was developed for those notorious militarists, the military. They purchased it with wasteful defense appropriations that could have been spent on homeless dolphins. Then the Hummer was used to oppress innocent third-world victims of American imperialism such as Manuel Noriega. Plus, Arnold Schwarzenegger owns one.

So Phil Donahue and Sinéad O'Connor will not be double-dating in a Hummer soon. But the odd thing is that Phil and Baldy are—for the first time in their lives—right. The Hummer is one of those overconceived and underconsidered Pentagon whatchamajigs. It's two-thirds muddle and three-fourths boondoggle and largely incapable of doing anything that couldn't be done by a four-wheel-drive Toyota pickup with a .50-caliber machine gun mounted on its roof.

The Hummer is fifteen feet long, seven feet wide, and weighs 6,200 pounds. That is fifteen inches longer, fourteen inches wider, and 2,749 pounds heavier than a Jeep Cherokee. The civilian model Hummer seats four in profound discomfort and costs $44,000. It has a Brobdingnagian 6.2-liter diesel engine that produces a Lilliputian 150 base horsepower and gets—excuse the pun—a not too *Swift* 13.5 miles per gallon. And the Hummer's sixteen inches of ground clearance and 60 percent grade capacity are nothing you can't get by putting great big tires and a winch on your Buick.

But I love the thing. I'd be proud and happy to own it. And I'll tell you why. I was an ABC radio correspondent in the Persian Gulf. When the ground war began, I went into Kuwait with a press convoy (mostly Mitsubishi Monteros, by the way) led by a group of affable but incompetent British officers. We called them the Desert Squirrels. We arrived in Kuwait City in the middle of the night, eight hours ahead of the Allied armies. Fortunately, the Iraqis had already retreated. But the city was in the hands of the "Kuwaiti Resistance"—armed high school kids who'd flunked their hunter safety courses. There was no electricity. We could hear small-arms fire nearby and large explosions in the distance, and we decided our little group ought to pull out of town until dawn at least, if not until next year.

The Desert Squirrels, however, had forgotten to bring maps. Thus

I and about forty other people wound up utterly lost in the pitch-dark suburbs of Kuwait City. We'd been listening to our shortwave radios and had heard that a large tank battle was being fought at the Kuwait International Airport. "Well, we'll steer clear of *that*," said the Desert Squirrel commander as he pondered, by dome light, a small, undetailed diagram of downtown Kuwait in a copy of *Fodor's Business Guide to Saudi Arabia and the Gulf Emirates.* We climbed back into our vehicles, turned a corner, and encountered a huge sign: "Kuwait International Airport." Then we heard something coming—clattering engine, crunching debris, and all the whines and clunks military machinery makes. I was about to collapse into one of mankind's truly spectacular fits of natural cowardice when I recognized it. Looming out of the ominous murk was an awkward, ridiculous, ill-designed, overpriced, and absolutely unmistakable Hummer. It was full of U.S. Marines. God bless it.

Surf and Turf Safari

Automobile, 1990

Day One

It was grim, cold February in Ann Arbor and we were pondering the question "What do readers want to know about the new Ford Explorer, the four-door versions of the Nissan Pathfinder and Toyota 4Runner, and the double-luxo Limited model Jeep Cherokee?" Then—suddenly as a memo from the editor in chief suggesting a corporate junket to Hawaii—the answer struck us: readers want to know how four-door sport/utility vehicles perform at expensive vacation resorts under conditions of all-day tropical fun.

And that is how nine *Automobile* staffers, loved ones, and pals

wound up around the luau pit wearing Magnum, P.I., shirts in the popular sudden-acceleration-at-the-Korean-vegetable-stand pattern and
making horrible come-on-I-wanna-lei-ya puns while drinking pink
and green things that come in coconut shells and have names like
Samoan Monkey-Muzzler.

Day Two

Shaking the gardenia petals out of our boxer shorts and retrieving our
skewered Top Siders from the remains of a flaming pupu platter, we bid
the dawn *aloha* (a Hawaiian word meaning "American Express or
Visa?"). We were on the Big Island, Hawaii proper, the place where
migrating Polynesians originally landed more than 1,500 years ago and
where Captain Cook died in 1779. Cook was the first *haole* (a
Hawaiian word meaning "person whose luggage is still at the Los
Angeles airport") to visit Hawaii. His crew spread venereal disease
through the islands, the Hawaiians beat Captain Cook to death with
clubs, and the tourist trade has continued with only minor alterations
to the present day.

Hawaii has so much scenery it's a wonder Congress hasn't passed
scenic quota legislation and bused some of these views to Nebraska.
There are pea green rain forests, black sand beaches, gorges plunging
like Hollywood morals, and cliffs rising higher than Japanese real estate
(which, in fact, some of these cliffs are). Active volcanoes abound,
behaving the same way in the earth's crust as last night's Kahlúa mai-
tais were in my stomach, plus there are crashing waves, snowcapped
peaks, and waterfalls so beautiful that Percy Bysshe Shelley himself
would have had to run down to the Roget's carryout and get a fresh
bag of adjectives.

We were not about to be distracted, however. Natural beauty has
been around forever, but this was our first look at the Ford Explorer.
Our consensus? Ford has hung the moon.

The Explorer's styling was a Museum of Modern Art industrial
design collection shoo-in, purposeful as a D-6 dozer but slick as an eel.
The size formula was correct—commodiousness factored by parkabil-

ity. The interior was as comfortable as Mother's living room but with better upholstery. And Mother doesn't have room behind her couch for a set of golf clubs, a boogie board, and a forty-horsepower Evinrude and wouldn't let you leave them there even if she did.

We loaded our sport/utility vehicles with a massive picnic spread and headed out the Saddle Road that cuts across the island between Mauna Kea and Mauna Loa, the tallest mountains in the Pacific. It's a narrow, snaky, potholed, jerry-patched off-camber route, so we drove it as fast as we could. After all, real-world sport/utes spend more time on bad pavement than they spend in the Paris to Dakar rally.

At the crest of the Saddle Road, in a parenthesis of awesome volcanic cones, we headed north into the cattle ranges on the lower slopes of Mauna Kea. World's foremost enduro rider (and darn nice guy) Malcolm Smith had scouted the ranch roads in this section. If an extra set of wheels gave Malcolm double vision, you couldn't prove it by his driving. He and his wife, Joyce, gazelled down the rut-busted, boulder-hogged cart paths in the Nissan Pathfinder. The rest of us kept up as best we could, yo-yoing in our inertia belts.

Off-road the Explorer was not quite so perfect. The dash-mounted push-button transfer case control seemed to have a mind of its own, a slightly retarded one. Sawed-off drivers like myself found the seat too low, and this, combined with a high, wide expanse of hood and vague power steering, gave an impression (fortunately false) that the front wheels could only be contacted by telephone. And in the rough stuff the transmission was maybe *too* sophisticated, not providing enough engine braking and giving the Explorer a teenage runaway feel downhill.

Along the first part of the ranch roads the land was sere and cactus pricked. It hardly ever rains on the western, Kona, side of the Big Island. But, when we crossed the shoulder of Mauna Kea onto the eastern, Hilo, side, the landscape changed completely to impossible lushness, a sort of Cambodian Ireland (and there's a scary thought). About 300 inches of rain a year fall over here, much of it at that very moment.

We lunched wetly but well in a eucalyptus grove, the air smelling like, I suppose, koala breath. Then we pushed on through misty, too-lush monkeypod forests and out into pastures greener than a rich Protestant's go-to-hell pants.

I was in the Toyota now, a different kettle of wahoo entirely. The 4Runner may call itself a sport/utility vehicle, but back in the old country its folks were plain trucks. You could tell from the interior, which looked cheap, maybe, but also like no kids, dogs, or washing out with a garden hose could ever hurt it. The transfer case shift knob and other controls were placed truckishly, without a hint of ergonomics, and the ride was as hard as an income tax form. But I liked it the best, at least in the rocks and dirt. Along with the tough ride came great "trail feel"—the only way to learn more about the surface you were on was to get out and lick it.

Opening some cattle gates on the back side of the mountain, we accidentally let a bull calf loose. Malcolm Smith headed out across hummocky meadows in the Nissan and I rode flank in the Toyota. For half an hour we git-along-little-doggied. The 4Runner was as nimble and sure as any cow pony and a lot better smelling.

Day Three

Next we ventured into the Waipi'o valley, once a center of ancient Hawaiian civilization but later wiped out, probably by the great vowel plague that devastated everything hereabouts. The valley is 1,200 feet deep and less than a mile wide and reached via a road that goes downhill at the same angle as a clothes chute. Our most boneheaded (a Hawaiian word meaning "P.J.") driver got so rattled by the 100 percent grade that he forgot to pump his brakes, thereby filling his vehicle with a smoke cloud thick enough to spur an air quality class-action suit in Mexico City. His girlfriend, Amy, spent the descent opening and closing the electric windows trying to decide whether it was better to slide off the edge of the cliff and die or slide off the edge of the cliff and die with her hair smelling like fricasseed brake pads.

The Waipi'o valley is gorgeous from a distance. It's the color of money and a pair of shimmering, thousand-foot waterfalls grace the far slope. But when you get there it's sort of like dating a fashion model—vacant, dim, and all wet. The road on the valley floor goes nowhere. And when we forded the Waipi'o stream an overage hippie popped out of his yurt and began screaming about the ecology, some of which he seemed to have been smoking.

I had the Nissan Pathfinder this time—a ute so relentlessly good that there's not much to discuss. The Pathfinder was almost as sweet in the bumps and dumps as the Toyota. Only the Nissan's mild hobby-horsing separated the two. The Pathfinder's five-speed transmission was perfect when I remembered to use it. The as-perfect engine (from the Maxima sedan) had a torque curve so broad that I kept thinking I was in an automatic. Then I would pull up to a stop sign and stall like a moron.

As experienced buff book readers know, now here comes the squawk: *Aloha,* Nissan, where'd the luggage space go? You've built a sports/utility vehicle that doesn't have room for any sports equipment much larger than the foil-wrapped equipment for a sport I'm too old to be playing in cars.

At the mouth of the Waipi'o there's a beautiful, though trash-flecked, black sand beach, where we had our lunch (being careful to leave our campsite cleaner than we found it). Then photographer Greg Jarem suggested that we run the cars around in the surf. He said he'd checked and there was no vicious undertow or immense drop-off. He also said that, even if he *hadn't* checked, and there *was* a vicious under-tow and an immense drop-off, his photographs of our drowning strug-gles would win him a Pulitzer.

As outrigger canoes, the utes proved pretty much indistinguish-able. But apparently we'd violated some local *kapu* (a Hawaiian word meaning "people who come over from the mainland and fail to spend every cent they own"). A number of native Hawaiians began yelling at us, saying that this was their country and what right did we *haoles* have to drive around like that and leave tire tracks all over the beach and . . . "and pick up your litter," pointed out Jean Lindamood.

I'd switched into the Jeep Cherokee, the original or paleo-sport/ute. In many ways the Cherokee was outdesigned and undercut by its newer rivals. The Cherokee's interior, even with the luxury tack-ons, felt skimpy and spartan. Off-road the Jeep seemed delicate and unhappy to be there. This isn't a wholly true impression. I've driven a Cherokee down the Baja to La Paz and back mostly by way of streambeds and goat tracks. But long, loopy, luggage-throwing ride motions, a touchy accelerator, and an automatic transmission that endlessly hunted for, but never quite found, the right gear made the Cherokee Limited our fourth choice for boondocking.

Back at the Hotel Royal Wickiwackiwoo, it was *Hawaii Five-O* night or some such. Hawaii must have been great before they did the place over in a "Hawaiian" motif. Anyway, the poor hotel employees had to all get dressed in thatch petticoats and Hiawatha diapers and walk around with frozen smiles, herding tourists to a forty-three-course traditional Hawaiian feast, which consisted of forty-two kinds of pork plus *poi,* a taro paste which tastes like paste made of taro.

After dinner three sensitive and intelligent young ladies with their shirts off performed the *hula,* an ancient Hawaiian folk dance which tells the story of three sensitive and intelligent young ladies with their shirts off who have too many strategically placed shell necklaces and cannot quite shake them loose although they try very hard. I found this important cultural event very artistic and absorbing right up until the moment Amy emptied the *poi* dish down the back of my neck.

Day Four

We decide to finish our visit to Hawaii by driving to the summit of Mauna Kea for no good reason. All four of the sport/utes were slower than Darwinian selection on the 13,797-foot climb, and we were proud they were making it at all until we were passed midway by an early-'70s Dodge Dart. We ourselves were starting to move and breathe like monsters in a B movie: WHEEZE/LURCH/WHEEZE/LURCH. The view from the top was extraordinary, but you know how fear makes everything vivid. A doghouse would probably look just as extraordinary if I were as afraid of dogs as I am of standing on a two-and-a-half-mile-high precipice with sixty-mile-an-hour winds at my back. Furthermore, it was at least as cold up there as it was in Ann Arbor. And I got the Explorer stuck in a snowbank and Mrs. Davis had to pull me out with the Cherokee—a pretty ironic ending to a vacation in Hawaii. "What are we *doing* up here?" said I in a small squeaky voice.

Maybe we were trying to improve on the inevitable anticlimactic finale to every piece of automotive journalism: "Then we had to give the cars back and go home." Maybe we were hoping for "Suddenly the ancient volcano came alive! Tongues of glowing molten rock made their devastating way down the slopes. Pele, the goddess of fire, would be the one to decide which sport/utility vehicle provided the most enjoyment and widest range of practical applications at an affordable price. Oh, no! Look out! AAAAAIIIIIEEEEE!!! . . ." (a Hawaiian word meaning "don't stand in the lava flow in your beach flip-flops").

And one more thing, we were being patrons of the arts. "Art" is the only thing I can think of to call the F-150 Lightning. Here is the most prosaic of utility vehicles unaccountably equipped with a 240-horsepower, 351-cubic-inch V-8—a Gran Turismo for lawn clippings, a funny car that carries home yard sale bargains. It can go 0 to 60 in 7.6 seconds and tops 110 miles per hour despite the aerodynamics of a Port-O-San. Why not drop a hemi into a forklift or build a land speed record rototiller? The Lightning's suspension is so sophisticated that Jackie Stewart was able to drive the truck around the Ford test track with a lap time only two seconds slower than the Mustang Cobra's. And I was able to drive it through the sheep shank curves and thank-you-ma'am frost heaves of northern Maine at speeds that would have been a lot less scary if Jackie Stewart had been behind the wheel.

It was fun to pull up at stoplights next to small-town Firebird owners and suck their moon roofs off with my wake turbulence. The Lightning was a bit harsh of ride but no more so than all sports cars used to be. And what pleasure to be able to do sports car tricks while upright and perched on high in a roomy and comfortable pickup cab. It was like driving a birdcage Maserati standing up.

But why would I want to do that? What is the Lightning's *purpose?* Are you going to clean out the barn at 110 miles an hour? Well, that's art for you. You could ask the same questions about a Jackson Pollock painting. "Jackson, that's some great abstract expressionism there, but . . . *why?* All that Sherwin-Williams—you could have painted the kitchen, the bathroom, the porch furniture, and Grandma's apartment over the garage."

The Lightning is absurd. However, freedom often is. And we'd fight and die for freedom, but not for sensible minivans. So don't think of our petrol-swilling sprint to the sea as a mere wastrel pleasure trip. Think of it as a freedom ride. We were protesting, demonstrating against such constraints upon human liberty as the damn gas guzzler tax. What possible justification do the plush-bottoms in Congress have for charging us a fee to spend our own money?

There is no oil shortage. Experts at *The Economist* magazine estimate that we have 650 years worth of global hydrocarbon reserves. (Of course, *The Economist* didn't know about this trip so we'd better knock a decade off that.) And price doesn't lie. Supply versus demand equals your MasterCard bill. According to Cambridge Energy Research Associates, if you adjust for inflation, gasoline prices are now 6 percent lower than they were before the "energy crisis" of the early '70s and 25 percent lower than they were in the lead sled days of 1963. In fact, gasoline costs less now than it did a hundred years ago, when the average vehicle owner had no use for the stuff and wasn't about to put it in his carriage horse.

Nor does imported oil threaten our national security. If the Chevrolet Suburban's thirteen-miles-per-gallon EPA city driving average leaves us at the mercy of people who wear their picnic tablecloths on their heads, then what's our army for? Excuse me, I forgot. The purpose of the U.S. military is to invade Haiti and distract the public's attention from the Whitewater scandal.

Civil disobedience is the only proper response. We were conducting a sit-in at twice the legal speed limit. And what better way to protest government intervention in the free market than by showing what that free market can do? What it can do is the Mercedes-Benz S600 V-12, which is a more wonderful thing than any government has ever produced. (Well, the Bill of Rights is nice, especially when you need to tell a highway patrolman that "excessive bail shall not be required, nor excessive fines imposed . . .")

The S600 was almost annoyingly perfect. Just when you thought the seat was too firm, you realized you'd been in the car for five hundred miles and your butt still felt like your own. No more had you decided the climate controls were excessively complex than you discovered that $68\frac{1}{2}°$F from the shoulders up and $72\frac{1}{4}°$F from the knees down was exactly how you wanted the cabin temperature set. And, as soon as you'd told yourself the sound system required a ham license to operate, you suddenly wanted to try all 5,000 of New England's National Public Radio broadcast outlets to find out if, on even one of them, you could hear Ollie North instead of Nina Totenberg.

Most annoyingly perfect of all was the S600's handling. As a life-long sports car devotee, I found it embarrassing to get into a 4,800-pound, seventeen-foot-long four-door sedan that went around corners as well as my 911 and with fewer surprise visits from a wandering hind end.

Does Mercedes want us to take the kids and the dog on the Targa Florio? No. The S600 is a serious car. That's the beauty of freedom. In the free market's big tent there's room for the existential absurdity of the F-150 Lightning, the intellectual gravity of the S600 V-12, and the occasional practical joke such as the Rolls-Royce Silver Spirit III. When I drove it, I couldn't stop laughing. It was my mother's Buick.

A 1965 Buick Electra 225 had a 401-cubic-inch V-8, was $18\frac{1}{4}$ feet long, and weighed 4,261 pounds. Thirty years later the Rolls has a 412-cubic-inch V-8, is $17\frac{1}{2}$ feet long, and actually tips the Toledos at half a ton more than the Deuce-and-a-Quarter. The handling hasn't changed much either. Want to go around a corner? Wet a finger, stick it in the crotch of a steering wheel spoke, and dial for dollars. Want to go fast? Just pick a straight stretch of track. There's plenty of coal in the tenders of these locomotives. The only thing different is stopping. The Rolls will. Braking, in an old Buick, was like evacuating your ski house during avalanche season—lock up and slide.

Some people weren't impressed with the Silver Spirit, but my family owned a Buick dealership. This is what I grew up driving. I heard the Rolls had lots of electronic do-funnies that didn't work right. But none of that stuff works right for me whether it's in a Rolls or not. My idea of a portable phone is yanking the thing out of the wall. This is being written on a typewriter. I not only can't figure out the timer on a VCR but can't figure out why to watch TV. The joke is what it costs to avoid progress. For the price of a Silver Spirit III, you could have bought forty-seven Buick Electras in 1965.

Of course, buying a Rolls is not the most expensive way of avoiding progress. You can let the government regulate it. Imagine if the DOT had evolved before the automobile did. An 1890s six-horsepower Daimler would have needed railroad ties mounted fore and aft to meet five-mile-per-hour bumper standards, two boys with bicycle pumps inflating animal bladders in case of a crash, and a pair of oxen trotting next to the running boards for side impact protection. Those tall, skinny wagon wheels were clearly a rollover hazard. They'd have been replaced with casters or maybe runners from a sleigh. A barrelful of wet charcoal would've been carried alongside to stick the exhaust pipe into for emissions control. Somebody would have had to pedal ahead on a velocipede to hold up the speed limit sign. And a hook and ladder company would have followed the Daimler everywhere in case of fire.

But what about pollution? The free market has an incentive to deliver safety features (dead people don't trade up), but doesn't the government have to control air pollution? We were discussing this in the marvelous Restaurant Bonaparte in Montreal midst garlic fumes, ripe cheese stink, flambéed dessert smoke, corona smog, and cognac breath miasma. It's hard to get too concerned about air pollution in a really good French restaurant. But, if the government insists, why doesn't it concentrate on the real causes of bad air? According to DOT studies, 10 percent of the cars on the road are responsible for half of all auto effluvia. The technology exists for instant tailpipe checks. The polluters should be made to pay. The money could be used to buy clunkers off the road—and put a bag over the Restaurant Bonaparte's Camembert. Instead, all of us have to pay thousands of dollars for government-mandated technology which is stuck on our automobiles whether they need it or not.

The cars we were driving, though they consume enormous amounts of gasoline, don't produce much pollution. Their engines—the Silver Spirit's included—are too modern and well tuned. What comes out the tailpipes of new cars is practically breathable. In recent testing in London and California, it was determined that the exhaust from the Saab 9000 was actually cleaner than the air it took in. How sad for the busted Wall Street punter trying to kill himself by running his Saab in a locked garage. The night wears on; he's out of cigarettes; the suicide note keeps getting longer; his wife is banging on the overhead door. "Honey, are you dead yet? The kids have to go to school."

Let us shake this mood with a ride in the 512TR. Ferrari has finally, with the Testarossas, wrestled beauty from the mid-engined atomic-doorstop supercar design. The new 512 has a snout predatory enough for a Mike Hawthorne—era GP car, a more elegant set of strakes to keep stray dogs from being sucked into the engine compartment and a finely curved Sandra-Bullock's-bottom-against-a-windowpane look to the rear. The puissance of the five-liter flat twelve makes one meditate on what the word *horsepower* really means. Suppose you had 421 Budweiser Clydesdales trained to do anything you wanted, such as run through your boss's office or crash your ex-wife's dinner parties. The 512TR is more fun than that. It is the most positive, neutral, direct, and well-grounded car I've ever driven. No matter how much the road surface resembled a pile of wet laundry, the Ferrari's tires stayed on it like spaghetti sauce stains. Acceleration was sufficient to leave earth orbit, and the brakes could stop time. Yet you could send your great-aunt to the yarn store in the 512, so easy was it to pilot. On a two-lane road near Noplace, Maine, I came around an off-camber upchuck of a curve at ninety, and there, not a lunch toss away, was one logging truck overtaking another. The whole road and both shoulders were blocked by twenty thousand pounds of diesel and tree. I came through unscathed. I don't know how. The Ferrari did it. I closed my eyes.

I did *not* close my eyes in the Viper. You have to pay attention when you drive the snake. The throttle steers, the bumps steer, the tires steer. You can even steer with the steering wheel. The cockpit has approximately the same creature comforts as a soapbox derby racer's. The pedals are offset so far to the left that you mistake your toes for oncoming traffic. Dodge brought the MG Midget convertible engineers out of retirement to design the canvas top, which blew loose at eighty and beaned Associate Editor Joe Lorio. And the sheet metal looks like a high school hot-rodder's study hall doodle. Who cares? The Viper is the original ugly date who's fabulous in the . . . You know what I mean. The four-hundred-horsepower eight-liter V-10 produces 450 foot-pounds of torque at fewer rpms than a Maytag spin cycle. So much force is available across such a range of the tachometer dial that the Viper, in effect, has an automatic transmission. There are six forward gears, but you can use any one you want to do anything you need.

And the reptile handles. For all its love of pavement hunting, it does go where it's put. You think you're launched off the high side. You think you're spinning out. You're holding on with all four paws and your tail. But you arrive alive and come through the curve on the perfect line at that. On I-95 outside Bangor I hit 150 miles an hour. With the top down. In fourth gear. It was better than catching Al Gore in flagrante delicto with Socks the cat.

There are people who don't want us to own these cars. They say we'll hurt the planet. They say we'll hurt ourselves. Do the eco-weenies really care that much about the whole earth, not to mention us? Or are they up to something else with all their caring?

The Green dweebs want a world where individuals don't count for much, where all the important decisions—such as whether to shift the Viper into fifth—are made in Washington. They want a world controlled by the political process. That's because the shrub cuddlers are, as individuals, so insignificant. They're losers, the three-bong-hit saviors of the earth, lava lamp luddites, global warming dolts, ozone boneheads, peace creeps, tofu twinks, Birkenstock buttinskis, and bed-wetting vegetarian bicyclists who bother whales on weekends. They have no money, sense, or skills. But they can make their mark on politics because the whole idea of politics is to achieve power without possessing merit.

Let's run them over with the GMC Suburban. Let's crush one of those electric vehicles the enviro-pests are always building and spill D batteries all over the highway. Let's blast through a crafts fair (the Suburban has 210 horsepower so it won't get snagged in any macramé) and drive into the middle of one of those men's liberation inner-warrior weekends and chase flabby guys in loincloths out of the woods.

That's the great thing about the Suburban, you can go anywhere you want. And you can take anything with you. There's room for your whole life in the Suburban. Say you can't bear to be separated from your favorite Barcalounger or Grandma's dinner china or the vegetable garden. Just throw them in the back. But tie them down. Because, on even the worst back roads of Maine and Quebec, the Suburban was able to keep up with everything except the 512 and the Viper. Maybe that had something to do with David E. driving. Still, it's a testament to modern tire technology and suspension engineering that real cornering can be extracted from something that's as tall as a fish story and as long as an excuse.

And, speaking of excuses, if we could have thought of one we would have just kept driving these juggernauts, descending upon the towns of North America like some benign (if you aren't an ecoweenie) and motorized version of Tamerlane's horde—spreading *Automobile*'s money in every direction and leaving bone-dry Mobil stations and pyramids of speeding tickets in our wake.

But the Atlantic was coming into view. And I realized I hadn't even honked the horn on the Jaguar XJ12. It turned out to be the best thing we had. At least the wallets said so. The Mercedes is almost double the Jaguar's price and the Rolls costs three times as much. But the XJ12, with its men's club interior and show-us-to-the-polo-grounds coachwork, seems more like a real luxury car than either. It wasn't as quick as the Benz, but it had all the power you'd ever use in a car you paid for with your own money. It will run at over a hundred all day. And, when you step on the accelerator, the V-12 has the sound and feel of that Viper date in little lacy things slipping between satin sheets. (But every now and then in the middle of the night the XJ's car alarm would go off for no reason other than to remind you that Jaguars are made in England.)

I loved this car. I loved the other cars. I love all cars, if the truth be known. We're told cars are dangerous. It's safer to drive through South Central Los Angeles than to walk there. We're told cars are wasteful. Wasteful of what? Oil did a lot of good sitting in the ground for millions of years. We're told cars should be replaced with mass transportation. But it's hard to reach the drive-through window at McDonald's from a speeding train. And we're told cars cause pollution.

A hundred years ago city streets were ankle deep in horse excrement. What kind of pollution do you want? Would you rather die of cancer at eighty or typhoid fever at nine? Cars have made us richer, freer, happier people. Life is better because of cars. Cars are good. If you don't think so, try making out in a country lane on Rollerblades, you eco-weenie.

Essays, Prefaces, Speeches, Reviews, and Things Jotted on Napkins

I t is the privilege of the seasoned journalist, when cobbling together an omnium-gatherum of his own work, to dump his desk drawers, empty his file cabinets, and rifle through the pages of the books in his library looking for every scrawled thought and odd scrap of discarded prose or poesy with which he might pad his tome. So far I have found these fragments of great works I forgot to complete:

- The first four lines of an epic poem on the bourgeois condition:

   When the gods would form an ass,
   First they make him middle-class,
   Give him comic cares and woes,
   And let his wife pick out his clothes.

- A caption for a cartoon to be submitted to The New Yorker as soon as I learn to draw. One housefly says to another, "I never acted that way when I was a maggot."

- The beginning of a genre novel

VOTE-OUT AT THE D.C. CAPITAL
A Tale of the Old East

In the first light of dawn an impressive figure rode southward at an easy pace, and he sat erect in his Pullman car as he rode. Chester Alan Arthur was his full handle, but once you get west of the Atlantic it isn't always healthy to inquire about a man's full name—just Chester A. Arthur was how he was known. On the horizon he could see the hazy outline of Washington, lone town in the District of Columbia. "Municipal statutes, county ordinances, state legislation, and the federal code are the only law around here, partner," said the grim conductor at his side. . . .

• *Notes for an essay describing how all of existence can be analyzed in terms of* The Three Stooges—*everything in life being either stupid and nasty (Moe), stupid (Larry), or very, very stupid indeed (Curly).*

• *And an editorial proposal for a* New York Times Book Review Swimsuit Issue.

Larger items of miscellany follow under their own headings.

Contribution to "Sixty Things a Man Should Know"

For *Esquire* magazine's Sixtieth Anniversary Issue,
October 1993

Get an education—a classical education filled with Plato, Cato, Pliny the Elder, Pliny Junior, and Cicero by the yard; with Marathons of an un–Boston kind and Hannibals who cross the Alps, not Jodie Foster; an education that includes Pythagoras's theorem, Zeno's paradox, Occam's razor, the rest of Occam's toilet kit, some basic science (nothing beyond a Bunsen burner), and a few of the mustier works of great literature. (What *is* Hecuba to him or he to Hecuba?)

The entire British Empire was built by young men who'd studied nothing but Latin, Greek, and plane geometry. They graduated from college, were sent out to rule India, and telegraphed home: "People here acting as though they were in the *Iliad*. Have figured all the angles. Send *pecunia.*"

Nowadays Oxford and Cambridge have courses in anthropology, sociology, psychology, political science, economics, and no telling what else. Meanwhile the British Empire has shrunk to three IRA informants, a time-share deal with the Red Chinese in Hong Kong, and that bed-and-breakfast of an island, Bermuda. *Sic transit gloria mundi,* as if anybody knew what that meant anymore.

There are, admittedly, things that can't be learned by studying the classics. But education is not just a matter of learning things. There's a difference between information and knowledge. It's the difference between Christy Turlington's phone number and Christy Turlington. There's also a difference between knowledge and meaning. Socrates wouldn't know grunge rock, but he'd know what it means. It means every flannel shirt in America should be dipped in Prozac. Furthermore, there is a difference between meaning and life. Hillary Clinton loves the "politics of meaning" and all it's gotten her is week upon week locked in a roomful of nerds figuring how to pay the country's doctor bills. What kind of life is that?

A classical education helps us unravel these, as it were, Gordian knots. It teaches us the lesson of continuity in human affairs. We read Juvenal's Sixth Satire:

> *Meantime she completely*
> *Ignores her husband, gives not a moment's thought*
> *To all she costs him. She's less a wife than a neighbor—*
> *Except when it comes to loathing his friends . . .*

And we realize first wives weren't born yesterday.

If we can do such reading in the original language, we can travel in time, go back two thousand years and find what's inside people's minds. . . . some pretty nasty minds, too, such as that of the poet Nicarchus:

You should certainly have made a sign saying which was your mouth,
   which' your asshole.
Just now when you were gabbing I thought you'd farted.

And a classical education gives us perspective. For instance, the fall of Rome is a melancholy tale, but careful readings in history show us that we happen to be the people Rome fell to.

A classical education provides no skills. But, personally, at age forty-five, I don't want a skill. If I had a skill I'd have duller work. I'd be a dentist. Instead, I get to pursue that career of the professional amateur called journalism. Besides, the skills I might like to have—getting on the green in three, pestering trout with lint on a pin—aren't gotten in school. And school is what I wish I'd gone to more of. Much stupid behavior could have been thereby avoided.

If I'd known how Plato came a cropper trying to put his *Republic* into practice under Dionysius II in Sicily or if I had had a better idea what caused the collapse of representative government in Rome and Athens, I would have been spared a decade of radical politics.

If I'd read the mush in Virgil's *Eclogues:*

. . . for you the Nymphs bring lilies,
Look, in baskets full; for you the Naiad fair,
Plucking pale violets and poppy heads . . .
et cetera, et cetera, et cetera

I would have been nauseated enough to escape all sorts of hopeless romances.

If I'd been led from Aristotle through Roger Bacon and Erasmus to the Enlightenment of the eighteenth century—if I'd realized what pains mankind had taken to achieve empirical observation, logical thought, and experimental methods of proof—I would have eschewed vibes, auras, mantras, astral projections, and all the other mental rubbish of the last thirty years.

And, if I'd read Petronius and François Villon, I would have given the feckless bohemian life a pass and gotten a bath and a job.

On the other hand, I *liked* being a hippie pretend guerrilla writing horrible long poems to Suzy and Moonbeam and Babs. I had a great time thinking I could end war and social injustice by letting my hair grow and dressing like a circus clown. And—though we're not supposed to say it these days—the drugs were swell.

Such follies are born of ignorance, but I've enjoyed them. So maybe you shouldn't get an education after all. I'm not well educated enough to know.

Foreword to *A Modern Man's Guide to Women*

Published in 1992, edited by Denis Boyles
t's an unusual preface which argues against the work it introduces. But there are some things in life better not faced head-on, and this book contains all of them. Mind you, you hold in your hands an excellent compendium of strategy and tactics. Mr. Boyles and his colleagues are the Carl von Clausewitzes of battles between the sexes. But, in a war where every victory is Pyrrhic, what use is concentration of superior force, flanking maneuver, diversionary thrust, or even a pincher movement on a crowded bus? And that's as if we had any victories. In those rare engagements of gender where the man comes out, so to speak, on top, the first thing that man does is surrender. On another front, have you ever won an argument with your mother? She has bested you in every debate and disputation from "Resolved: We Shall

Be Weaned" to "The Case Against Asking Your First Wife to Leave Her Drunk Second Husband in the Car at Your Daughter's Wedding." If you can't prevail over an aged woman whose every weakness and foible you know and with whom you have been contending your entire life, how do you expect to do against a team from out of town?

And then there is the question of whether publishing this book endangers malekind. The wisdom herein contained is normally a part of masculine oral tradition. These sagacious observations are wrung from the wet towel of interpersonal relationships by hands grown hornèd with the writing of child support checks. The droplets of hard-won perspicuity are then passed confidentially from man to man in smoky bars, muddy duck blinds, and country western song lyrics. Perhaps your own dad, when you were of a suitable age, took you into his den, loaded up his pipe, looked over the top of his reading glasses, and said, "If it flies, floats, or fucks—*rent it.*"

All over the world pudgy, balding, experienced fellows are telling callow youths:

"Cookin' lasts, kissin' don't."

"They all look the same if you turn 'em upside-down."

"When the groom farts in front of the bride, the honeymoon is over."

But now we have made the grave error of committing these dicta to print. They are not the sorts of things men should ever put in writing. Our mothers, sisters, wives, and girlfriends (the last two, we hope, not at the same time) are going to see this book, pick it up, start reading it, and . . . laugh.

Because we don't know what we're talking about. Men don't know anything about women. We never have. We never will. Oh, each of us knows a few specific things. I, for instance, know why most societies don't allow women in combat. Combat is just a battle to the death. You don't want to turn it into something really ugly like a marriage. But we don't know what makes women tick. Let alone shop. We can pool our knowledge and that is what this book sets out to do. Even then we are like the blind men trying to describe the elephant—after the elephant has moved to Boulder with its aerobics instructor. On the subject of women I'm afraid there's nothing to say. And I, for one, don't want to be caught saying it.

This business of males and females trying to understand each other is an odd phenomenon anyway, and a recent one. Maybe we would all—men and women alike—be better off admitting our bewilderment and returning to the ignorant ways of the past. In my father's day a man married the first woman who allowed him to unclasp her brassiere. And a woman married the first man she met who had a job and didn't wipe his nose on his suit coat sleeve. Then they settled down, had children, stayed together no matter what, and were miserable the same as us. But at least it was a peaceful, stable, unworried misery and never needed any self-help books written about it, just an occasional *Madame Bovary*.

The difficulty men have with women is really much worse than a clash of the sexes. The problem is not that 50 percent of people are females. The problem is that 100 percent of females are humans. Take a human of any kind or type, whisper nonsense to it, rub its private parts, flirt with its best friend, expect it to cook for you, and see what you get. We don't know anything about women because we don't know anything about *Homo sapiens*. Anyone who has studied psychology, sociology, anthropology, or any of the other wacko-and-wog disciplines knows the three great rules of the social sciences: Folks do lots of things. We don't know why. Test on Friday.

We know nothing about women. We know nothing about men. We don't even know anything about our own fool selves. (Although, if you want to find out some things about yourself—and in vivid detail, too—just try calling your wife "fat".)

There is no cure for the ill this book addresses. The authors can only make a few small practical suggestions. I have one myself. Girls should be given more realistic dolls—Betsy Wetsys that spit up, stink, and howl for hours, Barbies that sag and Kens that lose their jobs and hair. This would result, I posit, in less distaff whining later on.

But all such recommendations are trifling—a mere cleaning of the storm drains on the continent Atlantis. The basic conundrum remains. We are in love with members of a troublesome species.

Why don't we fall for dogs? They have *ten* tits. Small ones, true, but think of it—ten! Dogs are friendly, loyal, a little jealous sometimes but not possessed of any abstract ideas about monogamy (or anything else). They don't spend hours on the phone or put fuzzy covers on the toilet seat lid so that while you're standing there taking a leak the seat comes right back down aimed square at the principal organ of male thought. Dog jewelry is pretty much limited to a rabies vaccination tag. Dogs never want you to spend Christmas at their mother's house and can't insist on going to fancy restaurants because they aren't allowed inside. (Don't forget to bring home a wifey bag.) Dogs don't care if you shave and they actually like it when you leave dirty socks in the middle of the bedroom floor. Dogs do chase cars but that's better than asking you to buy them one. And dogs never own cats.

Dogs are good-looking. Their hair is beautiful. Albeit they have a little too much of it. But the typical dog probably has less hair in its armpits than the typical coed if the coed is a Nirvana fan. And that tail thing could probably be put to some interesting uses during . . .

I admit the dog idea of cuisine is disgusting. But many's the human bride who ought to have buried her dinner in the yard. Dogs smell, but so do we men. And, one more thing, the kids are going to be ugly. But when we're out in that muddy duck blind, telling our son the solemn truths about how it is between men and women, we will, if we marry a dog, be able to give the boy one truly important word of instruction:

"Fetch!"

On First Looking into *Emily Post's Etiquette*

Review of the fourteenth edition
for *House and Garden*, 1984

've been paging through the new, totally revised, terribly up-to-date version of *Emily Post's Etiquette* written by Mrs. Post's granddaughter-in-law Elizabeth L. Post. It's a big book, thorough, tidy of organization, and legibly printed. I have no doubt it would be handy if I were planning my wedding or funeral. And I'm sure it contains all manner of sound advice for conducting a new, totally revised, terribly up-to-date life. However, all the people I know have been left out.

Muriel Manners, Mr. and Mrs. Eminent, Sarah Stranger, and Mrs. Kindheart are nowhere to be found. The late Mrs. Post used these friends and acquaintances to illustrate her little dramas of courtesy and faux pas. She sketched her characters with marvelous economy—never a word about their physical appearance, inner conflicts, or personal history. Yet they came alive upon the page. I give this example from my mother's copy of the eighth edition, published in 1945:

NAMES LEGALLY CHANGED

Whatever may have been the reason for changing the name by which one has been known, social and business associates should be notified of the change if embarrassing situations are to be avoided. The quickest and simplest way of telling them is to send out formal announcements.

MR. AND MRS. JOHN ORIGINAL NAME

ANNOUNCE THAT BY PERMISSION OF THE COURT

THEY AND THEIR CHILDREN

HAVE TAKEN THE FAMILY NAME OF

BROWN

What subtlety there is in "embarrassing situations," social "associates," and "Whatever may have been the reason." One knows it didn't turn out well for the sad and rather pushing Name family (pronounced Nam-ay). Their import business was expanded with vain optimism and sank beneath a weight of bank debt. Today, John Original, Jr., is some sort of rapscallion Hollywood person and the Name daughter, on her fourth divorce, drinks before noon.

There are no such adventures in the new edition. The exotic Names have been replaced by the prosaic Milsokovichs, who are changing their handle to Miller, probably to get something that will fit on a Visa card. And that rapier thrust "may have been" is gone from the opening sentence.

In this and every other way Elizabeth L. Post's *Etiquette* is blunt and homely. It contains paragraphs on such subjects as BYOB parties, pregnant brides, illegal drugs, meeting people through personal ads, and unmarried couples who live together. To tell the truth, I already know how unmarried couples live together. I probably need to learn less. Anyway, Emily Post would never have broached the subject. She would have thought it, well, bad manners.

Nor would the elder Mrs. Post have held a respectable lady's past up to ridicule. But the new edition of *Etiquette* is decorated with facsimile quotations from the first edition of 1922:

Dishes are *never* passed from hand to hand at dinner, not even at the smallest and most informal one.

There are many places which are unsuitable for young girls to go whether they are chaperoned or not. No well-brought-up young girl should be allowed to go to supper at a cabaret until she is married . . .

Do not greet anyone until you are out on the church steps. . . . "Hello" should not be said on this occasion because it is too "familiar" for the solemnity of church surroundings.

Perhaps these weren't inserted for amusement but to show how manners change with time. I found them, though, neither funny nor informative. Instead they filled me with sad longing for the elegance, dignity, and sophistication I knew in my youth.

That is, the elegance, dignity, and sophistication I knew *about*. And the way I knew about it was from Emily Post. I was a bookish child brought up in a house with few books. What reading material we had was stuck on some shelves by the front door. One rainy Saturday when I was about eleven, I was sitting on the linoleum examining the spines of a New Testament, a Fannie Farmer Cookbook, *How to Win Friends and Influence People,* a *Reader's Digest* condensation of *Kitty Foyle,* a paperback *Bridge over the River Kwai,* which I'd already read, and a family snapshot album. It was then I noticed a large book on the bottom shelf. The binding was a deep, compelling shade of blue embossed with the single foreign-seeming word *Etiquette* in silver cursive letters. I pulled it out and cracked it open. I think the first thing I saw was a black-and-white photograph of delicate rattan chairs arranged around a low table in a little garden. In the background were brick gateposts with a small fountain visible behind them. The caption read, "AT TEA IN A CITY YARD. The inviting charm of a garden setting—even that of a city yard—is all too often overlooked." Undeniably true of the yards in the factory town where I was growing up. I turned the pages.

If you carry a stick, it should be of plain Malacca. . . . Above all—unless you are a dancer on the stage (like Fred Astaire)— avoid an ebony cane with an ivory top.

Boston's older ladies and gentlemen always dance at balls, and the fact that older ladies of distinction dance with dignity has an inevitable effect on younger ones, so that dancing at balls has not degenerated into the vulgarities of wiggling contortions.

Champagne glasses ought to be thin as soap bubbles . . . a thick glass will lower the temperature at which a really fine champagne should be served and spoil its perfection.

I was transported. Here was a world I did not know, had not even hoped, existed. Here was a society where beauty and grace were serious matters. Here were people who made studied efforts not to act like fools. I read on.

The endeavor of a hostess, when seating her table, is to put together those who are likely to be interested in each other. Professor Bugge might bore *you* to tears, but Mrs. Entomoid would probably delight in him, just as Mr. Stocksan Bonds and Mrs. Rich would probably have interests in common.

I didn't think I'd be bored to tears by any of them. They all sounded like preferable dinner companions to my two screaming sisters and fat, bullying stepfather. I was only a simple eleven-year-old, but I thought I'd get along all right. After all, Mrs. Post said, "Simplicity is not crudeness or anything like it. On the contrary simplicity of speech and manners means language in its purest form, and manners of such perfection that they do not suggest 'manner' at all." Simplicity

I had. As for the other guests, I supposed not even Mrs. Rich would tell me to get the hell out of the house or go soak my head. "The code of a thoroughbred," said Mrs. Post, "is the code of instinctive decency, ethical integrity, self-respect, and loyalty."

These people did drink (champagne, at least) but they didn't argue and back over my bicycle in the driveway afterward. And it wasn't just because they were wealthy, for I found my own mother described in *Etiquette*. She was "Mrs. Three-in-one," who had no servants and "must be cook and waitress and apparently unoccupied hostess." Her parties were said to be a delight and invitations to them eagerly sought. Why, my family could live in this world, I thought, if we but willed it. We wouldn't even have to move into the better neighborhood on the other side of Upton Avenue. Mrs. Post said, "A gem of a house may be of no size at all, but its lines are honest and its painting and furnishing in good taste . . . all of which may very well contribute as unmistakenly to the impression of 'quality' as the luxury of a palace." I resolved never to carry an ebony cane with an ivory ball top to my sixth grade class.

The *Etiquette* book had been a wedding present to my mother from exactly the kind of aunt who would give a twenty-eight-year-old woman an etiquette book for a wedding present. I doubt it had been opened before. I appropriated it to my own use and spent hours studying how to address a Duke (call him "Duke," "Your Grace" is for servants and retainers), what color waistcoat to wear with a cutaway (black), and when to use the "cut direct" (never, and I heartily wished the same were true for a punch in the eye in Toledo, Ohio).

But the people were what I liked the best, and they came to populate my fantasies. There was Mrs. Toplofty, very reserved and dignified but awfully decent once you got to know her and she invited you in for Kool-Aid. And Mr. Worldly, who always had something clever to say about the Detroit Tigers. Mr. Clubwin Doe was lots of fun at the YMCA. And the Oncewere family, though they'd fallen on hard times, still had plenty of style at kick-the-can and stoop tag. There were visitors, too, members of European noble families such as Lord Blank, and the vague and haughty Duke of Overthere (none of *us* ever called him

"Your Grace"). We always suspected these fellows of having designs on the "better situated" neighborhood debutantes, especially on the spoiled and willful daughter of Mr. and Mrs. Richan Vulgar. No one would actually "cut" the Vulgars, but we were rather cool to them when they wanted to borrow the leaf rake. Actually, certain members of our own set were a bit "fast" themselves. Mr. and Mrs. Uppal Knight, for instance, gave parties that went on until after 11:00 P.M. And the frankly naughty Cigret Colcreme was "separated" and had men friends who drove convertibles.

And thus it was that while my boyhood chums were pulling the wings off flies I was discussing ants and grubs with Professor Bugge and Mrs. Entomoid and handling three forks and four different kinds of stemware.

Of course, in the real world, I have never quite made my way to that perfect land of kindness, taste, and tact. Though I'd like to think, sometimes, I've been on the path. I hope to get there yet. But I wonder if any bored eleven-year-olds, sitting by bookshelf in trailer or tract house, will be inspired to undertake the same journey by the new edition of *Emily Post's Etiquette*. I fear not.

Book Tour

Essay for *Smart* magazine, 1989

Usually, writers will do anything to avoid writing. For instance, the previous sentence was written at one o'clock this afternoon. It is now a quarter to four. I have spent the past two hours and forty-five minutes sorting my neckties by width, looking up the word *paisley* in three dictionaries, attempting to find the town of that name on *The New York Times Atlas of the World* map of Scotland, sorting my reference books by width, trying to get the bookcase to stop wobbling by stuffing a matchbook cover under its corner, dialing the telephone number on the matchbook cover to see if I should take computer courses at night, looking at the computer ads in the newspaper and deciding to buy a computer because writ-

P. J. O'Rourke

ing seems to be so difficult on my old Remington, reading an interesting article on sorghum farming in Uruguay that was in the newspaper next to the computer ads, cutting that and other interesting articles out of the newspaper, sorting—by width—all the interesting articles I've cut out of newspapers recently, fastening them neatly together with paper clips and making a very attractive paper-clip necklace and bracelet set, which I will present to my girlfriend as soon as she comes home from the three-hour low-impact aerobic workout that I made her go to so I could have some time alone to write.

But there is one thing worse than writing (I mean, other than getting a real job or cancer). There is one thing which makes the most nightclubable roman à cocaine postliterate novelist long for a spell at Yaddo, which makes the most drink-addled free-press-buffet-gorged journalist dream of deadlines. The one thing worse than writing is promoting what you've written—going out on the yakking hack circuit to bamboozle the public, embarrass the self, and exasperate airline stewardesses.

There is no more miserable creature on earth than an "author" on a "book tour." Just ask him. Or ask the unfortunate public relations firm employee who has to meet that rumpled, hungover, smelly, querulous, fuddled creature—me—at the airport.

The book publishing industry doesn't have much money. And it doesn't deserve to have much money, being run by guys who were too dumb to go into something profitable like sorghum farming in Uruguay and who decided to try to make a living by publishing books instead. Because the book publishing industry doesn't have much money, when they send an author on a book tour the idea is to send him to as many possible places in as short a time possible via the least expensive mode of transportation known to man. Thus the author receives (on a day and at an hour just too late to make any changes in the arrangements) a "Book Tour Publicity Schedule" the size of a Wall Street insider trading conspiracy trial transcript, the first page of which reads:

Monday
Live television appearances, radio phoners, newspaper inter-
views, and bookstore signings in Indianapolis, Houston, Albany,
San Diego, Savannah, Detroit, and Seattle

Air West Virginia Flt. 25068
Super-Saver Double Economy Tourist Excursion Cheaper-
Than-Shipping-Your-Pet-in-a-Crate Fare
Seat 91Q   Warm Snack

LEAVE: New York La Guardia Airport 5:02 A.M.
ARRIVE: Chicago O'Hare sometime next February
et cetera

Gone are the days when air travel meant sitting next to a tired
businessman who spent the flight scribbling on a ledger pad quietly
destroying the value of your stock-market holdings. Airplanes are mass
transit now, sort of skyborne Greyhound buses but with longer lines
for the bathroom and fewer chances of survival in a wreck. Screaming
toddlers and enormously fat evangelical Christians seated next to you
fly free. With no businessmen to meet and marry, stewardesses just stay
on, growing old and hardened in their jobs. They're middle-aged
women with cares and worries of their own. "Sit down and shut up,
we're out of booze," they explain.

Author hotel accommodations are of two types. One is a huge
suite with breathtaking views, a King-of-the-World-size bed, a sauna,
a Jacuzzi, a fully stocked bar, and a 380-channel TV with all-day free
pornographic movies. This is the type of hotel accommodation the
author arrives in at 3:30 A.M. when he has to get on a plane at six the
next morning to go to another city. The other type of author hotel
accommodation is cramped, musty, noisy, and more nearly resembles
the author's own apartment except with somebody else's hair in the
sink.

Of course nobody in any form of media more sensible than book
publishing—such as radio, TV, newspapers, and all other forms of

media—wants to interview an author. That's the beauty of authors. They don't need to be interviewed. There's a whole great big silly book filled with the stuff an author wants to say, and, if people are interested they can read it. Politicians need to be interviewed because politicians have no other way to get their many worthwhile and intelligent ideas across except in political action committee–sponsored television ads that make you afraid of Negroes. And people whose mothers were murdered by gangs of wild Christmas carolers need to be interviewed because, otherwise, we won't know if these people can ever hear "O Tannenbaum" again without feeling weird inside. And rock musicians definitely need to be interviewed because rock lyrics don't give rock musicians adequate scope for full intellectual expression because so few words rhyme with *boogie*. But authors have had their say and should sit down and shut up the way airline stewardesses wish they would.

The people who do book tour publicity schedules are fully aware that nobody wants to interview an author. This is why they accept absolutely any offer to do so even if it means that the author has to fly to Indianapolis, Houston, Albany, San Diego, Savannah, Detroit, and Seattle on the same day in order to be interviewed by a local Renault Owners Club Newsletter, *Sassy* magazine, and the High-Fiber Gourmet on public-access cable TV.

The first stop in each city on a book tour is a thing called Morning Drive-Time Radio: "YO, HYUNDAI-HUMPERS, IT'S THE WDOA *MORNING SNAKE PIT* WITH BOOGER BOB WONZAK AND SCREAMING WEASELS STEVE McMUGGINS COMING AT YOU LIVE FROM 'DEAD ON ARRIVAL 95'— THAT'S HEY HEY HEY WDOA—95 ON YOUR DIAL!!! EVERYBODY HONK IF YOU HATE MONDAYS!!!!!!!!!!!"

I'm sure many people make their book-buying decisions during morning drive time while stuck in traffic, worried about being late to work, trying not to throw up in the ashtray, and listening to AC/DC songs.

Being on morning drive-time radio means an author has to get up at approximately the same time an author normally goes to bed.

Authors do not function well at this hour. They grasp a coffee cup between tremulous mitts and make little bubbling noises into the mike.

AUTHOR: gurgle

BOOGER BOB: MAN, ME AND THE STEVE-O, WE LOVE THIS BOOK! YOU ARE ONE WILD DUDE! THIS IS CRAAAAAAAAZY STUFF, MAN! YOU MUST HAVE HAD A REAL WACK-O-RAMA TIME WRITIN' STUFF LIKE THIS, HEY?

AUTHOR: Yes.

SCREAMING WEASELS STEVE: WHAT A MANIAC!!! WHAT A IN-SANE GUY!!! HERE'S THE TRAFFIC REPORT!!!

Booger Bob and Screaming Weasels Steve are, by the way, competent professionals and—when not bellowing at commuters—turn out to be better educated and better paid than the author. They are no happier to have me on their radio show than I am to be there. It's just that authors are the only people desperate enough for publicity to get up at five in the morning and have "Dirty Deeds Done Dirt Cheap" played into their earphones at 11,000 decibels.

After drive time, the author is dragged, deaf and humiliated, to a television station where he's put on one of those local TV morning interview shows much favored by the kind of local TV that can't afford *Mayberry R.F.D.* reruns.

Local TV is, for some reason, much more amateurish than local radio. I was on a book tour in Waco, Texas, in 1974 on the day that the Ethiopian government was overthrown, and I spent a fascinating twenty minutes watching the local TV newscaster attempt to say "Haile Selassie in Addis Ababa."

Local TV interviewers come in two varieties. One is a bulimic blond person with a deviated septum and a severe cognitive disorder who went into broadcasting because he or she was too emotionally disturbed for telephone sales work. The other variety is suave, sagacious, grossly overqualified for the job, and too depressed to talk to you. Good local TV people are always depressed because their field is so crowded. There are only a couple dozen real on-camera network television jobs, therefore the entire industry has to wait around for Dan Rather to pop a rivet so that everybody can move up a notch.

Local TV show producers are hired directly out of day care without much professional experience. A few years ago, I was on a morning interview show in New Jersey. I was made up, miked up, and seated in one of those bogus living-room places. "Ten seconds," said the local TV producer, age nine. The local TV interviewer bounded onto the set, looked at me, looked at his script, looked back at me, and said, "Who the fuck are you?" "You're on the air," said the local TV producer.

Because local TV can't get very good guests, they do the next best thing and get lots of guests and put them all on at the same time by category. My category is "humorist." I'm not sure why and neither are the thirty or forty people not related to me by blood who have purchased my books. Although I have noticed that whatever I write ends up on the same bookstore shelf with Michael Dukakis campaign biographies and *Two Million Very Hilarious Things to Do with a Frog You Just Sat On*, so I guess the categorization is fair. Anyway, on my current book tour I was sent to Boston to appear on local TV with four other humorists. Anybody who's ever had one humorist around knows that one humorist is more than plenty, or, as airline stewardesses often say to me, "Sit down and shut up, we're out of booze." Having five humorists around is like having five cats in a knapsack. There was one lady humorist in arrested middle age who had written a book of amusing stories you can tell to your houseplants and who had memorized her own entire book and talked through her nose so loud and fast that nobody else could get a word in sideways. And there was another lady humorist who was so shy and stricken by stage fright that she stole the whole show by knocking over half the furniture in the bogus living-room place and running off the set screaming in terror. And there was Dave Barry, who would be a great guy if he weren't a hundred times funnier than me and from whom I stole that paragraph about the types of hotel accommodations authors get on book tours. There was someone else. And there was me. This was not a recipe for great television.

Authors would like to go on "Trash TV" and throw chairs at Geraldo Rivera and Maury Povich and Morton Downey, Jr., but authors are never invited on these shows because most authors lead sedentary lives and can't throw a chair very far.

By 11:00 A.M. the local TV audience has been driven to Nintendo and the unfortunate public relations firm employee has noticed that the author is showing dangerous quivering symptoms and needs to drink lunch soon. Lunch will be at a prestigious restaurant on a local newspaper reporter's lavish expense account. (You want that for here or to go?) Most local newspaper editors consider the "book beat" to be somewhere in importance between scout meetings and Manitoba Provincial League curling scores. Reporters who are assigned to interview authors are either bad reporters who deserve no better than to interview authors or good reporters who have done something bad (usually to a bad reporter, e.g., releasing a box of live iguanas during her support group session) and are assigned to interview authors as punishment or they are young reporters who are assigned to interview authors because their editor doesn't know yet whether they are good enough to chase sensitive poetic types out of the newsroom with huge green lizards or bad enough to interview authors. The bad reporters ask bad questions such as "Can we go to a vegetarian restaurant?" and spend a lot of time pointing out that the author is no Cynthia Heimel and that this restaurant doesn't allow smoking or have a liquor license. The good reporters don't ask any questions because they are too busy getting drunk with the author. The only decent questions come from the young reporters, who ask, "Is writing really better than getting a real job or cancer?" And, "How can I get into something profitable like sorghum farming in Uruguay?"

Let's not even discuss bookstore signings, where the author gets to sit at a wobbly card table in the middle of a suburban shopping mall with a large pile of embarrassingly unsold copies of his book in front of him, and every hour or so somebody comes by and points out that he's no Cynthia Heimel.

After the author has been to the suburban shopping mall men's room three or four times to consult the pint of "liquid thesaurus" that authors carry at all times in case they have to go to bookstore signings in suburban shopping malls, it's time for talk radio.

Talk radio is the best part of a book tour because being on talk radio most nearly resembles regular talking, which is one of the four or five hundred thousand things I forgot to mention in the first paragraph that authors would rather do than write. Also, talk radio hosts are kindred souls to authors. That is, they keep authorish working hours in the middle of the night and have a career that involves a large amount of time wasting and few discernible job skills. Sometimes talk radio hosts have even read the author's book, which is a lot more than the author's publishing company's proofreader bothered to do. Thus authors love talk radio hosts or would if it weren't for the talk radio host tendency to ask authors questions based on the author's own work. Most authors who are not ladies in arrested middle age writing books of funny stories you can tell to your houseplants cannot remember anything they've written. This is because, if what the author wrote was fiction, it's just something he made up. And, if what the author wrote was nonfiction, it's just something he made up except for the names of celebrities. This is what authors get for not listening to their mothers, who said, "Always tell the truth, it's easier to remember."

The talk radio host will say something like "Now, here in your chapter about amusing stories Michael Dukakis can tell to a frog you just sat on you say . . ." (Talk radio host makes frantic "come on" "come on" hand gestures at author.)

AUTHOR: er . . . a lot of funny things about . . . um . . . frogs . . . and . . . uh . . . Michael Dukakis?

After a couple such attempts to lead the author, the talk radio host gives up and starts answering his own questions by reading from the author's book. This makes talk radio extra painless for authors, who can just sit there happily drunk in front of the microphone and listen to someone with a deep, authoritative radio voice read brilliant things the author has written or, at any rate, copied from Dave Barry.

So talk radio hosts are actually great human beings, the salt of the earth. But the people who call in on their telephone lines are strange. Apparently it's the same people night after night. "We've got Ned from Moline on line one," says the control room engineer, "and Susan from Wheaton on two and old Frank on three."

"Ned," explains the host, during a commercial break, "is the only black member of the Illinois Ku Klux Klan. Susan is an animal rights activist who bombed a calendar company because they printed an illustration showing barefoot boys cruelly torturing bluegills with fishing poles. And Frank drinks paint." Then you get to "talk" to all of these people.

But talk radio is still the best thing that happens on a book tour. The only thing that's better is if you can arrange your book tour so that it comes just after Hunter Thompson's book tour so that you arrive at airports, hotels, radio stations, television studios, newspaper interviews, and bookstore signings just after Hunter Thompson has been there. In the first place everybody will be so busy cleaning up the mess, calming hysterical employees, having the area searched by bomb-sniffing dogs, and so forth that there will be nobody left with the time or energy to pester you. In the second place, if you are—as Hunter Thompson is—an author, you will be treated with a lot of respect in any place Hunter Thompson has recently been. "Author!!! Author!!! Everybody into the southeast corner of the basement!!!" people will say as you approach. Hunter Thompson is so shy and stricken by stage fright that he knocks over half the furniture in the bogus living-room place and runs off the set screaming in terror like the lady humorist on the Boston TV show, except Hunter Thompson does this with a loaded .30-06 elk rifle and a quart bottle of whiskey on an IV tube and two immense Lebanese Shiite bodyguards.

This is the very best thing that happens on book tours, and it should happen on all book tours as it would restore the macho image authors used to have in the days of Kipling and Gertrude Stein, before the author occupation was overrun by the kind of panty-waist writing program graduates who are willing to go on book tours. Plus it would give the entire book publishing industry a much-needed shot in the arm or, maybe, head.

On the other hand, the very worst thing that happens on book tours is that the author gets a lot of attention by knocking over furniture and screaming in terror and suchlike and starts to think that being an author is something important like being a talk radio host or a person whose mother was murdered by a gang of wild Christmas carolers. Pretty soon the author is acting like a star and moaning and whining and even publicly complaining in print about going on book tours. The next thing you know the author calls up the unfortunate public relations firm employee and yells, "Can you imagine *Shakespeare* on talk radio with some guy who drinks paint?!" Which, as a matter of fact, I can.

TALK RADIO HOST JOHN EUPHUES: We have a knave on the phone from Ramsgate. Go ahead, villein.

KNAVE: Hello?

HOST: You're on the air.

KNAVE: Hello? This is a question for Bill Shakespeare.

SHAKESPEARE: Hi. How ya doing?

KNAVE: Great, Bill. Love your plays. Me and the fishwife are always in the pit at the Globe. Wouldn't miss one. That's us right down in the front, drinking paint.

HOST: What's your question, sirrah?

KNAVE: Yeah, well, one thing got us wondering, Bill. In *The Tragedy of Hamlet, Prince of Denmark,* what's with him and Ophelia? Why's he give her the go-by? She could've maybe helped him, you know? Like, maybe flirted with Claudius or something while Hamlet snuck up from behind and hit him on the head with a brick.

SHAKESPEARE: Whew, that's a good question. That's a really perceptive question. We had a much bigger part for Ophelia, a really terrific part, with a lot of meat on it vis-à-vis the plot. But then, two days before we go into production, the kid who's playing her, his voice goes and changes. Left us in deep yogurt, I'll tell you.

And I'll tell you I'd gladly change places with the Bard of Avon. He's only dead. I'm out on book tour.

Speech Given to Libertarians

At a Dinner Celebrating the Opening of the new Cato Institute Building, Washington, DC, May 6, 1993

The Cato Institute has an unusual political cause—which is no political cause whatsoever. We are here tonight to dedicate ourselves to that cause, to dedicate ourselves, in other words, to . . . nothing.

We have no ideology, no agenda, no catechism, no dialectic, no plan for humanity. We have no "vision thing," as our ex-president would say, or, as our current president would say, we have no Hillary.

All we have is the belief that people should do what people want to do, unless it causes harm to other people. And that had better be clear and provable harm. No nonsense about secondhand smoke or hurtful, insensitive language, please.

I don't know what's good for you. You don't know what's good for me. We don't know what's good for mankind. And it sometimes seems as though we're the only people who don't. It may well be that, gathered right here in this room tonight, are all the people in the world who don't want to tell all the people in the world what to do.

This is because we believe in freedom. Freedom—what this country was established upon, what the Constitution was written to defend, what the Civil War was fought to perfect.

Freedom is not empowerment. Empowerment is what the Serbs have in Bosnia. Anybody can grab a gun and be empowered. It's not entitlement. An entitlement is what people on welfare get, and how free are they? It's not an endlessly expanding list of rights—the "right" to education, the "right" to health care, the "right" to food and housing. That's not freedom, that's dependency. Those aren't rights, those are the rations of slavery—hay and a barn for human cattle.

There is only one basic human right, the right to do as you damn well please. And with it comes the only basic human duty, the duty to take the consequences.

So we are here tonight in a kind of antimatter protest—an unpolitical undemonstration by deeply uncommitted inactivists. We are part of a huge invisible picket line that circles the White House twenty-four hours a day. We are participants in an enormous nonmarch on Washington—millions and millions of Americans *not* descending upon the nation's capital in order to demand *nothing* from the United States government. To demand nothing, that is, except the one thing which no government in history has been able to do—leave us alone.

There are just two rules of governance in a free society:

- Mind your own business.
- Keep your hands to yourself.

Bill—keep your hands to yourself. Hillary—mind your own business.

We have a group of incredibly silly people in the White House right now, people who think government works. Or that government *would* work, if you got some real bright young kids from Yale to run it.

We're being governed by dorm room bull session. The Clinton administration is over there right now pulling an all-nighter in the West Wing. They think that, if they can just stay up late enough, they can create a healthy economy and bring peace to former Yugoslavia.

The Clinton administration is going to decrease government spending by increasing the amount of money we give to the government to spend.

Health care is too expensive, so the Clinton administration is putting a high-powered corporate lawyer—Hillary—in charge of making it cheaper. (This is what I always do when I want to spend less money—hire a lawyer from Yale.) If you think health care is expensive now, wait until you see what it costs when it's free.

The Clinton administration is putting together a program so that college graduates can work to pay off their school tuition. As if this were some genius idea. It's called *getting a job*. Most folks do that when they get out of college, unless, of course, they happen to become governor of Arkansas.

And the Clinton administration launched an attack on people in Waco, Texas, because those people were religious nuts with guns. Hell, this country was *founded* by religious nuts with guns. Who does Bill Clinton think stepped ashore on Plymouth Rock? Peace Corps volunteers? Or maybe the people in Texas were attacked because of child abuse. But, if child abuse was the issue, why didn't Janet Reno teargas Woody Allen?

You know, if government were a product, selling it would be illegal.

Government is a health hazard. Governments have killed many more people than cigarettes or unbuckled seat belts ever have.

Government contains impure ingredients—as anybody who's looked at Congress can tell you.

On the basis of Bill Clinton's 1992 campaign promises, I think we can say government practices deceptive advertising.

And the merest glance at the federal budget is enough to convict the government of perjury, extortion, and fraud.

There, ladies and gentlemen, you have the Cato Institute's program in a nutshell: government should be against the law.

Term limits aren't enough. We need jail.

Thoughts on the Prospect of a Sixties Revival

Written for *Rolling Stone* during the Twentieth Anniversary of the Summer of Love

There's a stench of patchouli oil in the air. The overrated, old Doors have a hit record. Hemlines are headed up. Sideburns are growing out. People are saddling their children with goofy names, like Zack. I see that the peace symbol—footprint of the American chicken—is giving the spray-paint industry a bad name again. Oh, God. The Sixties are coming back.

Well I've got a 12-gauge double-barreled duck gun chambered for three-inch Magnum shells. And—speaking strictly for this retired hippie and former pinko beatnik—if the Sixties head my way, they won't get past the porch steps. They will be history. Which, for chrissakes, is what they're supposed to be.

Who's behind this Sixties revival anyway? Is it the present generation, the kids who are twenty right now? If so, dudes, this is some twisted stuff you're into. What if me and my friends had revived the Forties? What if we'd gone around joining the Marine Corps, selling war bonds, and kissing soldiers good-bye at train stations while standing on tiptoe and kicking one leg up? I mean, we weren't *that* crazy. Of course you kids don't actually remember the Sixties. So, if you're responsible for this Sixties thing, we'll excuse you with a note from your mom. (God damn it, Sunshine, I *told* you not to eat peyote buds during pregnancy.)

But I suspect it's my generation, the forty-year-olds, who are dragging this mummified decade back into public and presenting it to everyone in the cheerful gift wrap of nostalgia. Are we psychotic amnesiacs, maybe? Did drugs fuse all our mnemonic brain cells together like strips of raw bacon left in the fridge? For a purely untrustworthy human organ, the memory is right in there with the penis. Sure, everyone says the Sixties were fun. Down at the American Legion hall everybody says World War II was fun, if you talk to them after 10:00 P.M.

Maybe we should freshen our recollections a bit. About drugs, for example. Personally I loved the little buggers. But we're only remembering the cool ones like marijuana, LSD (if you didn't have to talk to your folks on it), and psilocybin mushrooms. What about the STP, the PCP, the Thorazine, the crystal meth, and the little blue-green tab somebody laid on you in the park and you vomited so hard your socks came out your mouth? Then the mood police came. Your face had to go to jail. Not everybody can turn his toes into ten angry, hissing lizards with rows and rows of sharp little teeth. Quick! Help! Grab that chick, she just swallowed her superego. She could mellow to death at any moment. Ha, ha, ha, somebody left the lava lamp on all night and now the entire island of Oahu is gone. Wow, man, which way to the bummer tent?

And then there was the Sixties mortality rate—not only high but bizarrely selective. It was like some evil force was culling the citizen herd to produce a nation of intellectually and morally stunted goat mutants.

People Who Died During the 1960s	People Who Were Allowed to Live
John F. Kennedy	*Teddy Kennedy*
Robert Kennedy	*Lyndon Johnson*
Martin Luther King	*Don King*
Janis Joplin	*Bette Midler*
Jimi Hendrix	*Prince*
4 students at Kent State	*All the other students at Kent State*

I could go on but it would be more depressing than an old copy of *Look* magazine's "Youthquake" special edition.

Music? It wasn't all Country Joe and the Fish and the Beatles' "White Album." The Lemon Pipers were also part of the Sixties, as were Vanilla Fudge, Blue Cheer, the 1910 Fruitgum Co., the Cowsills, Dino, Desi, and Billy, Sonny and Cher, Ohio Express, the Partridge Family, Barry McGuire, the Archies, and whoever the asshole was who sang "Ballad of the Green Berets." Even some of Bob "Immortal Adenoid" Dylan's work doesn't get an A+ on the midterm test of time:

> Dogs run free
> Why not we?

Actually, that sounds like T. S. Eliot compared to most of the English spoken during the Sixties. Like, can you dig the whole riff, you know, heavy vibes with where it's at and really out of sight because I can get behind this far-out thing that's going down if you know where I'm coming from.

I've thought about this. I'm pretty sure, during the entire 1960s, I never once linked a subject to a predicate with a verb to create a sentence that meant anything. No wonder we were so interested in talking to dolphins. We sure couldn't talk to each other.

Plus we're forgetting all sorts of other, less important, awful things about the era:

crab lice
communal toothbrushes
Jerry Rubin
accidentally picking up hitchhiking Manson girls
brown rice
crashing
women who thought they "might be a witch"
happenings
getting your bell-bottom cuff caught in a motorcycle chain
    sprocket and having your leg yanked off
jail
Yoko Ono

But we can't re-create the Sixties, not even if we wanted to. We just don't have what it takes these days. There aren't any politicians left worth killing. Everybody's already been famous for fifteen minutes. Andy Warhol's gone to the big *People* magazine in the sky. So what are we supposed to do this time around, all be dead for a quarter of an hour? And too many of today's college students are majoring in Comparative Greed and Real Estate Arts. They'll never be able to come up with snappy slogans like "Tune in. Turn On. Drop Out." They'll probably bring their laptop computers to demonstrations and feed in:

Impact your data interface. Optimize networking at this point in time. Effect a core dump.

Even if we could get the Sixties cranked up again, how could we deal with them? How could we read those psychedelic posters through bifocal granny glasses?

Free love doesn't seem like a particularly good idea in the current epidemiological atmosphere. And love, real old-fashioned l-u-v love, means our teenage children will be sleeping with people like us. Think it over.

What about a war? We can't have a real Sixties if we aren't fighting a brutal, senseless war somewhere in the butt end of the third world. I'm over draft age so I don't mind myself. But what do the Nicaraguans think? Are they game? Shouldn't somebody ask them, just to be polite?

Miniskirts are every bit as dangerous. Miniskirts caused feminism. Women wore miniskirts. Construction workers made ape noises. Women got pissed off. Once the women were pissed off about this they started thinking about all the other things they had to be pissed off about. That led to feminism. Not that I'm criticizing. Look, Babe . . . I mean, Ms. . . . I mean, yes, sir, I *do* support feminism. I really do. But that doesn't mean I want to go through it twice.

I don't want to go through those inner-city riots again either. What with twenty more years of hopeless poverty, crack, and torture by government welfare agencies, they're tougher down in the ghetto than they used to be. We rile this bunch, we're liable to get our asses handed to us in a BMW hubcap.

And *Sixties II—The Story Continues* is going to rattle the redneck cage—just when they'd finally calmed down and started letting their hair grow like Willie Nelson. A lot of people out there still think *Easy Rider* had a happy ending. They could beat the shit out of us back then and they still can.

Giving all our possessions away is going to be more complicated than it was when all we owned was a hash pipe and a set of paperback Hermann Hesse novels. I'm not even sure the Haight-Ashbury Free Store is going to want my Toro rotary mower.

And will we have to have more huge fights with our parents? Some people remember the Sixties as the age of grooviness. I remember it as the age of screaming at the dinner table. Come on, we don't want to pester Mom and Dad anymore. They're old. They're sick. They're retired in Winter Park. We're going to have to fly all the way to Florida to shriek at our parents for not letting us share a bedroom with our girlfriend. (And, funnily enough, nowadays, our wives still won't let us do that.)

Then there were all those loopy Sixties beliefs—karma, Krishna, Helter Skelter, participatory democracy, who-knows-what. I remember when some people were so crazy they believed the president of the United States was a paranoid maniac who might phone-tap his own cabinet officers and wire the entire White House with voice-activated recording machines and use a bunch of lunatic-fringe Cubans to burglarize the National Democratic Party headquarters.

Why, if we had the Sixties back, some freaks and heads would probably tell us President Reagan made a secret arms deal with Iran and let a mentally unbalanced jug-eared lieutenant colonel run U.S. foreign policy.

But don't worry, the Sixties aren't coming back. At least I don't think so. Let's see what the *I Ching* says. Oh-oh. Weird hexagram. I don't know, folks, maybe we'd better get back to the land, set up communes, things like that—just in case. Because you remember what the terrible Sixties led to. That's right. They led to the loathsome, disgusting, repellent Seventies, which led to the unbelievably horrid, vicious, brutal, swinish now. And that's the worst thing of all about the Sixties— the one really unforgivable thing—that it's been straight downhill ever since.

Current and
Recurrent Events

Jim Fixx, *author of* The Complete Book of Running, *died of a heart attack while jogging. He was fifty-two. Among the manifold attributes of God, we must not forget sense of humor.*

Being a journalist, I had spent most of my career making things up. It was Michael Kinsley who first pointed out to me that the world is funnier than I am. In 1982 Kinsley was the editor of Harper's *magazine (which job he lost—I swear this is true—for not being enough of a pinko sap). Michael gave me an assignment to travel on a Volga River cruise with a group of aging American leftists. Watching this bunch try to put a good face on the butt-end of the Brezhnev years was . . . words fail me. I must resort, as writers will when words fail them, to quoting myself:*

> As we were going through the lock of the Don–Volga canal [an aging American leftist] came nattering up beside me at the rail. "Isn't it marvelous?" she said, staring at a gigantic blank wall of concrete. "They're such wonderful engineers in the Soviet Union." I agreed it was an impressive piece of work. "Marvelous, marvelous, marvelous, marvelous," she said. She peeked over the side. "And where *do* they get all the water?"

I had an epiphany. I realized that, for the rest of my life, I'd never lack things to write about. All I had to do was put myself in foolish situations (easy for me) and keep my eyes and ears open. Since then I have visited eight wars, two revolutions, half a dozen or so local uprisings, a number of third-world election campaigns (which combine the worst aspects of combat, civil disturbance, and the New Hampshire presidential primaries), plus any number of places exhibiting garden variety hatred and oppression (the New Hampshire presi-

dential primaries, for instance). I have found them all hilarious. Humor has nothing to do with the charming or the cheerful. Humor is how we cope with violated taboos and rising anxieties (rising gorges, too). Humor is our response to the void of absurdity. Humor comes to the fore when events render us impotent. And, as middle-aged men know, all events eventually do. We laugh when we don't know what the fuck else to do. Humor is not about a kitten tangled in a ball of yarn, unless—to steal a line from Michael O'Donoghue—the kitten strangles.

There's a joke about just such a dead kitten, a joke I heard when I was nine or ten years old, and it was another nine or ten years before I saw the humor in it. A kid discovers his kitten lying on the floor stiff and cold. He begins to cry. His dad tries to comfort the boy. "Look," says the father, "we'll give your kitten a big funeral. I've got a fancy wooden cigar box, and we'll put him in there on some velvet scraps from your mother's sewing box. Then we'll dig a hole in the backyard, and we'll write a special burial service and say it over the casket. And then we'll make a cross down in my workshop and put the kitten's name on it in gold paint." Just then the kitten begins to stir and wiggle and come back to life. The kid sees this and says, "Dad, can we kill it?"

The 1994 Mexican Elections

Make Lunch, Not War

Rolling Stone was traveling to Tuxtla, Chiapas, to pester the Mexicans during their presidential elections. On my flight was a group of high-minded women—void of makeup, wearing earthy-hued clothing, and shod in enormous swarthy footwear. What is it about high-mindedness and big black shoes? If tootsies peek out the ends of little white Joan and David pumps, does this cause toenail painting? Does toenail painting lead to tanning parlors? After tanning parlors, what? These women could wind up at a Jimmy Buffett concert if they aren't careful. Or maybe big black shoes are in the bylaws of People for the Ethical Treatment of Animals—so bugs can see your feet coming and avoid a horrible death by squashing.

I was about to ask why a crowd of earnest gals in Doc Martens was flying to provincial Mexico when I saw the laminated credentials hanging from their necks. Of course. They were pestering the Mexicans, too. They were international election observers. So, upon inspection, were lots of other people on the plane and not just women void of makeup. There were also men void of makeup. There were, in fact, observers of every ilk—from human rights organizations, labor unions, foreign policy think tanks, and democracy-boosting institutes funded by both Democrats and Republicans. They wore big black clogs, big black sneakers, big black Hush Puppies, and big black wing tips. Some six hundred "electoral visitors," as the Mexican government called them, had crossed the border to make sure our friendly neighbor to the south wasn't larding the ballot boxes and boiling the vote count.

We get the same sort of thing in the United States. You remember, during the Clinton-Bush race, how all those Saudi Arabians were hanging around our polling places, making sure our national referendum was on the up and up and asking our electoral officials questions such as "Is every man letting all four of his wives vote?"

I admit we Americans would hate having a bunch of foreign nosenheimers poking around in our political process. But you can't compare the United States with Mexico. Mexico has one political party that has stolen every election since 1929 while America has two political parties that have stolen every election since 1852.

Never mind. Mexico needs us buttinskies meddling in its plebiscite. We have to midwife self-government, nurse freedom in its cradle, train the toddler liberty to sit upon the pot of universal suffrage because . . . Because Mexico is an *emerging nation*.

But Mexico was home to the splendid Olmec civilization in 1100 B.C., when O'Rourkes were living in trees. And Mexico was settled by Europeans a full century ahead of what's now the United States.

Well, Mexico is an *underdeveloped country*.

Mexico has an annual gross domestic product $100 billion greater than Sweden's and its economy is growing faster than our own.*

---

*Note journalistic prescience about looming Mexican economic collapse.

Come on, Mexico is *part of the third world*. You can tell because they speak English with an accent and they're darker than we are.

And so all kinds of people dripping good intentions were on their way to grace the Mexican national elections of 1994 with their presence, myself included. Although you can't accuse me of high-mindedness. I'm a reporter.

What a story this was supposed to be. Mexico's ruling party, the PRI, is famously awful. Its very name—Institutional Revolutionary Party—is a list of disgusting things. The PRI dominates the labor unions, the mass media, and most of Mexico's businesses. What it doesn't control directly, it controls directly anyway, by bribery and intimidation. But public anger at the PRI has been growing for years. Mexican citizens are insisting upon open government. This time the PRI was getting real competition from PAN, the National Action Party—conservative, probusiness, and . . . actually . . . almost indistinguishable from the PRI, which has spent the past six years privatizing industries and promoting individual enterprise. Plus the PRI was getting real competition from the PRD, the Democratic Revolutionary Party—liberal, socialistic, and . . . almost indistinguishable from the PRI, which has launched a broad range of antipoverty and social spending programs.

But there was real competition even if you couldn't exactly tell the competitors apart. And in the middle of this three-way donnybrook the PRI presidential candidate, Luis Donaldo Colosio, was assassinated. Which goes to show just how backward is the Mexican attitude toward democracy. Everybody knows that in modern countries you don't shoot presidential candidates. You wait until they're elected.

Mexican law enforcement officials seem to have hired Oliver Stone to investigate the killing. Colosio's murder remains unsolved somehow even though the shooting was videotaped and the gunman was arrested and he confessed. The PRI was forced to come up with a new candidate, Ernesto Zedillo, who has the approximate charisma of Walter Mondale on NyQuil.

Just to make things even more interesting, the day NAFTA went into effect a group of peasant guerrillas wearing ski masks burst out of the jungle and took over four towns in Chiapas State, causing the whole world to ask, "Where did they get ski masks? The nearest bunny slope is two thousand miles away. And don't those things itch? It's ninety degrees out."

Yes, the situation was tense and dramatic when we do-gooders arrived in Mexico. Then nothing happened.

The campaign was peaceful. The polling went more or less smoothly. The vote count seemed close to fair, close enough for government work anyway. The guerrillas, who'd been chased into the mountains by the army, stayed up there. And the people of Mexico reelected the PRI. The PRI is corrupt, stupid, power mad, antiquated, undemocratic, and Mexicans returned them to power. They did this while all of us earnest big black shoe types were right there caring so deeply about political liberty. Where are the Mexicans getting their lessons in governance? Probably from Americanos. Think of Mexico as Dan Rostenkowski Nation.*

The fact that nothing's happening never stops a real reporter. I hired a translator, whom I'll call Rolando, and Rolando and I went straight to an open-air marketplace to do the *"hombre* in the *camino"* interviews which are the heart and soul of election news coverage the world over. I can't tell you why. We all know what happens when you stop the man in the street and ask him a question about anything other than elections. "How do I get to I-95 from the Lincoln Tunnel?" for instance. You wind up in Williamsburg, Brooklyn. But during political season this same randomly chosen schmo is supposed to possess the wisdom of Mary Matalin and James Carville combined.

I picked a fabulous-looking Indian woman in full native regalia, her kindly face riven and creased by life's long experiences and her black eyes sparkling with the ancient sagacity of her Mayan forebears.

---

*Note journalistic prescience about looming Rostenkowski electoral defeat.

Were the elections honest? I asked. Was she going to vote? What party did she favor? Which party would win? What changes did she expect from the new government? Would the advent of true democracy propel Mexico at last into the front rank of industrialized nations while increasing its influence on the international diplomatic stage and providing a reliable system of legal safeguards and a comfortable standard of living to its people?

"Who knows?" she said.

The second interview subject, a younger Indian woman in not quite as full native regalia, just giggled.

The third, a young man sitting by a pile of melons and fiddling with a comic book, answered *"sí"* to every question until someone in the crowd pointed out that he was too young to vote, way too young, twelve or something.

A man running a stall selling buttons, thread, and sewing needles said, "I hope the election will be fair because we deserve a change." He favored the PRD.

A woman leaning on a butcher block next to the severed head of a pig said, "I think the elections will be fair, but I don't know who will win." She favored the PRI.

An older woman making sausages out of parts of the pig even less appetizing than its head told Rolando and me, "Only God knows who will win. All I do is pray to God. I don't think to be on the side of a party will save the country. I don't go for any of the parties. I'm for peace." Then she began badgering Rolando. "So who are you for? Who do you think will win?"

"Well, that's kind of a private matter," said Rolando. "I mean, isn't this supposed to be a secret ballot?"

Peace was mentioned by a number of the interviewees. They were referring to the ski-masked uprising which began only fifty miles from Tuxtla. The insurgents call themselves Zapatistas after Emiliano Zapata, one of the heroes of the Mexican Revolution. Zapata believed in land redistribution. His idea was to redistribute land so that wealthy landowners had a small plot six feet deep. The Revolution lasted from

1911 to 1920 and killed an estimated one out of every fifteen Mexicans. So, in Mexico, when they say "peace" they aren't talking about disco medallions or Haight-Ashbury finger splits.

People were for peace, of course, but all over the market people were also selling little Zapatista figurines—handmade rag dolls wearing Indian serapes and Steamboat Springs–style knit headgear and carrying tiny carved wooden assault rifles. I talked to a pretty Indian woman standing behind a heap of Zapatista dolls, six pesos each. Who was she for? Her small son jumped up and trilled, "El PRI!"

Aside from some pre-Columbian raiment, occasional pig heads, and the Zapatista dolls (also Zapatista key rings and—seriously—Zapatista pen and pencil sets), Tuxtla was hopelessly normal. Though this is the capital of one of the most remote and impoverished of Mexico's states, its residents seem to have lost sight of their obligation, when foreign correspondents are on duty, to be foreign. The place looked like the affordable housing sections of Los Angeles except the streets were clean and the businesses weren't boarded up, burned out, or covered in grates, bars, and sheets of bulletproof Plexiglas. (Real revolutionaries apparently don't spend much time looting carryouts and beating truck drivers.)

Tuxtla seemed like a long way to go just to describe dull elections when we've got perfectly dull elections* of our own at home this fall. I tried hard to find something unusual and exotic. There was a marimba concert every evening from seven until nine in Tuxtla's central square. Well, they were really *big* marimbas. In fact, these marimbas were so big it took three or four guys to play them. The effect was like reading several years of *Playboy* Jazz Poll results: Lionel Hampton on the vibes, Lionel Hampton on the vibes, Lionel Hampton on the vibes. Outside town was a large cement building with a sign reading *"Instituto Nacional Indigenista"* which, considering what Mexico can do to the tummy . . . But *indigenista* turns out to mean "indigenous" in Spanish and the institute was the equivalent of our Bureau of Indian Affairs.

*Note even more journalistic prescience.

I gave up and went to the mall. The city had a brand-new big one with vaulted ceiling, glassed-in atrium, and peach-colored stucco walls. It possessed such non–third world touches as handicapped parking and wheelchair access and was called *Galería,* Spanish (also English, German, French, and Japanese) for "mall." How remote and impoverished is Chiapas supposed to be if it supports a store devoted solely to Hello Kitty products?

The Tuxtla Galería was slightly more fun than an American mall. You could smoke. And the rent-a-cops had guns. The cop hanging around in front of the jewelry store had an M-16. And the gigantic modern supermarket which occupied one end of the complex employed swarms of ten-year-old bag boys dressed in neat blue uniforms and matching piss-cutter caps. They packed the groceries with fervor, not so much for tips but because, as soon as they'd filled a customer's shopping cart, they got to shove it down the wheelchair ramp, jump on, and take a high-speed ride into the parking lot.

On the night before the elections there were thousands of people at the mall, panic buying for fear there would be rioting or even guerrilla war in the wake of the ballot. Americans would have been shopping for ammo and rottweilers. The Mexicans were shopping for food. Mexicans are by no means less violent than Americans. But they are better cooks.

Downtown Tuxtla was festooned with the highly colored symbols of Mexico's political parties. Plastic banners were strung on wires across the main streets and hung so thickly that I seemed to be in an environmentalist's nightmare, a triple-canopy petrochemical jungle. Most of the party symbols had been x-ed out. A good reporter can learn a lot by observing such details. The *x*'s across the banners of every political party showed that Mexicans were deeply dissatisfied not only with their present government but with the entire political establishment. The *x*'s also showed an intrinsic orderliness to the Mexican character because every *x* had been carefully drawn in trim, straight lines. "Interesting," I ruminated to Rolando while I wrote profound conclusions in my notebook, "the way nearly every party symbol has been defaced."

"They're *printed* that way," said Rolando. "That's how you mark your ballot in Mexico, with an *x.*"

"Oh," I said, erasing things.

Perhaps San Cristóbal would prove more fruitful. This is the second largest city in Chiapas and was the main target of the Zapatistas, who invaded the town center at 2:30 in the morning on January 1 and held the municipal palace, the radio station, and the principal square for twenty-four hours.

San Cristóbal is a two-hour drive east into the Chiapan highlands. It's 7,500 feet in the air. The highway loops and tangles like tape yanked out of a broken cassette deck. The cornfields rising from the roadside are nearly vertical, the way crops are painted in folk art, so much so that I thought maybe Grandma Moses wasn't a primitivist with no per-spective technique, maybe she was living in Chiapas and painting from life. It's impossible to imagine how the highland Indians could make a living from these fields. Even if they did manage to grow a crop it would just roll away and deliver itself to their downhill neighbors.

Since the time of the Spanish conquest the Indians have been treated like dirt. Not that well—arable land is scarce in Mexico. The Indians have been treated like living manure. They've been ignored or exploited, usually both. It is these impoverished people who form the rank and file of the Zapatistas though the most vocal leader, who styles himself Subcomandante Marcos, is a pale, urban mestizo. "I heard he maybe was a journalist," said Rolando.

I expected San Cristóbal to be as poor as the Zapatistas. But it wasn't. It was beautiful. Actually, it was cute. There were colonnaded plazas and teensy streets and Spanish colonial buildings attempting to look formal and Madrid-like though made of adobe. Old carved doors gave glimpses of green shaded courtyards and lots of those big terra-cotta pots with which all Latin countries seem to be plagued. Every third block held a cathedral, with all surfaces inside and out covered in the full canonical miniseries cast of angels, saints, lambs, doves, virgins, and baby Jesuses. I was told San Cristóbal had so many richly decorated ecclesiastical edifices because of the forced labor levied upon the Indians. Carving a snappy Mary Magdalene was better duty than working in the mines or the perpendicular truck gardens. So, every time a church was finished, the Indians would get religious visions and clamor for another church to be built.

Nowadays what the Indians did was sit outside these churches selling arts and crafts to hippies. San Cristóbal was full of hippies. There were way-back hippies growing gray, spreading out under their caftans, and straining the buttons on their embroidered work shirts. There were new-hatched neohippies fumbling with the icons of the Sixties wondering whether the peace symbol is supposed to be used mainly as a nose stud or also as a pierced eyebrow ornament. And there were smelly European backpacker hippies, age indeterminate, telling the locals, *"Ich bin ein Vegan."*

The hippies were excited by the Zapatistas. Mexico is, you know, so romantic. Ignored and exploited people under the command of a light-skinned Hispanic who might be a journalist took over a picturesque place full of handicrafts. To put it in American terms, a band of first wives led by Geraldo Rivera invaded Carmel.

But in Mexico they play for higher stakes. Witness the jewelry store guard with the automatic weapon. Or go to a bullfight. Imagine taking a confused and stupid animal and tormenting it to death for the sake of dramatic entertainment. (We'd never do that to cattle in the United States. We use celebrities.) In order for the Zapatista revolt to be a successful publicity stunt Mexico-style, blood had to be shed. The Mexican army came in and obligingly killed 250 people (according to the Mexican army), 500 people (according to the local bishop), and 1,000 people (according to all the hippies). Most of the casualties were, naturally, innocent. Guilty people are better motivated to hide. Also they fire back. When the army retook San Cristóbal and the other towns, Indian peasants who had the bad luck to be standing around looking too ignored and exploited got shot.

There was a cultural institute *cum* coffeehouse in San Cristóbal run by a very nice American of the Peter, Paul, and Mary generation. He'd come to the Chiapas mountains to make a new life. "I fought

American foreign policy for years," he said. "The Iraq war was the last straw." But he admired the Zapatista rebellion. He may have a good moral point here. I just don't know what it is. Would everything have been okay if the Iraqi army, rather than the Mexican army, had shot the Indians? Should George Bush have bombed Tuxtla instead of Baghdad?

A hand-lettered sign on the cultural institute's bulletin board offered a lecture on the Zapatistas and a tour of sites in San Cristóbal where principal events of the rebellion had occurred. The tour consisted of walking over to the main plaza and staring at the municipal palace. There were bullet holes, I was told.

"Where?" I asked.

"They've been patched." And there was revolutionary graffiti but the building had been painted.

The lecture audience was me, a Canadian college student with very long hair who wanted to be an "alternative journalist," and a denim-clad middle-aged woman who ran the cultural institute's bookstore and who must have heard all this before. We sat around one of the coffeehouse tables. Two Indian girls came in and showed some small pieces of embroidery to the middle-aged woman, who cooed extravagantly.

"You should get some soap," the woman said to me. "The Maya love soap. If you're going to be out in the remote villages, it makes a perfect little gift." Though I would have been inclined to give it to the backpackers.

The two Indian girls retired to the next table and ordered Coca-Colas. The college student had a homemade press card laminated in plastic. "You're a professional," he said. "Does this look convincing?"

The lecture was given by a grad student from Mexico City whom I'll call Juan. Juan was in San Cristóbal doing his anthropology thesis on the positive effects of tourism on indigenous peoples. His thesis was that there weren't any.

"But what about the money the Indians get from selling, um, small pieces of embroidery?" I said.

"That money only goes to the sellers," said Juan. Therefore Juan's argument was that people who don't make money from tourism, don't make money from tourism.

Juan said there were three basic causes of the Zapatista revolt. One was the nation's lumpy distribution of wealth. Juan claimed that, since 1988, Mexico had acquired twenty-four new billionaires, few of whom, I gathered, were Chiapan Indians. This seemed a bit abstract to me. You might be able to become a *thousandaire* exploiting the local impoverished peasantry, but richer pickings are required to make a billion. Even at his most predatory, Michael Milken was not seen peddling junk bonds in Chiapas State.

Then there was NAFTA. The Mexican campesino with machete, digging stick, and nothing in the way of a tractor but his wife now found himself competing directly with American agribusiness and all its federal subsidies, government price supports, and fishy tax breaks. "NAFTA was a certificate of death for the indigenous," said Juan. The Zapatistas really should have attacked the U.S. Department of Agriculture, but Washington's a long way and bargain airfares are hard to get at New Year's. (The good news is, between the billionaire problem and the NAFTA problem, we may have found something for Ross Perot to do with his life.)

The most important cause of the rebellion, however, was land reform, and here one's sympathy for the Indians ran headfirst into the lintel on that low doorway which is logic. You can redistribute the land in Chiapas in a way that's too fair for Mother Teresa and everyone still winds up with a bedspread-size patch on a forty-five-degree angle. Will the Zapatistas be less angry when they finally get their farms and it's a technical climb with ropes and pitons from the outhouse to the barn?

"The Zapatistas don't want to impose communism," said Juan. "They want to carry on with capitalism with social justice."

"They want to get social justice from *capitalism?*" said the college student, who was trying hard to be a leftist and was deeply shocked. "Do they want to become capitalists or do they want to continue on their communal land with just enough food every year?" His tone implied that the latter alternative was a goal to which all mankind might aspire.

Juan, sounding a bit disappointed himself, said the Indians wanted to have legal title and private ownership of individual plots.

Fortunately for revolution, the Zapatistas wanted lots of other things, too. "They have eleven basic demands," said Juan. "Suitable roof, adequate food, health, education, work, peace, justice, independence, democracy, freedom, and one other thing that I'm not remembering."

Which is a lot to expect from taking over a town square for twenty-four hours. "These are essentially human rights," said the young Canadian, reverently. And he was correct about the human part. It's hard to give democracy to cows. Not enough of them would vote to be hamburgers.

I had to drive back to Tuxtla that night, through fog banks and thundershowers, past swaying, skidding tractor-trailers and ancient, brakeless buses, down the curly, devious plummet of a road, which, in place of guardrails has little white crosses memorializing those who missed the turns. Supposedly there are 365 curves between San Cristóbal and the state capital. But Rolando said only two of them have names: the Monkey's Tail *(El Rabo de Mono)* and the Horseshoe *(La Herradura)*. What a waste of nomenclature opportunities. Hair in the Soup *(El Pelo en la Sopa)*, Argument with Jesuits *(La Disputa con Jesuitas)*, Tongue of My First Wife *(La Lengua de Mi Esposa Primera)*, and Now We're Fucked *(¡Ay Que Fucked!)* were just a few of the suggestions I made during two hours of terrorizing Rolando, myself, and a number of Indian pedestrians who were under the impression that the purpose of a double yellow line is to mark the path for women carrying firewood.

I needed to be in Tuxtla because the Mexican Federal Electoral Institute (IFE) had screwed up my press credentials royally (I mean freely electedly). The *Rolling Stone* staff had spent weeks on phone, fax, and Federal Express exchanges with the Mexican consulate, making sure my credentials would be waiting for me, which they weren't. But IFE officials in Tuxtla assured me the credentials would be sent on the next plane from Mexico City and the following plane and the plane after that—on more planes from Mexico City than Tuxtla gets.

My press credentials were not only not arriving from Mexico City they were also not arriving from Oaxaca, Veracruz, and Quintana Roo.

This made the IFE people sad. They were worried about me wandering around without proper identification. So they got out a Polaroid camera and a laminating machine and made me an ID at least as convincing as the Canadian college student's. It said I was a Mexican reporter. I look Mexican the way Steffi Graf does, and the only words I know in Spanish are *¡Ay que fucked!* The IFE officials considered this and grew worried anew. "Do you have a press visa?" they asked.

"I couldn't get a press visa without credentials."

"But you can't get credentials without a press visa."

Fortunately Mexico is a country where, though nothing works, everything can be fixed. IFE had an entire bureau of the Mexican Immigration Service in its offices for just such an eventuality. I spent an hour filling out forms in duplicate and handing them to a panel of young women who typed up more forms on large electric typewriters. San Cristóbal answered the question "Where did all the hippies go?" And the Mexican Immigration Service provided a definitive response to the query "Whatever happened to carbon paper?"

When all that was done, IFE got worried a third time. If I had an American passport with a press visa, how could I have press credentials saying I was Mexican? "This might confuse the authorities," they said even though they were the authorities, but I suppose they had a point because they *were* confused. They said I'd better come back the next day and get those credentials from Mexico City after all.

I was a little concerned about credentials myself. The army had checkpoints all around San Cristóbal, and plainclothes police were being sent into the areas formerly held by the Zapatistas. I saw a stakebed truck full of men in jeans and sport shirts, each carrying an automatic weapon. It looked like the Moody Loners Outlet Store was receiving a wholesale shipment of disgruntled postal workers. So I made my way down the wet, ugly, dark mountain road to Tuxtla, rushing to get to the IFE office before it closed. They said they'd thought it over, and the credentials I already had would be fine.

Anyway, no matter what kind of official papers you're supposed to have in Mexico, the official to whom you give them always seems completely perplexed, as though he were a traffic cop who'd stopped you for speeding and you'd handed him your college transcript. My Mexican press card and American visa bothered no one, but a soldier at a roadblock was very concerned by my passport. It's valid until the year 2000. The cover page reads "Date of Expiration 16 AUG 00." The soldier thought it had zeroed out.

Mexico is confusing. Mexico is confused. Vast complexity mixes with the simply inoperative. Speaking of traffic cops, I blew by one on the Tuxtla bypass going sixty in a thirty-mile-an-hour zone. "Oh, don't worry," said Rolando. "He's local police. This is a federal highway. Only federal police can bother you here." What is it with Mexico? Why are Mexicans so much in love with authority's forms while having so little respect for formal authority? "With precaution, every red light is a green" was Rolando's other piece of driving advice. And what does all this have to do with everybody saying *mañana* all the time? Is it something in the Mexican soul?

Mexicans have different souls than we do. There's a special heaven where Mexicans go—more brightly decorated, more highly spiced, and much cheaper than ours. But be careful of the milk and honey, you're safer with the bottled water.

No. It's just that their country has been run by party hacks for sixty-five years and that party is synonymous with the government and the government is synonymous with the economy and all life is a patronage plum. If you want to know why it takes so much red tape to accomplish anything in Mexico and why, after all that red tape, the thing isn't accomplished and why nobody is surprised when it isn't, think of a 763,000-square-mile, 78-million-employee New York City Department of Motor Vehicles.

Of course Mexico's Federal Electoral Institute has changed all that and brought the country U.S.-type democracy. This is the 1990s and the Mexican oligarchy knows it can't just steal votes to get elected. It has to lie to voters, too.

During one of my many visits to IFE, I watched a twenty-five-minute videotape explaining Mexico's free, fair, and totally honest election system. The background music was a bit too reminiscent of the *I Dream of Jeannie* theme for something purporting to describe a total lack of trickery. But, the video said, IFE was trustworthy because every one of its rules, decisions, programs, appointments, committees, employees, and public announcements has to be approved by all nine of Mexico's political parties. And there are some strange ones—such as the Authentic Mexican Revolutionary Party, led by a retired rancher from Coahuila notable for having started a campaign against cow ticks, and the Party of the Cardenista Front for National Reconstruction, named after the late Gen. Lázaro Cárdenas, father of the Cárdenas running for president on the opposing PRD ticket. The Cardenista Front didn't think Cárdenas was Cardenista enough.

According to the video, thousands of citizen poll watchers would be present to monitor the electoral performance. The poll watchers were chosen by lot. They had to be registered voters who were under seventy, were able to read and write, and weren't government workers or leading figures in a political party. Which brings us to an interesting question about true democracy. Why not let *them* run Mexico? And why not let them run the United States? Do you think a randomly chosen literate American voter who doesn't have Alzheimer's, isn't an IRS employee, and hasn't got an "Impeach Billary" sign stuck in his lawn would be a worse president than Clinton? Bush? Reagan? Carter? Ford? And let us not forget that, if the United States had an election system as free, fair, and totally honest as Mexico's, Nixon would have been president eight years sooner.

On election day Rolando and I went back up to the Chiapan highlands. I wanted to see the Indian towns around San Cristóbal, towns from which the Zapatistas presumably drew support. We were accompanied by an American anthropologist, whom I'll call Bill, who'd spent years in the area and had a pretty good idea what was going on. "Nothing much," said Bill.

Which was a problem because, when daring, intrepid foreign correspondents don't find trouble to cover, they risk turning into cloying, pathetic travel writers.

The town of Zinacantán is a must-see on any Chiapas vacation jaunt. Though modern amenities are few, the friendly, colorful Tzotzil Indian natives . . . Stop me before I describe the cathedral.

Zinacantán did have an impressive cathedral. Fortunately for readers, this has nothing to do with Mexican election conflicts. And the people of Zinacantán weren't having much to do with those conflicts either. I mean, they were standing in line to vote, but that was it.

The men and women were in separate queues. How much did this tell us about Indian society? What political and cultural significance did it have? Why were they lined up this way? "They felt like it," said Bill.

I tried interviewing again. Here is the most partisan response I got: "Whoever wins, good luck."

Then a busload of French tourists arrived. They'd come to see the cathedral. Who did *they* support? They conferred among themselves. Probably the socialist PRD, they agreed.

"But," I said, "I thought the socialists were unpopular in France right now."

"Oh, we don't want the socialists in *our* country," said the tour leader.

I asked Bill, "Who are the Zinacantáns really for? The Zapatistas, maybe?"

"I can't imagine the Zinacantáns being for anybody," he said. "They're pretty independent." And he told me that during the Gulf War they had invoked their most powerful supernatural protector, the Butterfly Spirit, to keep them out of the conflict. There are seven sacred peaks in the mountain rim around Zinacantán, and the shamans went from one to another holding a ceremony that had not been performed in living memory.

"Why were they so concerned about the Gulf War?" I asked.

"Because it was about oil," said Bill. "The way they saw it, Kuwait has oil and Mexico has oil and you never know."

If you think about it, their reasoning was very similar to the Bush administration's.

We visited a couple of other towns, Larrainzar and Chamula. Nothing happened there either. I did see lewd graffiti. Someone had spelled out the Tzotzil word *mis* in the dust on the fender of a tourist's car. *Mis* means "kitty" or "pussy." In Tzotzil, as in English, it's slang for the female genitals. "The Mayans love a pun," said Bill. Mayan kids are tickled by the idea that unmarried American women are called "Miss" and think nothing is funnier than to run down the street calling out to tourist ladies, "Miss! Oh, Miss! Hello, Miss!"

Bill felt that the national elections didn't impress the Tzotzil Mayans. "They have their own way of making decisions," he said. Apparently everyone in a community gets together, and they talk for days until complete consensus on a given issue is reached. Bill saw much to be admired in this. I thought it sounded even worse than regular politics. Bill admitted it had its shortcomings as a goal-oriented policy tool. He told me about a village up in the mountains so poor that the Indians used to say, "All we have are rocks." Then a corporation from Mexico City came and said the rocks could be turned into agricultural lime. The corporation offered to pay the village a large sum. The Indians got together and yakked and yakked. After weeks of deliberation they announced they were refusing the corporation's offer. "All we have are rocks," they said. "And, if we sell those, we won't have anything."

We drove into San Cristóbal late in the afternoon. The Zapatistas had not disturbed the election day peace. Although this was not literally true because a young man was selling Zapatista folk music cassettes on the street and using a boom box to play sample cuts—"Marcos's Song," "The Zapatista Hymn," "Ballad of Emiliano Zapata." Think of several tenor Leonard Cohens singing off-key with a mariachi band accompanied by your summer camp counselor on acoustic guitar. I hadn't taken the Zapatista invasion of San Cristóbal very seriously, but now, remembering that the rebels had held the radio station for a whole day, my heart went out to listeners everywhere in the broadcast area.

Rolando, Bill, and I were walking down the street—clutching souvenir Zapatista cassettes—when an American woman ran up. She was fully my age but dressed like a runaway teen and wearing a pair of the biggest blackest possible shoes. She was out of breath and nearly ecstatic with indignation. "I'm so glad the *media* is here!" she said. "The government is cheating on the ballots! There's trouble at the voting booths! There may be . . ." Her voice was filled with hope. ". . . a riot!" She pulled a small tape recorder from her purse and held it in the air, ready to make a permanent record of the cataclysmic events soon to transpire.

We went over to the central plaza, where about a thousand voters were standing in line. Some of them had been there since early morning and now it seemed as though there weren't going to be enough ballots for them all. They were irked.

This was a special polling place where people who weren't registered in San Cristóbal could place absentee votes. But, because San Cristóbal was a left-wing attraction at the moment and a tourist resort besides, an extra number of out-of-towners were on hand. Sure enough, the polling place ran out of voting slips. Then the people in line got very irked and pushed up onto the bandstand where the voting tables were and trapped a couple of IFE officials. One of those Frank Capra–type voices from the crowd rang out with stern reasonableness, "We demand an explanation!" A chant began, "We want to vote!" An awning over the voting table was torn down. A couple of loudmouths on the steps of the bandstand called for the ballots to be burned, which seemed beside the point since the problem was that there weren't any ballots. An enthusiastically outraged young Mexican journalist asked me, "Where are you from?"

"Rolling Stone," I replied.

"Right on!" he said, fabulously out of date.

Someone jumped on a chair and shouted that he had a plan. He said that anybody who didn't get to vote should write down his or her name and address and then they'd send a petition of grievance to Mexico City. This didn't sound like much fun. The fellow on the chair was booed.

"It's *almost* an ugly crowd," I said to another American reporter who was pressed against the bandstand railing next to me.

"This crowd is exactly as angry," said my compatriot, "as the crowd at O'Hare Airport on a holiday weekend when the flights to La Guardia have been canceled. If they'd get somebody up there announcing free frequent flyer miles . . ."

And that's practically what happened. The head of the Federal Electoral Institute in San Cristóbal elbowed his way to the voting table and began an aloud reading from IFE rules and regulations. It seems that Article Jillion, Section Zillion states that special polling places for absentee voters shall be supplied with only so-and-so many ballots and when those ballots are exhausted no more shall be given out, et cetera. A strange-looking man with a guitar and Zapatista stickers all over his sombrero tried to drown out the IFE official with one of those folk songs, but the crowd shushed him. When the man from IFE was finished reading there was a shuffling in the plaza and murmurs and mmm's and harrumphs. "Marcos!" yelled somebody. "Revolution!" yelled somebody else. I looked out at the throng. All the Mexicans were laughing. But scattered among the Indian and mestizo faces were the pallid mugs of gringo hippies, their mouths still frowning at injustice and eyes still bright with the dream that this might be Columbia University, 1968, all over again.

I arrived back in Tuxtla too late to catch the ten minutes of election night anti-PRI window busting which went on downtown. Some of the same happened in the national capital and a few other places. Then it petered out. Mexico may be a time bomb but it's also Mexico—plenty of fuse and somebody forgot the explosives.

By American standards there wasn't much election coverage on TV. Every now and then a special bulletin would interrupt the regular programming—*Prom Night III* dubbed in Spanish. Sometime after midnight the PAN presidential candidate gave a concession speech so long it would have taken him less time to serve a term as president.

The next morning Rolando and I were supposed to interview representatives from the three major political parties—listen to them as they poor-mouthed, mealy-mouthed, or big-mouthed. But nobody's ever on time in Mexico, me and Rolando included. By two in the afternoon the only person we'd talked to was a local PAN organizer, a personable young Ob-gyn. And, to tell the truth, I wasn't really paying attention to him until he'd walked us out the door of his modest office and was standing next to a VW Bug decorated with National Action Party bumper stickers. Then the doctor mentioned, with amused resignation, that in Mexico the big houses and big cars belonged to people who got into politics, not medical school.

From two to five, Tuxtla shuts down for midday meal and siesta. Rolando invited me to his house, a pleasant bungalow on a hill overlooking the city. A dozen people were there—cousins, in-laws, friends, kids, his mom. Rolando's wife had cooked three huge platters of roast pork on banana leaves, which she served with rice, guacamole, hot peppers, steamed onions, and fresh-baked flour tortillas. We drank a case of beer and then a bottle and a half of brandy. Rolando and I were the only English speakers, though thanks to "liquid Berlitz" we were all eloquent. But not a word was said about politics. And no one in Rolando's house was wearing big black shoes. Indeed, the women wore high heels and jewelry in the middle of the day. This is a civilized country. Rolando got out his guitar and played the sentimental, heartbroken songs beloved by Mexicans, such as "Margaritaville." Lunch lasted six hours.

I never did interview anybody from the other political parties. And who cares? Let us ponder a few questions about things political. When a reward or distinction goes to someone who doesn't deserve it, why do we say, "It was politics"? When we call a person "a real politician," is it a compliment? Are the words *office politics* ever used to describe anything good that happened at work? How often do we have occasion to call someone an "ethical hack," a "spiritual hack," or a "philosophical hack"? And what does the term *political appointee* bring to mind? Do you suppose Surgeon General Joycelyn Elders is much of a surgeon? Would you let her perform your vasectomy?

Mexicans had an election. Nothing happened. God bless them. Mexicans know that the world doesn't need more politics, it needs more lunch.

The 1987 Stock Market Crash

The American Spectator

On Monday, October 19, of this year, the stock market went to the bathroom. Since then a lot of us have been pretty busy— talking our broker pals down from window ledges and convincing friends in the junk bond business to shut off the Porsche and open the garage door. We've been so busy that we may not have noticed Black and Blue Monday marked the end of an era. Neopoverty means curtains for the Yuppies, a.k.a. the Me Generation, a.k.a. the Now Generation, a.k.a. the Dr. Spock Brats. Everybody born between WW II and the early Sixties is finally going to have to grow up. It's all over now, Baby Boom.

Of course the collapse of the Reagan Pig-out wasn't the only thing that did us Boomers in. There was massive drug taking, which turned out to be a bad idea. Maybe drugs make you a better person but only if you believe in heaven and think John Belushi could get past the doorman. And having sex with everyone we could think of—this broke up our first two marriages and gave most of us chronic venereal diseases and the rest of us obituaries. And then there was us, just being ourselves—"finding out who we are," "getting in touch with our feelings," "fulfilling our true inner potential"—frightening stuff. You'll notice that now we're all running out to rent the *Fatal Attraction* video so we can moon over a nuclear family and cheer for traditional morals. It seems like that boring middle-class suburbia where we grew up was swell after all. The problem is, we've spent all our money on cocaine and Reeboks and we can't afford it.

What went wrong? We were the generation of hope; the generation that was going to change the world; the biggest, richest, best-educated generation in the history of America—the biggest, richest, best-educated spot in this or any other galaxy. Nothing was too good for us. It took thousands of doctors and psychiatrists to decide whether we should suck our thumbs or all our toes, too. Our every childhood fad had global implications. One smile at Davy Crockett and the forests of the temperate zone were leveled in the search for raccoon-tail hats. When we took up hula hoops, the planet bobbled in its orbit. Our transistor radios drowned out the music of the spheres. A sniffle from us and *Life* magazine was sick in bed for a month. All we had to do was hold a sit-in and governments were toppled from the Beijing of Mao Tse-tung to the Cleveland of Dennis Kucinich.★ "We are the world," we shouted just a couple of years ago. And just a couple of years ago we were. How did we wind up so old? So fat? So confused? So *broke?*

The truth is our generation was spoiled rotten from the start. We spent the entire 1950s on our butts in front of the television while Mom fed us Twinkies and Ring Dings through strawberry Flavor

★Child mayor. Elected in 1977 at the age of thirty. Governed about as well as you'd imagine. Now deservedly forgotten.

Straws and Dad ransacked the toy stores looking for hundred-mile-an-hour streamlined Schwinns, Daisy air howitzers, Lionel train sets larger than the New York Central system, and other novelties to keep us amused during the few hours when Pinky Lee and *My Friend Flicka* weren't on the air.

When we came of age in the 1960s, we found the world wasn't as perfect as Mr. Green Jeans and Ozzie Nelson said it would be, and we threw a decade-long temper tantrum. We screamed at our parents, our teachers, the police, the president, Congress, and the Pentagon. We threatened to hold our breath (as long as the reefer stayed lit) and not cut our hair until poverty, war, and injustice were stopped.

That didn't work. So we whiled away the 1970s in an orgy of hedonism and self-absorption, bouncing from ashram to bedroom to disco to gym at a speed made possible only by ingesting vast quantities of Inca Scratch N Sniff.

Even this proved unsatisfying, so we elected President Reagan and tried our hand at naked greed. We could have it all—career, marriage, job, children, BMW, Rolex, compact disc player, another marriage, more children, and a high-growth, high-yield, no-load mutual fund. Actually, for a while, it looked like we *could* have it all. As long as we didn't mind also having a national debt the size of the Crab Nebula, an enormous underclass making its living from five-cent beverage can deposits, and currency that the Japanese use to blow their noses. But now our economy has the williwaws, and our Youth Culture has arthritis, Alzheimer's, and gout. Life's big Visa card bill has come due at last.

The Baby Boom has reached middle age. It's time for us to pause, time to reflect, time to . . . *OH, GOD, DARLING, DON'T DO IT WITH A GUN—WE JUST REDECORATED THE BATH-ROOM!!!* . . . time to evaluate the contributions that we, as a generation, have made to a world which presented us with so many unique advantages. Contributions such as . . . uh . . . um . . . BZZZZZZZZ! *Time's up!* Well, some of the Beatles' songs are really great. (Although, technically, the Beatles aren't part of the Baby Boom.) And there's that first Tom Robbins novel, *Another Roadside Attraction.* That was good, I think. I mean I was very stoned when I read it. And . . . And . . . New Coke?

Wait a minute, I hear dissenting noises. Civil rights, you say? But the Civil Rights Movement was founded by people a lot older than us. Harriet Tubman, for instance. We Boomers *did* start the Peace Movement. That was a big success. The Vietnam War only lasted another eight or ten years, once we got the Peace Movement going. Then, darn it, the Communists took over South Vietnam, Laos, and Cambodia and killed everybody they could get their hands on just like General Westmoreland, that pig, said they would. So I don't think we can count the Peace Movement as a major contribution, especially not as far as the former citizens of Phnom Penh are concerned. Our political commitment, however, really changed things. You can tell by the quality of the presidents that we used to have, such as Truman and Eisenhower, compared with the quality of the presidents that we got as soon as the Baby Boom was old enough to vote, such as Ford and Carter. And our idealism has made a difference. Ever since Live Aid all the Ethiopians have had to do the Jane Fonda workout to keep from larding up around the middle.

It is true that our generation was the first to take feminism seriously. That's because old-timey feminists used to worry about boring things like voting rights and legal status. But Boomer Women put some real life in the issue by emphasizing upscale grabbiness, pointless careerism, and insane arguments about pronoun antecedents. Fitness is another trend pioneered by the Boom. Millions of us are leading empty, useless, pitiful lives and lifting weights and eating fiber to make those lives last longer. Also the computer revolution—we invented a brilliant matrix of complex and intricate software programs which allow us to compile, cross-reference, and instantly access all the nothing that we know. Finally, there's our creativity—our wild, innovative, original artistic gifts—surely a legacy to the ages. Huh? Huh? Sorry, I couldn't hear you. I had the new L. L. Cool J *Bigger and Deffer* tape turned all the way up on my Walkman.

Let's face it, our much-vaunted rebellion against bourgeois values meant we didn't want to clean the bathroom. All our mystical enlightenments are now printed in Hallmark greeting cards. Our intellectual insights led to a school system that hasn't taught anybody how to read in fifteen years. All we've done for the disadvantaged is gentrify the crap out of their neighborhoods. And now we're about to lose our jobs.

Do we have any skills or anything? No. Complain, play Donkey Kong, and roll joints with E-Z Wider papers are the only things this generation has ever been able to do. Will anyone feel sorry for us? No. We've been making pests of ourselves for four decades, hogging the limelight, making everybody feel unhip and out of it. The earth has had a bellyful of us. We'll be selling kiwi fruit on the street and rattling microchips in a tin cup and people will *laugh*.

We're a generation whose heroes were Howdy Doody, Jerry Rubin, Big Bird, and Ivan Boesky. We deserve the stock market crash, and herpes and the Betty Ford Clinic besides. We're jerks. We're clowns. We're forty and still wearing jeans. Nobody takes us seriously . . .

Wait a minute. *Serious.* That's it. Oh, man, this will really bug the squares! What we do is we all start wearing dumpy corduroy sports coats and cheap, shiny navy blue wash pants and Hush Puppies. We get those stupid half-glasses and wear them way down on the ends of our noses. We read Schopenhauer, Wittgenstein, Kant, all those guys. We call it *The New Seriousness.* The media will wig out. We'll be all over network TV again.

Dig this—we start going to church, not Moonie church or born-again church but real Episcopalian church every Sunday. We invite each other over to afternoon teas and discuss the novels of Thomas Mann. We take up the cello. We do the London *Times* crossword puzzle in ink. We admire Woody Allen's *recent* movies. We vote in local elections.

We'll be *crazy* serious—international superstars of, like, heavy pensive eggheadery. We fire David Letterman and replace him with Jean-Paul Sartre. (Is he still alive? Well, somebody like that.) Shoot MTV videos for Handel and Rimsky-Korsakov. Do a feature movie about the life of Euripides with the sound track in ancient Greek. There are 76 million of us. Everybody's going to want a books-on-tape cassette of Bertrand Russell and A. N. Whitehead's *Principia Mathematica* for their car. We'll make a fortune! We'll be famous! And we'll change the world!

The New Seriousness—it's bitchin', it's far out, it's rad to the max, it's *us*. Gotta go now. Gotta call Merrill Lynch and buy stock in the Cleveland Symphony Orchestra.

Whitewater

Rolling Stone, 1994

This is twice in two years I've wound up on a fool's errand in Little
Rock. The last time I was supposed to be delivering a big wet kiss
of national approval to the Democratic presidential candidate. This
time I'm expected to give the same guy a popularily mandated
smackeroo of political death. Will you, the public, please make up your
mind? Do you want Bill Clinton covered in regular flowers or the
Gennifer kind?

You're always mad at us journalists. Back in early '92 you said we
were being too hard on the boy when we needled him for sleeping
through Vietnam, pointed out that he didn't know how to smoke marijuana right, and dredged up some tomato he hadn't canoodled with
for months and months. Then Clinton got the Democratic nomina-

tion. We members of the press clapped our hands raw at his speech about how he had a childhood like a whole week of Oprah Winfrey shows. We patted his back until his suit jacket shoulder pads popped for picking Al Gore to hand out mints after state dinners. And you said we were being too kind. You said we ignored Clinton's history of double-shuffling the issues and playing ally-ally-out-in-free with the truth. You claimed we didn't tell you his staff still wore diapers. We cuddle-bunnied him right into office. "Every time Bill Clinton sits down, *The Washington Post* gets a broken nose," you said. Now we're all in Little Rock vowing we've got enough dirt to keep network camera crews riding John Deeres until Colin Powell runs for office. Our rakes drip muck. Our slings groan with mud. And we've got a giant clothes hamper chocked with soiled first family business apparel—Phew! Cattle market socks! We're hearing an ominous noise of rattling femurs among the White House coat hangers. And you're still not happy.

You say we're distracting Clinton from the business of government. Well I hope so. Distracting a politician from governing is like distracting a bear from eating your baby. Or like getting a dog to quit chewing on your wallet, anyway. But what *do* you want us to do? Come on, you're the customer. You tell us. Should we go back to Washington and write hundred-column-inch cerebrum-snuffing, eyeball-fibrillating articles on health care reform? How about some NAFTA follow-ups? A nine-part series on the Republic of Kyrgyzstan? Or maybe we should come over to your house and investigate *you*.

So leave us alone. Sure, we're down here hunting the president in a pack. But that's because we journalists are social animals. We're just having fun. Actually, nobody but other journalists will have anything to do with us. You want us to mate and breed, don't you?

Besides, Bill Clinton can take care of himself. Witness his Whitewater press conference. He is good. He managed to work his dead mother into the first paragraph of his speech. Note the way Bill's accent goes all country when he's in trouble, though Hot Springs is a boutique resort town and as down home as Martha Stewart. Bill's stepfather was the local Buick dealer. "When Clinton talks about an outdoor toilet, he means he was peeing in the swimming pool," somebody in Hot Springs said to me. But Bill's a big, good-looking, lovable goof. "I forgot I bought my mother a house." You can't help liking him. And he keeps just a hint of a smirk on his mug to let us know he's not a complete cement-head.

"By the standards of Arkansas I was honest compared to Richard Nixon" is pretty much what Bill argued at the press conference. And he carried it off. Bill almost had me convinced Republicans caused Whitewater until I remembered that Arkansas only has about one Republican and he had to stay home that week because his wife accidentally used the sheet with the eyeholes in it to make the bed.

I swear I'm going to get to hell and find Bill has talked his way out. "Uh, Moloch," I'll say, "did you have a president down here, kind of a large one, Democrat of course, with lots of hair, who sounded like Clint Black on cold medication?" And Moloch will say, "Well, he *was* here, but he got talking to the boss and . . . Wait a minute, where's my car?"

Maybe I don't have a whole lot of sympathy for Bill Clinton. But since coming to Little Rock I do have sympathy for his waistline, which mine now exactly resembles. Not only is Bill honest by the standards of Arkansas, he's skinny by the standards of Arkansas, too. On my first night in town I went to a restaurant called Cock of the Walk, where they had deep-fat-fried catfish and deep-fat-fried every other thing you can think of on earth including—seriously—deep-fat-fried pickles. They're delicious. So is all the other food in Little Rock. The booze isn't bad either. Arkansas is a state where people still drink, smoke, and eat deep-fat-fried pickles. There are worse places that journalists could be stuck for the next . . . Next quite a while. We don't want to drive the president out of office until we know for sure whether Al Gore is an alien cyborg. Sure, he looked human when he debated Perot, but I understand it blew out two-thirds of his circuits. Since then, you'll notice, the administration hasn't let Gore do anything more complicated than interface with a tornado warning system in Georgia.

Anyway the media horde is in Little Rock. We go to Doe's for steaks as big as Hillary commodity trades, get cocktails as strong as White House denials at the (we couldn't resist the name) Whitewater Tavern, do some line dancing as messy as Madison Savings and Loan balance sheets at Midnight Rodeo, and then we go back and go to sleep at the glorious old Capital Hotel in rooms with ceilings as tall as the tales we'll tell the next day in print and on TV.

Little Rock by night may not be quite so much fun for the non-journalists. Several times, driving around town on a toot, I've noticed lights burning late in the offices rented by Special Prosecutor Robert Fiske. And Little Rock by day isn't much fun for anyone. There's nobody on the downtown streets. The city has that dead look of places where people make their money behind closed doors. Every third building seems to be a lawyer's office. The Rose Law Firm occupies a whole block. Its windows are dark. The curtains don't move. It's a sinister place in a friendly, red brick colonial way, as though the Continental Congress had a Ministry of Fear.

The governor's mansion is also "Early American" though built more in the semisuccessful country western singer style with masonry that's a little too pink and a pseudo-Tara portico larger than the house. There's a chiropractor next door. The south Little Rock neighborhood is going to seed. Just a couple of blocks from the mansion you can see abandoned houses, surly teens in giant pants and catty-cornered baseball caps, and stores with so many bars on the windows that you'd think they were selling take-away jail time. The federal program to get cars up on blocks in people's front yards has been a real success here, as it has throughout the state of Arkansas.

Clinton's intense desire to get into the White House may have been motivated by real estate savvy. The White House has great location. Clinton didn't do well on the Whitewater deal, but perhaps he's learned from his mistakes.

To take the pulse of the Arkansan polity I keep the radio of my rented Chevrolet Lumina on the AM band. Little Rock talk radio talk is all about Jesus or politics. And each talk show caller knows the whole name of every legislator, city councilman, county commissioner, school board member, appellate court judge, highway superintendent, and chicken inspector in the state. I have never heard so much discussion of wire-pullers, highbinders, jacklegs, ballyhoo men, and boodle artists. Arkansans have politics like other people have hives.

As for Jesus, there must be a lot of sin in Arkansas to support this much forgiveness. All sorts of Christian enterprises advertise on the radio shows. There are Christian bookstores, Christian day care centers, Christian drug and alcohol counseling centers. For all I know there are Christian strip joints. The girls don't disrobe. They don't dance or wear makeup either. I mean, this is Baptist territory. They sit in pews and take their clothes off in their hearts.

Sometimes the Jesus and the politics get mixed together. "Now if Clinton were found out to be secretly Catholic," someone told me in the Capital Hotel Bar, "*then* we'd be talking scandal." And I heard one preacher reading from the Book of Daniel, chapter 11, verses 20 and 21:

> Then shall stand up in his estate a raiser of taxes *in* the glory of the kingdom: but within a few days he shall be destroyed, neither in anger, nor in battle.
>
> And in his estate shall stand up a vile person, to whom they shall not give the honor of the kingdom; but he shall come in peaceably, and obtain the kingdom by flatteries.

Call it simple piety if you like, I think he was dissing the 1992 presidential election.

During the daytime in Little Rock there really isn't much for a reporter to do except pester sources and I don't have any. So I went to the Old Statehouse, a handsome Greek Revival structure. It's now a museum devoted to Arkansas history, this history being a straightforward affair: Arkansas was all mountains and swamps. Indians lived there. Rednecks took it. Yankees whupped 'em. And Tyson Foods moved in.

A diorama depicting pioneer days was introduced with a quotation from one Thomas Bang Thorpe dated 1842:

> Happen! Happened in Arkansas: where else could it have hap-
> pened but in the creation state, the finishing up country. . . . Its
> airs—just breathe them and they will make you snort like a
> horse . . .

Which is one way to put it. Nearby was an exhibit of matched pistols
with another quote, this one from a (wisely) anonymous member of
the irresponsible, sensationalist media of 150 years ago:

> Down in Arkansas, when a man cannot be gotten rid of at the
> polls, he is immediately killed off in a duel.

Bill Clinton should be thankful that the worst thing he faces is some
kidding in the press.

One room in the Old Statehouse held a display of the inaugural
ball gowns of all the First Ladies of Arkansas. There was no Hillary
Rodham Clinton dress. There were, however, a bunch of panties that
Bill had collected. Just kidding.

I bought a book at the Old Statehouse gift shop, *Territorial
Ambition, Land and Society in Arkansas, 1800–1840* by S. Charles Bolton.
Ethical imbroglios of the Whitewater type seem to have long tainted
the horse-snorting airs of the creation state. Mr. Bolton cites an 1819
letter from Robert C. Henry, a carpetbagger from Kentucky who is
urging his brother to trot down to Arkansas and get a snout in the
trough. Writes Bob:

> Should I be favored with the appointment of judge, I shall have
> it greatly in my power to serve my friends. . . . we could do
> almost as we pleased. In fixing the seat of government we can
> have an eye to some desirable tract of country. . . . All our fam-
> ily & friends could settle there . . . and should thus acquire
> standing & consequence in the Country.

And, sure enough, on Tuesday, March 29, Jim McDougal—partner of the Clintons in the Whitewater development deal and owner of
the defunct Madison Savings and Loan—decided he'd acquired the

requisite amount of standing and consequence in Arkansas and filed to run for Congress on the Democratic ticket.

The filing took place at the new Arkansas Statehouse. This dates from 1911, is modeled on that great legislative edifice in Washington, and contains all its prototype's architectural features in compact form— a Tonka Toy U.S. Capitol. Jim McDougal was sallow-skinned, peaked, and dropsical. He walked with a cane. His head was shaved and he was wearing a three-piece suit with pronounced pinstripes and lapels on the vest. He looked like a member of the Addams Family who'd gone off to run a small-town savings and loan.

McDougal greeted each member of the press with gracious charm and then tore into us as a group. He said the financial figures show Whitewater is nothing. "A sophomore accounting class would know it. But the arithmetic is beyond the comprehension of a gaggle of Yankee reporters." The gaggle of Yankee reporters wrote this down.

McDougal denounced Clinton critic Rep. Jim Leach as "a fascist" and said that he, McDougal, was running for Congress because "the Republicans have been starving America for a hundred years. I dislike them intensely." He said he'd been "fighting the forces of oppression" since he was twelve and held up a snapshot of himself as a kid dressed in a soldier outfit.

It costs $5,000 to file for a congressional race in Arkansas. McDougal has declared bankruptcy. He paid the filing fee with a $3,000 check and $2,000 in cash. He said the money came from small contributors. McDougal didn't seem to know who the incumbent was in his district. I asked an attractive young woman who was standing in the Capitol rotunda wearing a gold donkey pin in her blazer lapel. "Jay Dickey," she said. "A Republican—I can hardly say it, but he is."

Which brings me to another book I bought at the Old Statehouse gift shop, *Ozark Mountain Humor*, a selection of local folktales edited by W. K. McNeil. The following was collected in 1973 in Fayetteville, Arkansas:

> The politician was campaigning through the South and stopped at one cabin. "My, you have a fine family—eighteen

boys!" he told the man in the cabin. "All good Democrats, I suppose?"

"Well," the man said, "I tried to bring 'em up right, and they're all good Christians, and all but Sam is Democrats—that ornery cuss, he got to readin'."

The next day I drove to Whitewater. "Better bring your checkbook . . . this kind of place won't stay a secret long," said the brochure that the McDougals and Clintons had printed in the mid-1980s.

The development is three hours north of Little Rock. Outside town the lawyers' offices disappear. Instead, every third building seems to be a church. Most are built from cement block, bear the names of denominations no Yankee has heard of, and have signs out front with messages such as:

CH CH
What's Missing?
UR

The other two out of three buildings are trailers. Rural Arkansas is poor. Although you do see better-off areas. You can tell because the trailers are double-wides. There's a $1,000 fine for littering the highway in Arkansas, but if you throw car axles, old tires, beer cans, and broken furniture all over your front lawn you apparently get a gold watch. The natural scenery is beautiful, however. Those rock ledges that stick way out into the air in a Snuffy Smith comic really do exist in the Ozarks. And so does an amusement park called Dogpatch U.S.A.

The 220-acre Whitewater parcel turns out to be a fine piece of land, a hardwood-forested bluff overlooking the White River, in which there is some of the best fishing in the South. Bill and Hillary's own special lot was right on the water. I'll bet they planned on some real good times out here in the woods—taking Ira Magaziner and Lani Guinier on possum hunts, catching catfish on dough balls with George

Stephanopoulos, throwing a block and tackle over a shade tree limb and dropping a new engine into Donna Shalala's Camaro.

I had a little trouble finding the road into Whitewater. There's something about stopping to ask directions at homes with parked Harley-Davidsons, loose chickens, and signs saying "Awful Dog." Arkansas happens to be the number-one state in the nation for fatalities per mile driven. And I was convinced that most of those fatalities occur while flatlanders are being chased out of driveways.

But I was wrong. All the people I met in Arkansas were friendly, even after they found out I was a reporter. Either Arkansans are the most congenial folks in the world or they are so bored that talking to me seems interesting.

I lean toward the latter explanation because everywhere I stopped, on the way to Whitewater and back, folks wanted to discuss my Chevy Lumina. "You like that car there? Heard it was a good car. Thought about getting one instead of a truck. Now what color would you call that?"

"Red?"

Not much happens in Arkansas no matter what Thomas Bang Thorpe said.

Except at the bar in the Capital Hotel. Come the end of the day everyone shows up—lawyers, clients, judges, defendants, businessmen, bankrupts, political rivals, reporters, the people reporters report on, Friends of Bill's, and Bill's worst nightmares. It's like a softball league after a Saturday in the park.

We have a few drinks and share deep insights:

"You know what the real lesson of the Clinton presidency is? Always be nice to the fat kid who plays a stupid instrument in the high school band."

"It's a good thing we didn't reelect George Bush—we'd be paying higher taxes, Congress would be deadlocked, and we'd all be bored to death with some incomprehensible Iraqgate scandal."

"You stole that nose breaking joke from Jay Leno. 'Tonya Harding came to an abrupt halt and Connie Chung broke her nose.' I heard that on *The Tonight Show.*"

Then we have a few more drinks and listen to the Arkansans talk politics: kickbacks, rake-offs, payola, and lined pockets; hush money, slush funds, booty and swag; bond deal pork and tax break plums; contract grift, construction graft, sweetheart legislation of every kind, plus jobbery, junkets, and palm grease. If one-tenth of what I've heard is true, everybody in the state of Arkansas is going to spend eternity in perdition. And if none of what I've heard is true, they're all damned to hell anyway for being the biggest liars ever.

After quite a few more drinks yet, the real inside stuff gets spilled. You probably already know that Vince Foster was a lesbian. Chelsea's real father is House Banking Committee Chairman Henry Gonzalez. Robert Fiske has subpoenaed Eleanor Clift. And Roger Clinton shot Judge David Hale. Whoops! I didn't say it. That's not going to happen until next week.

Then we have nightcaps.

L. J. Davis wrote a long piece about Arkansas political corruption in the April 4 issue of *The New Republic.* Davis told *The Washington Times* that he'd been warned to leave Little Rock. But, he came to grief before he could get out of town. "All I can say," said Davis, "is I remember unlocking the door. Four hours later I woke up on the floor of the hotel room with a knock on the head, my kidneys hurt like hell . . ." And I'll bet that is exactly what happened to me, too. Some Clinton administration thug sapped me on the noggin. That's why I feel so darned rotten this morning.

But what did Bill and Hillary really do? Did they break any laws? Are they sleazebags or what? Well, I'm a Republican. I'm in favor of sleaze. That's not what bothers me about Whitewater. What bothers me is here we have Bill being governor and Hillary a partner in a heavy-hitting law firm and their friend Jim McDougal running Arkansas's most aggressive savings and loan. They've got the government, the legal system, and the banking business wired. They're right in the middle of the largest economic boom in the history of the United States. And they *still* can't make money. I'm thinking, "We're going to let these people tell us how to save on our medical bills?"

Then, however, I hear about Hillary Clinton in the cattle futures market. She takes $1,000 and turns it into $99,540 in ten months. And I'm sitting on a CD trying to turn $1,000 into $1,000. She must have quite an eye for beef on the hoof. (I'll hear no Bill weight jokes until I've jogged off these deep-fat-fried pickles.) All of a sudden Hillary has appeal that I hadn't previously noticed. Seems like quite a gal, in fact. Say, Hil, are you busy after '96?

Yet aren't the Clintons a little embarrassed about that "gilded age of greed and selfishness" stuff? Bill, during the '92 campaign, said, "For twelve years of this Reagan-Bush era, the Republicans have let S & L crooks and self-serving CEOs try to build an economy out of paper and perks." As opposed to mortgage flips and margin trades. Turns out the Clintons' yuppie bashing consists of standing in the Rose Garden whacking themselves on the head with their own Gucci loafers.

But it's all right. They're liberals. Liberals are supposed to be self-flagellating. And, if liberals are going to feel guilty, they need to have something to feel guilty for. Furthermore, redistributing the wealth is what liberalism is all about. Bill and Hillary were just a little ahead of the curve.

You have to understand that liberals are better than the rest of us. They care. Any money that the Clintons made, they spent to further their life of public service. If I made a bundle on leveraged real estate, timely broker tips, and legal fees from clients who wanted favors from my spouse, I'd use the money to buy a big car. Not the Clintons. They'd use the money to get elected to the White House, and there's a big car there already.

Bill Clinton's record shows what a governor who cares can do. When Bill was first elected in the late Seventies the state of Arkansas ranked forty-ninth in median income. And now it's forty-eighth, all because West Virginia doesn't have a governor who cares the way Bill does. Same thing with education—in 1978 Arkansas was ranked forty-fourth in per pupil public school spending. And now, well, actually now it's ranked forty-sixth. But the point is Bill *cares* about this. Over in fiftieth-ranked Mississippi, their governor probably just doesn't give a hoot.

Is Bill honest? Hmmm, let's imagine for a moment what it would be like to have a totally honest president of the United States. "You want to know what's wrong with this country? If you voters would quit hanging out in bars, drinking, talking trash, and eating deep-fat-fried pickles, if you'd go get a real job, there wouldn't *be* anything wrong with this country!"

Is Bill corrupt? We're talking politics. Think about what politicians do. Imagine a big, likable guy in a fancy suit comes up to you on the street and says, "I don't know you from Adam, but I'm going to do all sorts of wonderful things for you for free." And think about what journalists do. Imagine a smaller, less likable guy in a worse suit comes up and says, "I don't know you either, but I'll tell you the complete truth about everything for a modest fee."

So don't worry about Bill and Hillary. And don't worry about the bunch of us down in Little Rock. We were all humans in a previous life. They were reincarnated to run for office. We were reincarnated to chase politicians all over the map. If we catch one, I'll let you know whether deep-fat-fried Democrat is as good as those pickles.

Health Care Reform

The Wall Street Journal, 1993

I can't seem to learn anything about President Clinton's health care reform plan. I watch the network news and discover that the plan cannot be summarized briefly. I read the papers and find the plan cannot be explained at length. I listen to the president himself and he seems at least as confused as I am, though less succinctly.

I also don't know why I'm supposed to take health advice from a man with a waistline like a Beautyrest mattress, the jogging pace of a beached sea lion, and the sleep habits of a teenage slumber party.

I gather, from the president's sales pitch, we're supposed to come up with a large sum of money to invest in a vaguely described deal that's going to have a huge payoff someday. Isn't the SEC trying to crack down on this sort of thing?

But our ignorance of the Clinton health care plan is of little import. Understanding government programs is like looking at the *Sports Illustrated* swimsuit issue. Form is more important than content. The plan is 1,400 pages long, detailed specifics to come. You can stand on this thing to paint the ceiling. In my copy of *The World Almanac,* the U.S. Constitution and the Bill of Rights occupy $4\frac{1}{2}$ pages. That's $4\frac{1}{2}$ pages to run an entire country for more than two hundred years and three reams of federal pig Latin if I slam my thumb in the car door.

Of course I haven't read this health care reform plan. I suspect Ira Magaziner has "read" the document only in the sense that you or I "read" the book of instructions that comes with a basement dehumidifier. And, anyway, says the president, this might not be the real or final plan because he's an open-minded guy and wants to be bipartisan and hasn't had a chance to get everybody's input. Roger Clinton may have some bright ideas. Socks the cat may, too. Though the plan does not cover veterinary expenses. Yet.

We can, however, be certain of some facts about the health care reform plan. It won't work. No government proposal more complicated than "This note is legal tender for all debts, public and private" ever works. And that doesn't work. Health care reform hasn't even started and it isn't working. The administration's first step was to present the nation with 1,400 pages designed to reduce paperwork. The plan won't work and will be expensive. All comprehensive government entitlement programs grow vastly larger and more costly than they were meant to be. Witness Medicare, Medicaid, FDIC, and so forth. And the one time our country *did* have a comprehensive government entitlement program that was cheap—the Homestead Act— it involved the death or exile of nearly all the native people on the continent.

Our health care system is too complicated and expensive. So, to fix it, President Clinton is proposing the most complicated and expensive piece of legislation in our nation's history. There is a much simpler way of making American medical treatment less expensive. Just make it worse. And this, too, can be accomplished under the Clinton plan.

Federal health care reform will drive the best people out of the health care professions. What type of person is going to become a doctor, a nurse, or, for that matter, a health insurance executive just to wind up as a bureaucratic goat or government hack? Students with straight A's can get more entrepreneurial freedom (and cheaper health care benefits) tarring roofs. There will come a day when you'll be wheeled in for a heart bypass operation and the surgeon will be the same fellow who's now behind the counter when you renew your car registration at the Department of Motor Vehicles.

But let us not forget the moral dimension of health care reform. Everyone, rich or poor, needs health care to live. And everyone, rich or poor, needs food to live. Therefore, next year, the Clinton administration will introduce legislation mandating federal preparation of everybody's breakfast.

Members of the public have a lot of questions about the president's health care plan. Will it cost me less? Can I keep my own doctor? If my kid gets an exotic disease can I go broke looking for a miracle cure and then land a big Hollywood movie contract when Junior's hair grows back? We can divine the response to all these queries. As it is with spouses, so it is with government spokespersons (and let us remember Hillary is both): If an answer is more than three words long, it's No.

Which brings us to Hillary Rodham Clinton herself and the salient point of the health care reform. The president has put a *lawyer* in charge of making *doctors* cheaper. Next he'll be trying to get our grass mowed for less by calling the plumber to come have a word with the boy who does the lawn.

Ms. Clinton's lawyer-led health care advisory panel did not, however, just leap in and suggest that doctors start to charge by the minute, conduct physical examinations in front of juries, and get paid for doodling on pads of yellow paper. Instead, the panel carefully examined medical practices in a host of other countries that are going broke from excessive social spending.

If Canada's health care is so great, how come more Americans aren't apprehended at the border trying to sneak into Ontario to get free liposuction? Such comparisons are of limited value anyway. Canada is a sparsely populated nation with a shortage of gunshot wounds, crack addicts, and huge tort judgments. What can we really learn from a medical system devoted to hockey injuries and sinus infections caused by trying to pronounce French vowels?

We can learn, apparently, to fix prices. Price fixing worked so well in the old Soviet Bloc. And it's still working with New York City's rent controls. Everyone knows how easy it is to find an inexpensive nice apartment in a safe neighborhood in New York. And, by the way, why is price fixing a public service when Democrats in the White House do it but a crime when Republicans try it on the golf course?

President Clinton is attempting to convince the American voters that they're going to be able to get sick cheaply. He's right. Getting sick has always been cheap, often free. It's getting well that costs a whole lot of money. When the price of an item is fixed above market value, there is a surplus of that item—as the Arabs discovered with oil. When the price of an item is fixed below market value, that item disappears—as the Russians discovered with everything. We have here a basic law of economics. The price of health care will be fixed below market value. And we're all going to die.

The Caribbean Refugee Crisis

The American Spectator, 1994

E d Crane, president of the Cato Institute, the redoubtable libertar-
ian think tank, and I were having a cocktail hour chat about
whether the Clinton administration should be sewn up in a sack
full of cats or locked in a small, warm room with Michael Dukakis.
After a few sets of eighty-six-proof curls with the liquid free weights,
Ed made a perspicacious comment about the Cuban rafters and Haitian
boat people currently being persecuted by our Coast Guard on orders
from the commander in chief. "Damn it, P.J.," said Crane. (I'm quoting from memory so excuse me, Ed, if I don't do your eloquence justice. I understand trace amounts of vermouth have been found in the
brains of Alzheimer's victims. I've got to quit putting that stuff in the
gin.) "Damn it," he said, "these people get onboard things made out of

oil drums, orange crates, balsa wood, and cardboard boxes; they cross hundreds of miles of shark-infested ocean, suffer hunger, thirst, and exposure, and brave treacherous currents, high seas, and storms just to come to America. *I say they're citizens.* Give them their passports right on the Florida beach—no oaths, no exams, no forms to fill out. These are the kind of people we *want* in America!"

But these are not the kind of people our infinitely compassionate, sharing and caring, hug-mongering sop of a president wants in America. Bill Clinton has blocked the only exit from the totalitarian nation of Cuba, closed an escape route held open by every U.S. administration—Democratic and Republican—for thirty-four years. What would we have thought of Konrad Adenauer if each person who came over the Berlin Wall had been shipped to a—give me another name for it—concentration camp? Then suppose that, once those East Germans were packed behind barbed wire, they were told they'd have to go back to East Germany to apply for West German visas?

As for Clinton's attitude toward the Haitians, why he's glad to invade their country. He's perfectly willing to shoot Haitians. But let them drive cabs in New York City? Oh no.

In Clinton's Caribbean refugee policy we get a glimpse of the president's true nature, a look at the Inner Bill, a peek at the scum beneath the flab.

Clinton's excuse for refusing sanctuary to the Haitians and Cubans is that they are economic refugees. Yes, these people are seeking real freedom, material freedom, freedom to do, have, and be. And they're probably not as interested as Bill is in the liberal idea of freedom—freedom to hand out child-size condoms at day care centers and so forth. Haitians and Cubans want to come to the United States, get jobs, work hard, start their own businesses. If they start their own businesses, they'll vote Republican. Of course Bill Clinton hates them.

Bill hates them and he fears them, especially the Cubans. Bill knows the Cubans are crazy. Only crazy people would flee from a country with free medical care, guaranteed employment for life, and first-rate gun control. The president and his sanctimonious twit of a wife have worked for decades to build a society like this, and here people are taking their lives in their hands to get away from it.

"Taking their lives in their hands"—one more reason for Bill to despise our island neighbors. These people are mastering their fates. They're going to America to start a new life. Haitians and Cubans must think there's such a thing as free will, maybe even individual responsibility. But any good liberal knows we're part of a collective enterprise. Which is run by Bill. To achieve our common destiny we need leadership. That's where Bill comes in. And all our ills are the result of society's sickness. Calling Dr. Bill.

Let's face facts about our disgusting political opponents. We've been nice to the liberals for too long. They're thugs. The liberal dream is to control people, to oppress and exploit them for some "higher" goal. And how are the liberals ever going to be able to control people brave enough to sail to Florida in a rum carton? In fact, even people of far less mettle than Haitian and Cuban refugees are difficult to control. This is why liberals hate people.

A civilized person should no more tolerate the presence of a liberal than the presence of a member of the Ku Klux Klan. Indeed, it may be argued that liberalism is worse than the KKK insofar as Klansmen only hate some people while liberals hate them all.

You can see the liberal hatred of people in the enormous liberal excitement about abortion and contraception. If people are hard to control then ipso facto more people will be harder. And this is why liberals are always championing laws and social programs which are theoretically good for a class of people while being provably disastrous for people themselves: racial quotas, busing, welfare, my goddamned taxes. Liberals don't just lose sight of the individual or ignore his needs in the pursuit of broader goals, liberals detest, abhor, and spit upon the human being.

The core of the liberal belief is that the mass is more important than the man. As if God created not Adam and Eve but a Recovering Fruit of Knowledge Taste Test Support Group.

Liberalism, however, dressed in "sharing and caring" modernity, is ultimately about the primitive, ignorant, tribal idea of collective life. And about human sacrifice—liberals like that even better. The will, the conscience, the very existence of the person must be destroyed for the benefit of the mob. Liberals have the same morals as Fascists, Communists, Crips, and Bloods. The worship of collective power always ends in some kind of drive-by shooting. Pearl Harbor, for example.

There may be—measured by some cold and pointless statistical means—such a thing as a greater common good. The power-grubbing, self-regarding Bill Clintons of the world tell us so. But there is no such thing as a greater common bad. Pain cannot, no matter what the unctuous creep in the White House says, be shared. Only individuals suffer.

In this case those individuals are packed into sad, unseaworthy little crafts trying to make it to that ultimate bastion of individualism, America. But, when they get here, they're going to discover that the only person welcoming them is Ed Crane. And maybe me, if I recover from this hangover. Look for us on the sand, with our trousers rolled, holding aloft the sacred prize of freedom—shaken not stirred. (Do Haitians like their martinis with one olive or two?)

100 Reasons Why Jimmy Carter Was a Better President than Bill Clinton

The American Spectator, 1993

1. Jimmy Carter had a nicer wife,
2. A smarter baby brother,
3. A less frightening mom,
4. And a . . . No, we can't bring ourselves to make fun of the first daughter, especially since some of us have been going through an awkward adolescent stage for nearly four decades. But we can say: "Damn it, Hillary, quit fussing with *your* hair and do something about Chelsea's."
5. And, speaking of coiffures, Jimmy Carter never in his life got a haircut that cost more than $2.50, if appearances are anything to go by.
6. Carter had governed a more important state.

7. Carter had once held a job.
8. He came from a more cosmopolitan hometown,
9. And had a more charismatic vice president.
10. It took Carter months to wreck the economy.
11. It took Carter weeks to become a national laughingstock.
12. Carter committed adultery only in his heart.
13. And, if we know anything about female tastes, Carter was telling the truth about that.
14. As for military record, Carter was, comparatively speaking, a regular Audie Murphy.
15. They were on drugs in the Carter administration—they had an excuse.
16. *We* were on drugs in the Carter administration—*we* had an excuse.
17. Carter looked—think back carefully, we promise we're telling the truth about this—less foolish in his jogging outfit.
18. Jogging actually *worked* for Carter. Say what you will against the man, he's no double-butt.
19. Carter passed out while jogging and the nation was safe for a moment.

Compare and Contrast

CARTER ADMINISTRATION	CLINTON ADMINISTRATION
20. Pardoning draft dodgers	Draft dodgers
21. Women integrated into the military	People dressed like women integrated into the military
22. Return of canal to Panama	Return of Haitians to Haiti
23. Bailout of Chrysler Corp.	Jobs in White House travel office for hick cousins from Arkansas
24. Creation of Departments of Energy and Education	Can't find enough gay disabled women of color to head the departments he's got already

25. President successfully treated for hemorrhoids — Hillary still heading health care reform panel
26. Russians in Afghanistan — Brit Hume in White House press corps
27. Jody Powell with feet on desk — George Stephanopoulos with feet not quite touching floor
28. Kidding Mexicans about Montezuma's revenge — Kidding Mexicans about NAFTA
29. Boycott of Moscow Olympics — Not seeing as much of the Bloodworth-Thomasons lately
30. Hostage rescue attempt in Iran — Trying to get Zoë Baird confirmed at Justice
31. Mt. St. Helens — Air Force General Harold Campbell
32. Peace Between Israel and Egypt — Peace between Bob Dole and Pat Buchanan
33. Elvis dead — Barbra Streisand all too lively
34. SALT II — U-2
35. Three Mile Island — Sam Nunn
36. Hyman Rickover — The Ty-D-Bol Man
37. Wimping out in the face of the second most powerful military force in the world — Wimping out in the face of Slobodan Milošević
38. Gas shortage — Gassiest administration since who knows when
39. Mariel boatlift — Which one is she? Does Hillary know about this one?
40. Proposition 13 — (Write your own Clinton libido joke in the space provided:_____ _____)
41. Carter was a good man to have onboard when your canoe was attacked by a swimming rabbit.
42. Carter hardly ever hugged or kissed anyone in public except Leonid Brezhnev.

43. The FBI didn't kill anybody at Jonestown.
44. Bert Lance could make a bigger splash doing a cannonball into the Camp David pool than Webb Hubbell.
45. Hamilton Jordan could beat Mack McLarty at arm wrestling.
46. Plus Jordan could get into Studio 54.
47. Joseph Califano was prettier than Donna Shalala.
48. And he opposed abortion.
49. Warren Christopher was young and full of pep during the Carter administration.
50. And Warren Christopher's initials look funnier on a briefcase than Cyrus Vance's did.
51. Zbigniew Brzezinski is worth more points in a Scrabble game than Anthony Lake.
52. Jimmy Carter didn't play any Fleetwood Mac songs on the campaign trail.
53. Or any Judy Collins records at home.
54. Or any saxophones anywhere.
55.   THE UNDEAD

CARTER ADMINISTRATION	CLINTON ADMINISTRATION
Miss Lillian	VAT

56. No one can say a word against any Carter Supreme Court appointee.
57. Carter did not use Bloomsbury, Mayfair, Pall Mall, Hackney, Notting Hill, Shoreditch, or any other London neighborhood as the name of his child.
58. One thing about Carter-era inflation, the money may have been worthless but at least we had some.
59.   ENDANGERED SPECIES

CARTER ADMINISTRATION	CLINTON ADMINISTRATION
The Snail Darter	The DLC

60. Jimmy Carter's nervous smirk was less demanding of a punch in the snoot, even if it did present a larger target.

Major Foreign Policy Questions

CARTER ADMINISTRATION

61. Should Red China have a seat in the UN?
62. Does Nicaragua have strategic importance for the United States?
63. What type of relationship with Israel best serves America's interests?
64. Is it time for America to relinquish its global leadership role?
65. Would economic sanctions on South Africa be effective?
66. Should we sell wheat to Russia?
67. Is deployment of the neutron bomb immoral?

CLINTON ADMINISTRATION

Is Macedonia what Macedonia is supposed to be called?

Is it "Ukraine" or "The Ukraine"?

If those guys are so Jewish how come they aren't on the staff of *Tikkun*?

Should Chelsea go to Japan with Bill and Hillary?

How about economic sanctions on white males right here in the USA?

Let's just give them a bunch of money.

Does appointing Jean Kennedy Smith ambassador to Ireland put the Kennedys in their place or what?

68. Language Which President Would Not Shut Up In

CARTER	CLINTON
Spanish	English

69. Navy's football team can whip Oxford's

P. J. O'Rourke

Worldview

WHAT IDEAS LOOMED LARGE INSIDE THEIR RESPECTIVE
THICK SKULLS?

CARTER	CLINTON
70. Human rights	Partnership role for the First Lady
71. Moral equivalent of war	Partnership role for the First Lady
72. National malaise	More mayonnaise
73. Diminished expectations	David Gergen

74. Carter did not, as part of focusing his agenda, address himself as "Stupid." He let us do that for him.
75. Carter wore real blue jeans and not the Levi's 550 roomy in the buns kind.

Compare and Contrast Part II

CARTER	CLINTON
76. *Mork & Mindy*	Mary Matalin and James Carville
77. *Laverne & Shirley*	Cokie Roberts and Anna Quindlen
78. *The Dukes of Hazzard*	Various half brothers
79. *Three's Company*	Gennifer Flowers
80. *Happy Days*	1980–1992
81. *The Incredible Hulk* and *Wonder Woman*	Marriage seems stable for the moment but superpowers are fading
82. WKRP	NPR
83. Star Wars	Defense cuts
84. *Annie Hall*	Anita Hill
85. *Grease*	Mousse

86. *Saturday Night Fever*   Saturday night working late at
                                        the OEOB
87. *The Goodbye Girl*   Kimba Wood
88. *Midnight Express*   Bus Trips
89. *La Cage aux Folles*   The Marines
90. *All the President's Men*   *Home Alone*
91. Abbie Hoffman   Socks the cat
92. Carter's poll ratings were higher (in Iraq).
93. Carter walked the *whole* inaugural parade route.
94. Carter saved America from a plague of Misha the Bear Olympic mascot toys.
95. Has Bill Clinton helped the shah of Iran get medical treatment?
96. Carter spent his time doing things like figuring out the White House tennis court playing schedule—the man *knew* his intellectual limitations.
97. Carter had enough clout to get Lani Guinier appointed to the Justice Department (and anyone who gets shot down for holding Menckenish views about the excesses of democracy has to be some kind of friend of ours even if she doesn't know it).
98. Carter let the Soviets have Angola, Ethiopia, and South Yemen. And, in retrospect, the Soviets deserved no better.
99. Carter wasn't a throwback to the Carter era.
100. And let us not forget that Jimmy Carter gave us one thing Bill Clinton can never possibly give us—Ronald Reagan.

Republicans Take Control of Congress

The American Spectator, 1995

AUTHOR'S NOTE: This article was written for *Rolling Stone* and rejected by its editors, who said (honestly) that they wanted "a more serious exposition of conservative beliefs." And—pals of mine though they are—they need it. So I plagiarized as much of Friedrich Hayek's *The Road to Serfdom* as I thought I could decently get away with, weaving a few jokes into the denser sections of the text to put my own stamp upon things, and sent that to *Rolling Stone.* This, on the other hand, I gave to *The American Spectator,* which has been generous over the years in providing a home for wayward or exiled compositions.

Introduction Written for *TAS*:
Mr. and Mrs. American Spectator Reader, Let P. J. O'Rourke Talk Sense to Your Kids

Do you have a mopey young person in your family? Does he or she possess an all-ebony wardrobe, have a lopsided haircut, and know what "latte" is? Is this "slacker" lying on your couch all day listening to Nine Inch Nails CD's? Or making a lifetime career out of going to college? Or still working in a Kinko's Copy Center at the age of twenty-eight? Or trying to get an NEA grant to write a film script about all of the above? And the nose ring—is negotiating a temporary removal for Grandma's visit going to require the intervention of Jimmy Carter?

You may have a larva- or pupa-stage Democrat in your home. Try this test. Get the child's attention (extra latte helps). Now say, "Newt Gingrich." Did you receive the following reaction?

"Mom! Dad! [theatrical sigh] It's like . . . [eyes roll toward ceiling] Oh, man . . ."

Yes, a conservative tide is rising all across the political landscape of America, but some members of "Generation X" have climbed onto the outhouse roof of intellectualism and managed to keep their Doc Martens dry.

As a special service to our readers, *TAS* has enlisted P. J. O'Rourke to have a word with the youngsters. P.J. is the International Affairs Desk Chief at the with-it and trendy *Rolling Stone* magazine. He speaks their lingo. He knows Dr. Hunter S. Thompson personally. And he claims that he can actually tell the difference between Nine Inch Nails and the noise a washtub full of cats makes when you throw it down the cellar stairs.

Clip this article and hand it to your progeny. It explains, in language young people can understand, what's happening in Washington now that Republicans are in charge and why what's happening is a good thing even for people with facial tattoos. Who knows? Maybe the kid will buckle down and become *manager* of a Kinko's Copy Center.

Republican hordes have descended on Washington. They rove where they will, sacking and looting, or, as it were, voting and golfing. Also talking on C-Span, listening to Rush Limbaugh, and signing enormous book deals. It is a frightful scene. Men risk having their taxes slashed in broad daylight. No woman is safe from dinner table conversations about unfunded mandates. Pathetic groups of unemployed Democrats huddle on Capitol Hill, homeless. House-less, anyway. Senate-less, too.

The National Endowment for the Arts is threatened. "See here, Mr. Subsidized Dramatist, can't your characters die of something besides AIDS? How about a sword fight once in a while?" Public broadcasting is also at risk. Underprivileged children may be deprived of *All Things Considered*. Woefully imperiled are all the accomplishments of the Clinton administration, such as . . . such as . . . Bill can forget about midnight basketball.

The Republicans want to do away with whole sections of government. The Department of Education *doesn't have a prayer*. (Ha, ha, a little Christian Coalition joke. Who says right-wing religious zealots don't have a sense of humor?) Numerous congressional committees have already been eliminated causing a severe business downturn in America's snoozing, doodling, and yawn suppression industries. The president was forced to make a conciliatory State of the Union speech, the short version of which was "Hillary, you'd better go home and fix dinner." And heartless welfare reformers will soon be erecting grim, drafty orphanages all over the country. Speaking of which, now that Rose is dead, Ted Kennedy is technically an orphan. In you go, Teddy. And . . . *whack* . . . mind the nuns.

Everyone in the thoughtful, progressive, sensitive, compassionate, objective, and fair media world which I inhabit is awful upset about these darn Republicans. And I would be too except I am one.

I hear thoughtful, progressive, sensitive hissy noises in the audience. "Tsk. Tsk. You write for *Rolling Stone*. We assumed you were too hip to be Republican." Yeah, hip, that's me. I'm hip from Hip Street and it gets hipper as you go along and my pad is in the last crib, Daddy-O. Navel ring? Tongue stud? Man, I went out and bought a three-foot barrel hoop and got one whole butt cheek pierced. Where I come from even the circus clowns dress all in black, and the only reason a dozen of them get in that little car is to show kids how miserably cramped life is for veal calves.

Call earth. I'm a forty-seven-year-old middle-class male with a job. Every hippy-dippy thing that's thought up—from heroin addiction to special vegan lunch lines in the local high school cafeteria—I get to pay for. Of course I'm a Republican. But there is one shred of beatnikery to which I cling. I still detest authority. I always did. My every bedtime was a Bataan Death March. Cleaning my room, an exile to the mines of Siberia. I cannot see a school crossing guard without wishing for a grisly hit-and-run. Some credit their loss of faith to a beneficent deity permitting the existence of evil. I rail against God because I was told to stop eating paste in Sunday school class. To this day I will not bring the car home before eleven, even though it's my car and nobody lives in the house but me. And when I'm sent back through an airport metal detector, I scream that I have a steel plate in my head. "I'll sue you under the Americans with Disabilities Act! You'll be court-martialed! You'll be busted to the lowest rank of the Airport Security Service and made to sit in front of a PA system microphone all day endlessly repeating, 'The space by the curb is for immediate loading and unloading only'!"

I spit on dominion and control. And the greater the power, the more my abomination. Which brings me to the subject of government. Great, hulking, greasy, obese, gobbling, omnivorous, ever-aggrandizing, fat-witted government—I am not its friend. In Washington, the Republicans are (in their wing-tip-hobbled, suspender-entangled, Old Spice–befogged way) trying to destroy big government. The Republicans I like okay. The destruction I adore.

Think of what big governments have gotten up to in this century: not one but two world wars, the gulag, the holocaust, aerial bombing of civilian population centers, the Berlin Wall, nuclear explosions, the post office. A wicked individual might want these, but he wouldn't have the cash and connections to get them. A villainous corporation could afford them but has to market the products. The

Vietnam draft would be a tough sell for even the most fiendish businessmen. "Get shot! Get killed! Get diseases from foreign women who
despise you in their hearts!" And never mind the thirty-two-cent
postage stamp.

Governments do terrible things. All right, I sympathize. I do terrible
things myself. Although it's getting harder to find somebody to do them
with now that I'm forty-seven and a Republican. What bothers me is
how the terrible government things are always for the greater common
good. Communists, Nazis, and more than a few democratically elected
leaders of the free world have told us in plain language that their loathsome acts were justified by felicific calculus—the most good for the
greatest number. Censorship, genocide, the Volstead Act, wholesale
expropriations of private property, segregation, religious persecution,
mass deportations, and vaporizing Nagasaki have all been "for the good
of the nation," "good for mankind," "good for us in the long run,"
"good for future generations."

Amazing how well-meaning, how virtuous, how *good* the people
in authority always are. I guess good people are just naturally attracted
to government. You remember them from high school—the Senior
Class President, the Sophomore Class Secretary, the Chairgirl of the
Junior Prom Decorations and Refreshments Committee. They weren't
like some kids I could name, keeping the car out till all hours looking
for crossing guards to run over. The kids in school government were
good kids. Teachers liked them. Parents liked them. Why, you could take
one of those kids—pry his suckerlike mouth off the career counselor's
behind—and, heck, make him president of the United States. And we
did.

The thing I like about Republicans is that they're no damn good
at all. I know, I'm one of them. A Republican just wants to get rich,
buy oceanfront property, dump the old wife, and get a new blond one
who'll listen attentively while the Republican talks about unfunded
mandates over the arugula salad.

Now Republicans aren't really evil. They'll save the rain forest if they have to. Tell them that's where the golf ball trees grow. They'd better do something about the Amazon or they'll be teeing off with their kids' hacky sacks. And if Republicans notice that their oceanfront property is all ocean and no front, they'll pass a law against polar ice cap melting in a minute. But these guys in the lime green pants hammering at bean bags with Ping three woods don't *really* care about global issues, much less social justice. The GOP majority in Congress is going to spend most of its time tinkering with the New Blond Wife Act of 1995. And the rest of its energy will be devoted to giving Dutch rubs and (those insensitive Republicans) Indian rope burns to the enormous system of government which has been created over the past sixty years by the good people in authority who *do* care.

The activists, the advocates of worthy causes, the idealistic leaders, the self-sacrificing organizers—all the good people—care even more than you enlightened youth. They say, "Oh, you? You just buy Newman's Own salad dressing, give some money to PETA, wear a red ribbon on your bridesmaid's dress at your sister's wedding, and applaud for Barbra Streisand, and you think you've done your bit. Sure you care. But you only care about things like high-tension power lines when they're causing childhood cancers in your neighborhood. We care about high-tension power lines in places that don't even have electricity. We care so much we can't sleep. We can't eat. It wrecked our marriage. And because we care more than you do we're better people than you are. And because we're better people than you are we have the right—no, the duty—to tell you what to do."

Telling you what to do being the entire idea of big government, with its agencies, experts, courts, laws, regulatory codes, and powers of taxation to fund health care reform so that if I have a traffic accident while trying to run over school crossing guards you pay my doctor bills. And the people who control that big government, the people who care so much, really are better than the rest of us. Consider Harry Truman. You can tell Harry Truman was better than us because when he vaporized Nagasaki it was for the greater common good. If you or I did that we'd just be killing a lot of Japanese.

Harry was in the right line of work. Politics is the ideal profession for good people like Harry Truman and for the many other good people who have followed in his path such as Lyndon Johnson, Bill Clinton, and Washington, DC, Mayor Marion Barry (who only became good a couple of months ago, but, to judge by the size of the government in the District of Columbia, he's real good now). You see, it's hard for us not-so-good people to accomplish things. If we want to prevent childhood cancers caused by high-tension power lines, we have to quit our jobs, go back to school, and earn degrees in medicine, biochemistry, physics, and electrical engineering. Then we have to do years of research to determine whether or not high-tension power lines actually cause cancer. And, if they do, we have to remove all the high-tension power lines and convince 250 million people to light their homes with the little candles left over from the last big birthday cake the kid got before he died.

All a politician has to do is care. Staff and assistants handle the rest.

This is why it's so important for big government to get bigger. So it can help you. For instance, you can't find a good-paying job. That's because, in the 1980s, rich people took all the good pay and used it up. But big government can find a good-paying job for you because, when government gets bigger, there are more jobs in the government. These pay well. And, if you need money in the meantime, the government can print some for you because one of those good-paying government jobs is running the mint. That's just one way the government can help. And you need help, too. Because people are trying to do horrible things to you all the time. Like the big food companies that put poison in your food so that you'll never buy food from any competing big food companies. The same thing with the car companies and all those dangerous cars they make. GM knows you can't go to a Ford showroom if you're a paraplegic and brain dead. You should sue. Big government means there are always plenty of judges and juries available. And you're a victim. You're a victim of lots of things. A victim of prejudice against racial minorities. Just look at all those smug white people with the good-paying government jobs. What did they do to deserve them? And so what if you're a smug white person yourself? With black and Hispanic birthrates going through the roof, you'll soon be a minority, too. Plus you're disabled. You may not know it. That would mean you have a cognitive disability exhibited by not knowing you're disabled. Perhaps you don't recall any difficulty walking, talking, seeing, et cetera. So you're suffering from repressed memory syndrome, too. Therapy can help. You were probably molested as a child by a beloved member of your household. It's all coming back now. Remember how Rover would run up and jam his nose into your . . . You need a government program. And so does Rover. So do all the earth's animals. Whole species are facing extinction. Democrats just for starters. Awful things are happening everywhere. Only government can stop them. The ozone's breaking out in holes. The atmosphere is so polluted that pretty soon we're going to have to get our air in little bottles from the Evian company. The greenhouse effect is running out of control. Is it warm in here or is it . . . EEEEEE!!! THE END OF THE WORLD!!!

Did you ever wonder if Chicken Little had an agenda? I mean, was Chicken Little running around telling all the other chickens that the sky was falling out of pure, disinterested altruism? Or was there something Chicken Little wanted? And once Chicken Little had all the other chickens convinced that the sky was falling was there, all of a sudden, a Federal Department of Falling Sky? And did Chicken Little get appointed Secretary of Things That Hit You on the Head?

A cabinet post is an excellent springboard to higher office. You can almost hear Chicken Little's New Hampshire primary speech. "My feathered friends, our coops are guarded by foxes! All our eggs are in one basket! We're living on chicken feed! Massive layoffs are threatened at KFC! Plus, the sky is falling! In these troubled times, who better to lead us in squawking and fluttering and running around after our heads have been cut off than the Honorable C. Little—a real *chicken!*"

You must know that the politicians loathe you. They think you're a moron. They have to make rules and regulations or you'd screw up everything. You'd fall right out of the car if it weren't for seat belt laws. And you can't be trusted with money. You'd spend it on fatty foods and cigarettes or a powerboat that would harm the environment. The politicians need to get that money away from you. They have to raise taxes quick. Better let the government look after your cash. Government will do worthwhile things with your paycheck such as lend it to Mexico. And fund educational TV. Because you'd watch nothing but football and *Melrose Place* if it weren't for serious and informative nature programs about how Democrats are facing extinction. And you're as mean as you are stupid. You're too selfish to help the poor. So politicians have to take even more of what you earn and give it to poor people. Well, of course, politicians can't actually *give* that money to poor people. Then the poor people wouldn't be poor and would turn into Republicans or something. Poor people don't really need money anyway. They need government programs. And housing projects. And a large welfare bureaucracy to make sure they stay in the housing projects and don't get out and start wandering around the parts of town where politicians live.

Damn them all, these ballot lice with their jiggery-pokery of compassion and their pimping for virtue on the stump. The greater common good should get a good one right where it will *do* some good. And here's another for those who say they care—something for them to care *about* that's big, shoe shaped, and black and blue. To hell (and a job in the private sector) with the lot of them. Politics is the work of parasites, condescending parasites at that. We are being patronized by our own ear mites and liver flukes. Politics is . . . Wait, there's a rumbling from the National Affairs Desk . . . *"Better Than Sex"?* Hunter, Hunter, you're supposed to be alone in the voting booth. What kind of sex are we talking about here?

And politics doesn't work. Look at the parts of America where government has had the most power, where government has spent the most money. Look at those housing projects we've got the poor people in. Then say to yourself, "What the government has done for folks in the inner cities, it can do *that* for spotted owls."

But all my Republican buddies cavorting on Capitol Hill, aren't they politicians, too? Alas, you betcha. It would be nice if they stuck to the lovely task of destroying government. But there's no such thing as politicians who can mind their own business. Republican congressmen are going to want to make some positive contributions to our political system, and you may not feel too positive about that. For one thing, some of us Republicans are antiabortion on the theory that every fetus is a Republican or, if adopted by a nice, rich family, will be when it turns thirty. And some Republicans want children to read a prayer before school. Although whether it is the Republican insistence on children learning to pray or the Republican insistence on children learning to read which has the National Education Association so upset, I'm not sure. There are certain Republicans who would like to get rid of immigrants (these Republicans being under the impression that Pat Buchanan is a Cherokee name). If Republicans have their way, poor people in crime-ridden neighborhoods will no longer be given squalid housing, they'll have to buy it. And, under the Republicans, certain large corporations and business interests no doubt will be allowed to run wild—as opposed to the way the Clinton administration cracked down on Tyson chicken and cattle futures trading.

But that's about it in the way of Republican innovations. We don't have that many ideas. Democrats have lots of them. Every time a politician gets an idea it costs you money, and sometimes, in the case of wars, it costs you your skin.

Republicans are cheaper. We leave you alone. And when Republicans pull some sleazy thing like Whitewater at least it works. You didn't see Michael Milken going to jail for *not* selling junk bonds.

Plus you know where you stand with Republicans. Everybody realizes we're SOB's. Not like the Democrats, always claiming to be the spiritual scions of Mahatma Gandhi. You don't want a politician trying to drown you while the whole world thinks he's giving you a bath.

And one more extremely important thing about Republicans. We're against gun control. You can shoot us.

Bad Sports

As was mentioned before, ignorance is valuable to a humorist. But clumsy, incompetent, useless idiocy is a treasure beyond price. A joke needs a butt. Folly needs a fool. And each item of comical writing needs someone in it of whom merciless fun can be made. The problem is finding a person like that who won't sue. The author has been enormously lucky in this regard. Whenever he sat down at the typewriter, he found himself close at hand.

Fly-Fishing

Rod and Reel, 1987

'd never fly-fished. I'd done other kinds of fishing. I'd fished for bass. That's where I'd get far enough away from the dock so that people couldn't see there was no line on the pole, then drink myself blind in the rowboat. And I'd deep-sea fished. That's where the captain would get me blind before we'd even left the dock and I'd be the one who couldn't see the line. But I'd never fly-fished.

I'd always been of two minds about the sport. On the one hand, here's a guy standing in cold water up to his liver throwing the world's most expensive clothesline at trees. A full two-thirds of his time is spent untangling stuff, which he could be doing in the comfort of his own home with old shoelaces, if he wanted. The whole business costs like sin and requires heavier clothing. Furthermore it's conducted in the middle of blackfly season. Cast and swat. Cast and swat. Fly-fishing may be a sport invented by insects with fly fishermen as bait. And what does the truly sophisticated dry fly artist do when he finally bags a fish? He lets the fool thing go and eats baloney sandwiches instead.

On the other hand, fly-fishing did have its attractions. I love to waste time and money. I had ways to do this most of the year—hunting, skiing, renting summer houses in To-Hell-and-Gone Harbor for a Lebanon hostage's ransom. But, come spring, I was limited to cleaning up the yard. Even with a new Toro every two years and a lot of naps by the compost heap, it's hard to waste much time and money doing this. And then there's the gear needed for fly-fishing. I'm a sucker for anything that requires more equipment than I have sense. My workshop is furnished with the full panoply of Black & Decker power tools, all from one closet shelf I installed in 1979.

When I began to think about fly-fishing, I realized I'd never be content again until my den was cluttered with computerized robot fly-tying vises, space-age Teflon and ceramic knotless tapered leaders, sterling silver English fish scissors, and thirty-five volumes on the home life of the midge. And there was one other thing. I'm a normal male who takes an occasional nip; therefore, I love to put funny things on my head. Sometimes it's the nut dish, sometimes the spaghetti colander, but the hats I'd seen fly fishermen wear were funnier than either and I had to have one.

I went to Hackles & Tackles, an upscale dry fly specialty shop that also sells fish print wallpaper and cashmere V-neck sweaters with little trout on them. I got a graphite rod for about the price of a used car and a reel made out of the kind of exotic alloys that you can go to jail for selling to the Soviet Union. I also got one of those fishing vests that only comes down to the top of your beer gut and looks like you dressed in the dark and tried to put on your ten-year-old son's three-piece suit. And I purchased lots of monofilament and teensy hooks covered in auk down and moose lint and an entire L. L. Bean boat bag full of fly-fishing do-whats, hinky-doovers, and whatchamajigs.

I also brought home a set of fly-fishing how-to videotapes. This is the Eighties, I reasoned, the age of video. What better way to take up a sport than from a comfortable armchair? That's where I'm at my best with most sports anyway.

There were three tapes. The first one claimed it would teach me to cast. The second would teach me to "advanced cast." And the third would tell me where trout live, how they spend their weekends, and what they'd order for lunch if there were underwater delicatessens for fish. I started the VCR and a squeaky little guy with an earnest manner and a double-funny hat came on, began heaving fly line around, telling me the secret to making beautiful casting loops is . . .

Whoever made these tapes apparently assumed I knew how to tie backing to reel and line to backing and leader to line and so on all the way out to the little feather and fuzz fish snack at the end. I didn't know how to put my rod together. I had to go to the children's section at the public library and check out *My Big Book of Fishing* and begin with how to open the package it all came in.

A triple granny got things started on the spool. After twelve hours and help from pop rivets and a tube of Krazy Glue, I managed an Albright knot between backing and line. But my version of a nail knot in the leader put Mr. Gordian of ancient Greek knot legend fame strictly on the shelf. It was the size of a hamster and resembled one of the Woolly Bugger flies I'd bought except in the size you use for killer whales. I don't want to talk about blood knots and tippets. There I was with two pieces of invisible plastic, trying to use fingers the size of a man's thumb while holding a magnifying glass and a Tensor lamp between my teeth and gripping nasty tangles of monofilament with each big toe. My girlfriend had to come over and cut me out of this with pinking shears. Personally, I'm going to get one of those nine-year-old Persian kids that they use to make incredibly tiny knots in fine Bukhara rugs and just take him with me on all my fishing trips.

What I really needed was a fly-fishing how-to video narrated by Mister Rogers. This would give me advice about which direction to wind the reel and why I should never try to drive a small imported car while wearing boot-foot waders. (Because when I stepped on the accelerator I also stepped on the brake and the clutch.)

I rewound Mr. Squeaky and started over. I was supposed to keep my rod tip level and keep my rod swinging in a ninety-degree arc. When I snapped my wrist forward I was giving one quick flick of a blackjack to the skull of a mugging victim. When I snapped my wrist back I was sticking my thumb over my shoulder and telling my brother-in-law to get the hell out of here and I mean right now, Buster. Though it wasn't explained with quite so much poetry.

Then I was told to try these things with a "yarn rod." This was something else I'd bought at the tackle shop. It looked like a regular rod tip from a two-piece rod but with a cork handle. You run a bunch of bright orange yarn through the guides and flip it around. It's supposed to imitate the action of a fly rod in slow motion. I don't know about that, but I do know you can catch and play a nine-pound house cat on a yarn rod, and it's great sport. They're hard to land, however. And I understand cat fishing is strictly catch and release if they're under twenty inches.

Then I went back to the television and heard about stance, loop control, straight line casts, slack line casts, stripping, mending, and giving myself enough room when practicing in the yard so I wouldn't get tangled in my neighbor's bird feeder.

After sixty minutes of videotape, seven minutes of yarn rod practice, twenty-five minutes of cat fishing, and several beers, I felt I was ready. I picked up the fin tickler and laid out a couple of loops that weren't half bad if I do say so myself. I'll bet I cast almost three times before making macramé out of my weight forward Cortland 444. This wasn't so hard.

I also watched the advanced tape. But Squeaky had gone grad school on me. He's throwing reach casts, curve casts, roll casts, steeple casts, and casts he calls squiggles and stutters. He's writing his name with the line in the air. He's making his dry fly look like the Blue Angels. He's pitching things forehand, backhand, and between his wader legs. And, through the magic of video editing, every time his hook-tipped dust kitty hits the water he lands a trout the size of a canoe.

The videotape about trout themselves wasn't much use either. It's hard to get excited about where trout feed when you know that the only way you're going to be able to get a fly to that place is by throwing your fly box at it.

I must say, however, all the tapes were informative. "Nymphs and streamers" are not, as it turns out, naked mythological girls decorating the high school gym with crepe paper. And I learned that the part of fly-fishing I'm going to be best at is naming the flies:

> Woolly Hatcatcher
> Blue-Wing Earsnag
> Overhanging Brush Muddler
> Royal Toyota Hatchback
> O'Rourke's Ouchtail
> P.J.'s Live Worm-'n-Bobber

By now I'd reached what I think they call a "learning plateau." That is, if I was going to catch a fish with a fly rod, I either had to go get in the water or open the fridge and toss hooks at Mrs. Paul's frozen haddock fillets.

I made reservations at a famous fishing lodge on the Au Sable River in Michigan. When I got there and found a place to park among the Saabs and Volvos the proprietor said I was just a few days early for the Hendrikson hatch. There is, I see, one constant in all types of fishing, which is when the fish are biting, which is almost-but-not-quite-now.

I looked pretty good making false casts in the lodge parking lot. I mean no one laughed out loud. But most of the other 2,000 young professionals fishing this no-kill stretch of the Au Sable were pretty busy checking to make sure that their trout shirts were color coordinated with their Reebok wading sneakers.

When I stepped in the river, however, my act came to pieces. My line hit the water like an Olympic belly flop medalist. I hooked four "tree trout" in three minutes. My back casts had people ducking for cover in Traverse City and Grosse Pointe Farms. Somebody ought to tie a dry fly that looks like a Big Mac. Then there'd be an excuse for the hook winding up in my mouth instead of the fish's. The only thing I could manage to get a drag-free float on was me after I stepped in a hole. And the trout? The trout laughed.

The next day was worse. I could throw tight loops. I could sort of aim. I could even make a gentle presentation and get the line to lay right every so often. But when I tried to do all of these things at once, I went mental. I looked like Leonard Bernstein conducting "Flight of the Bumblebee" in fast forward. I was driving tent pegs with my rod tip. My slack casts wrapped around my thighs. My straight line casts went straight into the back of my neck. My improved surgeon's loops looked like full windsors. I had wind knots in everything including my Red Ball suspenders. And two hundred dollars worth of fly floatant, split shot, Royal Coachmen, and polarized sunglasses fell off my body and were swept downstream.

Then, mirabile dictu, I hooked a fish. I was casting some I-for-get-the-name nymph and clumsily yanking it in when my rod tip bent and my pulse shot into trade deficit numbers. I lifted the rod, the first thing I'd done right in two days, and the trout actually leaped out of the water as if it were trying for a *Field & Stream* playmate centerfold. I heard my voice go up three octaves until I sounded like my little sister in the middle of a puppy litter, "Ooooo that's-a-boy, that's-a-baby, yesssssss, come to daddy, wooogie-woogie-woo." It was a rainbow and I'll bet it was seven inches long. All right, five. Anyway, when I grabbed the thing some of it stuck out both ends of my hand. I haven't been so happy since I passed my driver's license exam.

So I'm a fly fisherman now. Of course I'm not an expert yet. But I'm working on the most important part of fly-fishing technique—boring the hell out of anybody who'll listen.

Bird Hunting

Men's Journal, 1994

Some of the best bird covers in New Brunswick are old garbage dumps. The word *cover,* used in the sense of hunting ground, is a variant of *covert* although there is nothing MI-6ish or Mossad-like about game birds as far as I can tell. Birds do not go to the dump because they're thinking that's the last place I'd look for creatures of natural beauty and untamed grace. Nor do they need to. Given my faculties as a sportsman and the skills of the dogs with which I hunt, birds could hide in the foyers of New Brunswick bed-and-breakfasts, in bowls of wax fruit.

Birds go to the dump because—I hate to break this to Friends of the Earth—animals have no aesthetics. Eels congregate in the sludge on the bottom of New York harbor. Trout bite on feather, fur, and tinsel dry flys as ugly as Barbie clothes. To a raccoon a trash can is Paris in May. Rabbits desert the most elaborate nature refuges to visit your ill-planned and unweeded vegetable garden. Wild geese adore golf courses, even the unfashionable public kind. And there is nothing, it seems, more gorgeous and fascinating to a deer than the headlights of an oncoming car.

Considering animal taste, I'm not sure I want to know why birds are attracted to dumps. And considering my own taste—gin slings, madras pants, Ed McBain novels, Petula Clark LPs—I'm not sure I want to know why I'm attracted to bird hunting. But I will try to make sense of the matter.

I've been shooting in New Brunswick for a decade. Usually eight or ten of us make an outing in the fall. We are an ordinary lot, halfway through life's actuarial leach field and pretty well fixed. We're not likely to be tapped for a Benetton ad.

Some of us are avid hunters and deadly shots, and some of us had a gun last year that didn't fit and needed a different choke and the safety kept sticking. I was using the wrong size shot and too light a load. I'm beginning to get arthritis in my shoulder. I had a new bifocal prescription. My boots hurt. The sun got in my eyes.

This is not one of those men-go-off-in-the-woods hunting trips full of drink, flatulence, and lewd Hillary Clinton jokes. For one thing, some of us aren't men. A couple of us aren't even Republicans. We pack neckties, sports coats, skirts, and makeup (although I don't think anyone wears all four). There is little of the Cro-Magnon in this crowd. Though there *is* something about three bottles of wine apiece with dinner and six-egg breakfasts . . . Did somebody step on a carp? And you've heard about Hillary whispering to Bill, "Give me ten inches and hurt me!" So he made love to her twice and appointed David Gergen White House communications director.

Our New Brunswick sojourn is not a wilderness adventure either. We're no Patagonia-clad apostles of the Rio Summit out getting our faces rubbed in Mother Nature's leg hairs. And we're too old to need a thirty-mile hike, a wet bedroll, and a dinner of trail mix and puddle water to make us think life is authentic. If we'd wanted to push human endurance to its limits and face the awesome challenges of the natural elements in their uncivilized state, we could have stayed home with the kids.

No. We spend the first half of the shoot in the deep woods but at a good lodge with an excellent chef. The chef not only cooks six-egg breakfasts and Bordeaux-absorbent dinners but packs delightful lunches for us, for example moose sandwiches, which are much better—also smaller—than they sound.

For the second half of the shoot we drive to the Bay of Fundy and stay at a handsome inn where the sensible innkeepers bring out the old bedspreads and second-string towels so there will be no need to apologize for the mess left by gun cleaning, dog brushing, and male pattern baldness. The innkeepers also let us into their kitchen to cook what we've killed. Some of us may not be brilliant shotgunners, but we are all serious game cooks even though I'm not really used to cooking on a commercial gas range and those copper-bottom pans the inn has heat up, I think, too fast and shouldn't there be some kind of government standards or warning labels or something concerning brandy flammability?

What we are hunting in New Brunswick is mainly woodcock, *Scolopax minor,* a chunky, neckless, blunt-winged, mulch-colored bird with a very long beak and a body the size, shape, and heft of a prize beefsteak tomato. Rereading that sentence I see I have failed to capture in prose the full measure of the woodcock's physical attractiveness. Probably because it looks like a knee-walking shorebird in urgent need of Jenny Craig. It does have lovely eyes. And a wonderful personality, too, for all I know. Anyway, the woodcock is, in fact, a cousin of the sandpiper and the snipe but makes its home on less expensive real estate.

Woodcock live in the alder patches which occupy, in horizon-knocking profusion, the numberless streambeds and vast marsh bottoms of New Brunswick's flat, damp topography. Alders are a pulpwood shrub whose branches grow in muddled sprays like bad flower arrangements. Hunting in young alder thickets is like walking though something with a consistency between Jell-O and high hurdles. Old alder thickets, which grow as high as twelve feet, present grim, decaying vaults of face-grabbing, hat-snatching limb tangles. But the alder thickets where the woodcock nest and feed are those, like us, in their middle years. And these have all the bad features of alders young and old plus a greasy mud footing and foliage which, even in late fall, is as dense as salad.

Once such a mess of alders has been entered it becomes impossible to tell the time of day or where you are supposed to be going or from whence you came, and the only thing you know about your direction is it's not the one the dog's headed in. Every now and then you come upon a dump. The overturned cars and abandoned refrigerators are, at least, landmarks. And if you've been in the alders long enough, they're a positive delight to the eye. The old woodsman's adage about getting lost is "always go uphill." This is a problem in New Brunswick, which doesn't have much in the way of uphills; indeed the entire province seems to be on a downhill slope. Anyway, from my own experience, the only thing going uphill when you're lost does is give you a terrific view of no place you've ever seen before.

The woodcock are in the alders because the soil there is full of earthworms, which is what woodcock eat. The flavor of all birds is notably influenced by diet. A Canada goose shot in a field of corn is a treat. A Canada goose shot on the fourth green and filled with fertilizer and lawn chemicals is disgusting. Fish-eating ducks taste like fish that have been eaten by ducks. And I'm told "eating crow" is not an empty phrase. Woodcock are delicious. This raises the worrying thought that we should really be hunting and frying night crawlers. They are certainly easier to find and kill. But worm digging gear is not going to look stylish in an Orvis catalog.

You need a dog to hunt woodcock. Most pointing dogs can be trained to do it, but the breed of choice is the Brittany, a knee-high orange and white canine about as long as he is tall with no tail worth the mention and looking like an English springer spaniel with a better barber and a marathon running hobby.

Brittanys were bred in the eponymous province of France about 150 years ago specifically for woodcock hunting. They have a character that is both remote and excitable—yappy and grave at the same time, something like a John Simon theater review. Brittanys are very intelligent, whatever that means in a dog. Does a very intelligent dog have a unified theory of table scraps or a good and logical explanation for humping your leg?

What a Brittany has, in fact, is an intense, irrational, foolish, almost human desire to hunt woodcock. He possesses several techniques. He can run into the alder cover and flush a bird that is much too far away. Flushing is what a hunter calls it when a dog scares a bird silly and makes it fly. It will then fly in any direction that your gun isn't pointed. This as opposed to pointing, which is when a dog scares a bird even sillier and makes it sit down. The Brittany can also run into the alder cover and *point* a bird that is much too far away. When a Brittany points he goes absolutely rigid and still (and does so in a way that makes him look like he's about to hike a dog football or moon a dog sorority house rather than in that paw up, tail out, King Tut tomb painting posture dogs have in *Sports Afield* photographs or on place mats from the Ralph Lauren Home Store). The Brittany is wearing a bell around his neck. The idea is to keep track of the dog in the woods by following the noise of the bell. Then, when the dog goes on point, the bell will stop ringing, and you're supposed to head directly toward . . . You understand the problem. Brittanys may be intelligent, but the people who thought up the bell were, to put it bluntly, French.

The Brittany can also do what it's supposed to do and hunt right in front of you—"working close" as it's known—in which case he'll walk over the top of the woodcock leaving you to flush it yourself by almost stepping on the thing, whereupon it will fly straight up in your face with an effect as nightmarish as a remake of Hitchcock's *The Birds* starring Ted Danson and Whoopi Goldberg.

When everything goes exactly right, which is none of the time, the Brittany will go on point someplace where I can see him do it. I'll "walk up" the woodcock, which will take flight at an obliging distance. The woodcock has powerful breast muscles and is capable of almost vertical ascent. It will rise above the alders beating its wings so fast that its feathers make a loud whistling sound. Then, in a motion called towering, the bird will pause for a moment before flying away. This is when I take my shot. And, assuming that the alders haven't jammed my hat down over my eyes or knocked the gun out of my hand and assuming that I remembered to load the gun in the first place and that I haven't stepped on the dog while walking up the bird and gotten myself bitten on the ankle, then—if my hand is steady and my aim is true and nothing blocks the way—I'll miss.

I regard it as armed shopping, a tame pursuit when you think about it. It's going to the grocery store that's bloodthirsty. Consider all those Perdue oven stuffers you've bought for dinner over the years. How many of them had any chance at all? You mighty nimrod, you. Every one you stalked you killed. Whereas for me, there's hardly a bird that comes before the barrels of my gun that doesn't get away free. Nay, better than free. The bird receives an education about what those orange and white and hairy—and pink and winded and pudgy—things are doing in the woods. I am a university for birds.

Birds, of course, do get shot on these trips, even if not by my gun. And the dog is actually as important to finding dead birds as he is to missing live ones. Woodcock possess almost perfect camouflage, and, while difficult to see when living, they—for some reason—disappear completely into the leaf mold once they've been killed. It is hard to imagine what Darwinian benefit there is to an invisible corpse. Though there may be one. If the thing that eats you can't find you when you're ready to be eaten, maybe that gourmand will give up on the whole enterprise. It's a modification of the oyster defense mechanism, which is to look incredibly snotlike at mealtime. Anyway, there are a number of interesting evolutionary questions about woodcock. How'd they lose the beachfront condo? Why would anyone migrate to New Brunswick? And how come they eat worms? Is it a bet or something? According to Guy de la Valdéne's authoritative text on *Scolopax minor, Making Game* (Clark City Press), the woodcock has lived in North America since the middle Pleistocene, for a million and a half years. But there were no earthworms on this continent until the seventeenth century. They were introduced in potted plants from Europe and Asia. Before 1600 were the woodcock sending out for Chinese? Also, birds are supposed to be direct descendants of dinosaurs. So why aren't woodcock extinct? My guess is it's because whatever killed the dinosaurs was wearing new bifocals. I don't suppose we'll ever know for sure. Any more than we'll ever know for sure whether the apatosaurus went:

PEEP

At least it makes me feel good to think that every time I dine on poultry I'm getting even in some small way with *Barney & Friends.*

That dogs are able to find birds, alive or dead, is not surprising. Dogs more or less "see" the world through their olfactory sense. (Therefore what I look like to a dog after a long day in the alders is something I won't dwell on.) Woodcock—to judge by our dogs' behavior—must smell to a Brittany like coffee in the morning or Arpège at night. The surprising thing is rather that hunting dogs don't leap on the live birds or gobble the dead ones. The whole point of breeding bird dogs is to come up with a pooch who—contrary to every imaginable predator instinct—*doesn't* catch his prey. He lets you, with your shotgun, do it for him (or not as the case may be. It is a fact known only to bad shots that dogs smirk). Suppose you sit a six-year-old boy on the end of a dock with a fishing pole and every time the bobber goes under you grab the rod and land the fish. Suppose you get the child to put up with this all day and not only that but like it. V. S. Naipaul, in his history of Trinidad, said (apropos of what I don't remember and God knows why V. S. Naipaul, of all people, would bring up the subject) that Sir Robert Dudley, circa 1600, illegitimate son of the Earl of Leicester, was noted "for being the first of all that taught a dog to sit in order to catch partridges." A remarkable bastard was Bob.

And pointing is only half of what dog breeders have accomplished. The dog also retrieves. Imagine—to put this in terms comprehensible to the lowest common denominator of male readers—you found a Victoria's Secret model in your front yard, wearing her professional attire, and intensely interested in affection. And suppose you carefully picked her up, being sure not to hug her too tightly or return any intimate caresses, and delivered her to your next-door neighbor, the guy who's had your Skill saw since last February and always lets his crabgrass go to seed.

I have no idea what dogs get out of hunting. And once I started to think about that I realized I didn't have much of an idea what people get out of hunting either.

Partly it's a social thing. All of us on the trip are good friends, and it's nice to be off together in a place for which our bosses and offices can never quite figure out the area code. ("Where was that you said you were going? New Zealand? New Orleans? New Guinea? New Jersey?") But we could go to each other's houses and turn off the phones and run through the shrubbery in our old clothes, if we wanted.

There's nature appreciation. But, though New Brunswick has some appealing coastal vistas and some handsome salmon rivers, the province is not a scenic wonder, and the land we hunt is no prettier than the average Ohio cornfield. Still, we do appreciate it. There's something about being out in nature with a purpose—even if that purpose is only to torment dogs and scare feathered creatures—that makes you pay more attention to the outside world. A hike is such a pointless thing, no matter how wonderful the view. You might love the way your house looks but you wouldn't just walk around and around in it. When you hunt you have to keep a careful eye on weather, terrain, foliage, and dangerous animals such as me if I happen to be in the cover with you swinging my gun around in every direction trying to get the safety to release. There's even a religious aspect to detailed examination of the outdoors. The universe, on close inspection, seems hardly to have been an accident. Or, if it is an accident, it's certainly a complexly ordered one—as if you dropped mushrooms, ham, truffles, raw eggs, melted butter, and a hot skillet on the kitchen floor and wound up with a perfect omelette. That said, alder patches are something God created on a Monday, after a big weekend.

Hunting also produces a good, solid sense of false accomplishment. After a long day of bird getaways and gun bungles, of yelling at dogs and yourself, you really think you've done something. You don't get this feeling from any other recreation. Probably it's a throwback to the million years or so that man spent thumbing through the large stone pages of the Paleolithic L. L. Bean catalog. The cave paintings of Lascaux, after all, depict bison hunts, not tennis matches.

The fact that my friends and I don't have to hunt to get food may actually be our reason for hunting. Fun can be defined as "anything you don't have to do." Or is that right? You have to eat. And eating is the one sensible (if you're not counting calories or the fire extinguisher mess from the little problem I had with flambéing) thing that we do on this trip.

Woodcock, like most game meat, is almost fatless and can be cooked as rare as steak without a chicken tartare effect. Woodcock has a slightly liverish flavor, but it is liver to make a neoplatonist of you. This is the cosmic ideal of liver, liver in the mind of God or, anyway, in the mind of Mom—liver that tastes like your mom thought you should think it tasted.

The only real meat on a woodcock is the breast. When cleaning a woodcock you can split the breast skin with your thumbs and pull the muscle off the carcass. Take this, cut it in half, and roll the halves around in a hot frying pan in good olive oil with a little salt and pepper and maybe a dash of Worcestershire sauce and a sprinkle of rosemary, and you've got . . . something nobody else in the house will touch. It's ugly as a sea slug and smells like tripe, but it tastes superb. We use the drumsticks as hors d'oeuvres, a kind of snob's answer to Buffalo wings. Really serious woodcock cooks sauté the "trail," the intestines, and serve them on toast. We're not that serious.

We have meals of high-savored woodcock. And we have meals of delicate tasting ruffed grouse, whose meat is to Kentucky Fried as the fresh-baked baguettes of Provence are to ballpark hot dog rolls. And we have meals of wild duck, the piquant flesh of which bears not the slightest resemblance to the Donald-flavored item that's bought in stores. Served with all these are steaming heaps of fiddlehead ferns picked from the nearby woods and bowls of piping New Brunswick potatoes, small as golf balls and sweet as pies, and rolls and buns and scones and jiggling plates of wild foxberry jelly and pots, tubs, and buckets of strong drink and desserts aplenty besides.

Here at last is something I really *am* good at. I can tuck in with the best of them. And I get better every year. I have the new holes punched in my belt tongues and the let-out pants seats to prove it.

When dinner is over we yaw and waddle away from the table and back to our rooms for one more drink or five and to make some truly inventive excuses for our shooting—"I was thinking about my ex-wife and I pulled the trigger too soon"—and to tell each other various bits of highly improbable avian lore. Then we are up again at dawn to hunt.

Ruffed grouse, or partridge as it's called in New England, *Bonasa umbellus,* is an airborne special forces commando chicken. It's about the size of a chicken. It looks like a chicken. It acts like a chicken—scratches, pecks, and does a chicken walk. But it's decked out in camouflage khakis and browns. And it can fly, which is something a chicken can't do. (I know because a fighter pilot friend of mine was once in a furious argument at the officers' club as to whether chickens couldn't fly or just didn't want to. Someone drove to a local chicken farm, bought a chicken, got in an open cockpit biplane, took the biplane to three thousand feet, and tossed the chicken out. There is a large dent in one of the Quonset huts on that air base. But the story's better after dinner.)

Grouse prefer a more gentlemanly sort of country than woodcock. Grouse like old apple trees on overgrown farmland, brushy edges of conifer forests, and patches of hawthorne shrubs. These last are filled with sinister barbs, but you don't have to go into them. You can send the dog. Nicer hunting ground does not mean nicer hunting however. I have been consistently outwitted by ruffed grouse. Not that this is any compliment to the bird's intelligence. I have been consistently outwitted by my VCR and my tuxedo bow tie. Nonetheless, for an animal with a . . . well, with a bird brain, the grouse is sagacious. Three of us were hunting a field one afternoon, and the man on the right put up a grouse. Instead of flying away and inviting a shot, the grouse hopped over the man's head and flew straight for the middle hunter at eye level, thereby keeping either from being able to shoot without hitting the other. Repeating the tactic, the bird darted around the middle hunter and flew at me. And, when the bird got past me, it broke into every-which-way flight maneuvers and reached the woods untouched. A grouse can walk almost as fast as it can fly and will trot away from most encounters, silent and invisible. The bird rarely holds. And grouse droppings, or "chalk," smell more like grouse than grouse do so you'll often find your dog has spent ten minutes pointing bird shit. When the grouse does get up, it flies with a tremendous bass note flutter of wings, a tremolo played on a tuba, a noise so startling that you're likely to shoot your hat.

As do many game animals, grouse seem to check the calendar. They can be flapping around in scads and passels the day before hunting season opens, and the next morning they're as rare as intelligent television. The locals in New Brunswick hunt grouse on the ground, waiting until the birds come out on the country roads at dusk to gravel, that is, to swallow the small stones that birds need for their gizzards, to break up food in lieu of chewing. Then the locals blow the heads off the grouse with full-choke twelve-gauge shotguns. It's very unsporting to shoot a game bird on the ground, and we disdain this manner of hunting utterly. Unless we need the grouse for dinner. Or we've had a bad day. Or it's after 3:00 P.M.

The peculiar thing about grouse is their learning curve. Savvy as they are where they're hunted, in locales where they're rarely or never shot, they are sap-green patsies. Some of our usual party went to northern Maine a dozen years ago to hunt grouse at a lodge where most of the customers were after deer, moose, or bear. We found the grouse sitting in rows on tree limbs. Spruce grouse, which are darker and differently marked, are famous for this kind of behavior. Spruce grouse not only look like chickens but are dumb enough to fly to a Sunday dinner and surrender. But these were ruffed grouse and no amount of shouts and dog barks would budge them. We had to throw sticks to make them fly, and, when even this didn't work and we broke down and shot one off its perch, the next bird in line just shuffled over and took the deceased's place.

One of our New Brunswick guides, Tom, who is Indian, says that when he was a kid his family was too poor to afford shotgun shells and he used to hunt grouse by sneaking up behind them with a noose on the end of a stick. I wouldn't believe this from anybody but Tom, who is a chief of one of the local bands of Micmac and a practitioner of traditional medicine and spent a year traveling around the United States on a Ford Foundation grant, comparing tribal religious ceremonies. Tom has a shocking ability to see things in the woods and get up close to them. And he can walk through an alder patch without getting poked in the eye by a stick. Tom is a very convincing man.

Unfortunately, Tom is also a very convincing man when you're out with him in the far middle of those god-awful gloomy alder thickets and the sun has gone down and you've got no idea how to get back to the car and he starts telling you about the *Tjno,* a giant Indian who turned wild and if you stumble into his territory he'll catch you and make you work for him. That is, if you're a woman or a child. "Husbands," said Tom, "the Tjno eats." Tjnos are now, I suppose, mostly employed as divorce lawyers.

There are also *Pugalatmooj* in the woods—little people who taught the Micmac how to make canoes and arrowheads. They sound a bit like leprechauns but more useful and less likely to make fools of themselves appearing on St. Patrick's Day cards. Tom said you can hear the *Pugalatmooj* whistling. And I believe you can, especially if you're completely turned around in a sea of alders and it's getting real dark. "How do *you* keep from getting lost out here?" I asked Tom.

"Oh, Indians never get lost," he said, looking on every side with an expression as perplexed as my own. "However," said Tom, "sometimes the path wanders away."

Another of our guides, Robert, is a retired RCMP officer and an expert on ducks. He can call ducks, shoot ducks, make duck decoys, name from memory every kind of duck found in North America, and give each kind its Latin moniker. Robert can tell you everything you want to know about ducks except why anyone would ever go hunt them.

The idea of duck hunting is to get up about the time that people who are having fun go to bed and get dressed in dirty flannels, itchy thermal underwear, muddy hip boots, clammy rain ponchos, and various other layers of insulation and waterproofing, then clamber, trudge, wade, paddle, stumble, flounder, and drag yourself miles into a swamp while carrying coolers, shell boxes, lunch buckets, flashlights, hand warmers, Buck knives, camp stoves, toilet paper, a couple of dogs, and forty or fifty imitation ducks, then sit in a wet hole concealed by brush cuttings and pine boughs until it's dark again and you can go home. Meanwhile the weather will either be incredibly good, in which case the ducks will be flying in the clear sky thousands of feet above you, or incredibly bad, in which case the ducks will be landing right in front of you but you won't be able to see them. Not that any actual ducks are required for this activity, and often none are sighted. Sometimes it's worse when they are. The terrible thing about duck hunting is that everyone you're with can see you shoot and see what you're shooting at, and it is almost impossible to come up with a likely excuse for blasting a decoy in half.

Last year I was in Bosnia covering the war there for *Rolling Stone.* And I was hunkered down in a muddy trench behind a pile of shrubbery and tree branches watching tiny Serbs attack in the distance. "This seems familiar," I thought. It was, indeed, the very image of duck hunting (although for some reason, this time, the ducks had the guns).

And sure enough, one month later to the day I was hunkered down in a muddy trench behind a pile of shrubbery and tree branches with Robert and my pals. It was pissing down rain. I'd forgotten my pocket flask. Somebody had left the sandwiches in the bottom of the canoe and they'd turned into bread and mayonnaise soup. The glass liner had broken inside the coffee thermos. Everybody was out of cigarettes. And the dog had rolled in something awful. Of ducks, there were none. Not even any bottom-feeding coot, the recipe for which is:

PLANKED COOT
Arrange bird on a 1″ thick kiln-dried oak plank. Roast in oven
for two hours at 350°, basting every 20 minutes with a red

wine, olive oil, vinegar, and garlic clove marinade. Throw the
coot away and eat the plank.

It is only natural that war and hunting are of a kidney. Hunting
has been intimately connected with warfare since the beginning of civilization. And before the beginning of civilization there probably wasn't
a difference. The traditional leisure activity of archers and lancers and
knights and such, when not killing people, was to kill other things.

We don't need hunting in the modern world. It makes the wilderness so primitive. It upsets actresses and sensitive undergraduate types.
And, anyway, we can easily bag a cheeseburger out the window of our
car. But we do need war. At least I assume we do—to judge by the
amount of it that's going on in the world at any given moment. And
it's my theory that the entire purpose of the annual hunting trip is to
make war look, comparatively speaking, like fun.

Deep-Sea Fishing

Men's Journal, 1992
magine a serious, highly competitive, physically demanding outdoor sport that you can play while sitting in a chair drinking beer. Deep-sea fishing is as close as a middle-aged man gets to heaven—unless he's not watching his cholesterol.

I was on the boat *Lucky Too* with Captain Jay Weed and Mate Scott Genereux. We were sixteen or eighteen miles out of Key West, just past the big coral reef that runs from left to right below the Florida Keys like the line under an arithmetic problem. The seas were tall and disorderly. The water was such a deep Brooks Brothers suit color that it looked false—blue-tinted contact lenses on a brown-eyed woman. The wind was up and the sky was filled with tumbling dryer-loads of clouds. The *Lucky Too* is a thirty-four-foot fiberglass cabin cruiser with a 212-horsepower diesel engine. It's purpose-built for sport fishing. But even with this much size and power the boat was topping and bobbling and slobbering around.

Captain Jay was looking for fish. I have no idea how. Maybe he knows their ways from years on the open sea, or maybe they leave their phone numbers on channel buoys. Mate Scott was walking on the heaving deck as though it were so much Kansas sidewalk. He was baiting hooks and tending lines and generally exhibiting the kind of nautical competence that makes such land-lubbing forty-four-year-olds as myself feel like shoes for an eel.

Everybody on the boat had a job. My job was to not throw up. This is the one, entire skill to being a deep-sea fisherman—not punting your bran muffins. Though you have to have a thick spot in your wallet, too. Deep-sea fishing isn't cheap. A good boat charter costs between $400 and $550 a day plus six-packs and a lunch to blow and a minimum 15 percent tip to the mate if you expect to go out on that boat again and not wind up trolling schools of pizza anchovies. I must admit I was good at deep-sea fishing. What with a prescription anti-seasickness patch behind my ear and *Men's Journal* footing the bill, I was, in fact, a regular damn athlete.

We were fishing with four rods, seven-foot-long fiberglass poles as thick as rake handles at the butt. Until something bites, these rods sit in holders built into the side rails of the boat. Captain Jay trolled at four or five knots (a knot being pretty much like a mile per hour, but more expensive). The lines from the rods are baited with fish bigger than what I used to catch and cook in my midwestern boyhood. Two lines drag directly behind the boat, one on the surface and another weighted on a "deep troll" rig to fish sixty or eighty feet under water. The remaining two lines are held away from the boat by a pair of steel outriggers, which lean over the ocean like high-tension wire towers built by drunks.

The *Lucky Too* has, on its aft deck, a pair of fighting chairs—barber chairs without the barbers. At the front of a fighting chair's seat cushion, in line with your crotch, is a socket to hold the base of the fishing rod. Now and then there'd be a sizzle, and line would start hurling off one of the reels. Scott would grab the rod, make sure it was a fish on the hook and not a lobster pot or an overboard beer cooler, then hand it to me. I'd fit the rod into the socket and get busy.

There's a lot of excitement when a fish strikes, most of it for the fish, of course. Some game fish leap out of the water when hooked. Some even leap as high as fish do in the photographs on charter boat brochures. And a big fish will run the monofilament out like a teenage daughter on a Visa card credit line. You reel a few times first, to set the hook. After that you "work" the fish with a pumping motion—pulling back on the rod with all your weight then reeling like the world's champion egg white stiffener as you bring the rod back down. It's important not to give the fish any slack, though we're talking strictly in physical terms. You can have any kind of emotional relationship you want with the fish.

As soon as you've reeled as much line as you can, the fish will run it out again and you'll pull back on the rod and start over. You do that between a dozen and a hundred times while trying not to think to yourself, "If it weren't such a big fish and I weren't paying so much to catch it, this would be as much fun as pushing a stalled car to the nearest turnpike exit."

We were fishing for sailfish, which, had we caught any, we would have thrown back. There aren't enough sailfish anymore, and they are so prized as a catch that most sportsmen let them go. This probably sounds insane if you're not a fisherman, but that's the "catch and release" philosophy: don't kill these animals, just annoy the hell out of them. We were also fishing for mackerel, especially the big king mackerel or kingfish. These would be sold cheap on the dock because mackerel are, frankly, very mackerel flavored. Smaller fish such as cero mackerel, little sharks, et cetera, would also be thrown back. There is, all told, a certain futility to deep-sea fishing. But it's a satisfying futility, like having sex with birth control.

Hooking a big barracuda was very satisfying indeed. Very futile, too. I mean, I wasn't going to eat the thing. Barracuda taste like a cat-food salad, and they give you ciguatera, an awful disease. And I wasn't going to get it mounted as a trophy. Why would I have something that's as ugly as a divorce hanging on my wall? I just wanted to haul this scaly SOB up to the stern and give him a fish version of an IRS audit.

I'd been losing kingfish to barracuda all afternoon. A thirty-pound king mackerel would take the bait, jump in the air in a manner spectacular enough to be worth exaggerating later, and put up an admirable (if you admire fish) fight. Then I'd begin reeling it in and here'd come the barracuda. They'd snap and flash and trouble the water. By the time I got my mackerel into the boat, I'd have only half a fish and not the cheerful half either. If I got a barracuda itself on the line, its own brothers, its pals, its school-of-fish mates would do the same thing, gobbling cannibal chunks of flesh. Barracuda are the lawyers of the sea.

But the big barracuda I caught must have come off the William Kennedy Smith defense team. There wasn't a bite mark on him. He was about three and a half feet long. And he weighed twenty-some pounds, most of which was jaw muscle and the rest of which was teeth. Of course we let him go. Anything as nasty as that must serve some purpose in maintaining the balance of the earth's ecosystem. Probably it eats ecologists.

You see, deep-sea fishing has nothing to do with the enchantments of nature. Our friend and fellow intellectual the dolphin, for instance. With the help of various activist groups he has achieved everything except the vote and abortion rights. But out in blue water the dolphin is a fish thief and welfare cheat. A hooked game fish is an easy mugging, a finned food stamp to a dolphin. Barracuda take a percentage, *vigorish*. But a dolphin makes one swipe at a kingfish the size of a golf bag—a kingfish you've been fighting for half an hour—and leaves nothing but the head. Anybody who's seen this will think again before getting into the Sea World swim tank with smiling, playful Flipper.

Nor does deep-sea fishing have anything to do with nature's brilliant design. I watched for an hour while the same tern flew down and snatched our bait and then flew away until the monofilament line yanked the fish from its beak. Then the tern would come back and do it again. Like a modern American with a government benefit, the tern couldn't figure out there was a string attached.

Deep-sea fishing is about nature that is mean and stupid. And let

P. J. O'Rourke

us not forget futile. I suppose this is what Hemingway was getting at in *The Old Man and the Sea*. (Though Ernie could have sent in a dolphin as soon as the codger hooked the marlin and saved us all some reading time in high school.)

Mean, stupid, futile—nature and middle-aged men have a lot in common. This is one clue to the pleasures of deep-sea fishing. And another clue is that, in order to deep-sea fish, you have to travel to someplace far away from wives, children, jobs, bills, and stationary exercise bicycles—Costa Rica, Cabo San Lucas, Bimini, Cozumel, or the like. I picked Key West because I'd had fun there in the 1970s. At least I think I did. It's all blurry now. But I remember catching record-size hangovers in bars with three bathrooms: "Men," "Women," and "Drugs." It was a dirty little island back then, populated with the flotsam of the seven seas and the jetsam of trailer parks uncounted.

But I hadn't seen Key West in almost ten years. The place has changed. Time-share resorts have been built where historic liquor stores once stood. Tennis courts blot the swamps. And there's a Santa Fe–style restaurant where a perfectly good parking lot used to be. Key West has become a "travel destination," filled with—of all things—families. There are families everywhere, ambulating in sunburned clumps: fussing mom, bored kids, dad with his eyeball fused to the camcorder. And they're wearing clothes in colors from the spectrum of visible light's, dreaded "vacation band." These are resort clothes, clothes with too many zippers, too many drawstrings, too many pleats, buttons, pouches, snaps, pockets, buckles, straps, epaulets, and elasticized hems; clothes so divorced from normal sartorial function that the Bermuda shorts might as well have three leg holes. And every item of apparel is covered with designer logos like smallpox scars.

Scattered among the families are double-scrubbed, peach-faced college students, fun-having as hard as they can, getting mirth filled and perky on three light beers. It's amazing how decent, middle-class Americans, enjoying themselves in a harmless way, create a more repulsive atmosphere than dope smugglers, drunks, sex deviants, and coke heads ever did. Key West's main street, Duval, used to have five or six terrible bars, two flophouses, and a Cuban lunch counter. It is now flanked with unbroken lines of souvenir T-shirt stores. Sample slogan: "My Buns Got Toasted in Key West."

In the midst of these emporiums is local sing-along king Jimmy Buffett's Margaritaville,™ a sanitary and wholesome nightspot with menu items named after Jimmy's songs. It is so different from the places in Key West where Buffett actually used to drink that the device of simile is strained. Suppose the present-day Elizabeth Taylor were given her original part in a remake of *National Velvet*. It is that different.

Margaritaville™ has a souvenir T-shirt store of its own, naturally, where all manner of Buffett memorabilia may be purchased. What a shame this never occurred to the great musicians of the past. Think what Wagner could have done with a Götterdämmerung Outlet— adjustable Valkyrie hats with foam rubber horns, life-size inflatable Rhine Maidens, and personalized, gold-plated Nibelungen rings.

Better to be out with nature however mean and stupid. And she was particularly so the next day, with a sky like the bottom of an old frying pan and waves as big as hospital bills. The first thing we caught, though it was large and full of fight, wasn't even a fish. A poor pelican snatched our bait and had to be pulled to the boat and unhooked. It was a wet and difficult business for Scott to get a hold of so much angry bird without bird or Scott being too badly hurt. When the pelican was freed it turned as perverse as a human and hung around the *Lucky Too,* looking expectant.

We caught nothing else that morning except a couple small yellowtail snappers, which displayed the same color combinations as Key West tourists. The boat was being shaken like a bad dog. And the real excitement was trying to take a leak in the *Lucky Too*'s tiny head. I attempted to wedge myself into position, pushing a hand against the ceiling and a foot against the deck, another foot against one bulkhead, and the other hand against the wall behind me, but this left no appendage free to undo my zipper. The only comfortable way to piss would have been to sit down on the toilet and have the john filled with Styrofoam packing peanuts to hold me in place.

I tried to eat lunch but the cooler was chucking ice cubes into my lap, my sandwich got blown out of my hand, and my beer leapt out of its gimbal holder and spilled into my Top Siders. I didn't have a chance to vomit; my food was doing it for me.

There are times, deep-sea fishing, when even the meanest and stupidest middle-aged man wonders if he wouldn't be happier back at the office losing a fortune in leveraged buyouts. Then we got into the blackfin tuna. We found them just on the edge of the reef, where the ocean turns from abysmal blue to a perfect grass green as though you'd been watering the lawn and just couldn't stop and now the front yard is thirty feet deep. Blackfins aren't very big fish, never more than forty pounds. They weigh less than the paperwork from a real estate deal, but they've got as much fight in them as any condo salesman. Blackfins don't do any graceful leaps or acrobatics, either. No one ever made a 1950s table lamp with a ceramic base in the shape of a battling tuna. They strike in a quiet, solid way as though you'd hooked the dock. And working the fish, pulling it back to the boat, is a matter of enough sit-ups to make Jane Fonda ditch the exercise business and marry a rich guy. Tuna are deadweight when you're reeling them and torpedoes when you aren't. One moment of inattention and your line is headed for Cuba. And, when you finally do get the tuna to where it can be gaffed, it shakes its head back and forth like a girl meeting William Kennedy Smith in a bar and dives, going for the bottom faster than T-bill yields.

We caught a bunch of them—beautiful fat parabolas of fish, dark-spined with brass highlights along the flanks. The sun came out and the wind went down a little. Flying fish sped down the valleys between the waves. A loggerhead turtle swam by, brown as a Havana cigar and big as a breakfast nook. The boat quit rocking so badly or I quit minding so much. I had another two or three beers. Scott took a fillet knife, grabbed one tuna by the tail, and cut out long, thin, garnet-colored strips of meat—the freshest sushi in the world. Captain Jay turned the *Lucky Too* toward Key West, and I settled into a haze of exhausted and slightly alcoholic bliss. One of the quiet joys of middle age is knowing exactly where you are in the food chain—above tuna, below souvenir T-shirt stores.

Golf

Men's Journal, 1992

The smooth, long, liquid sweep of a three wood smacking into the equator of a dimpled Titleist . . . It makes a potent but slightly foolish noise like the fart of a small, powerful nature god. The ball sails away in a beautiful hip or breast of a curve. And I am filled with joy.

At least that's what I'm filled with when I manage to connect. Most of my strokes whiz by the tee the way a drunk passes a truck on a curve or dig into the turf in a manner that is more gardening than golf. But now and then I nail one, and each time I do it's an epiphany. *This* is how the Australopithecus felt, one or two million years ago, when he first hit something with a stick. Puny hominoid muscles were amplified by the principals of mechanics so that a little monkey swat suddenly became a great manly engine of destruction able to bring enormous force to bear upon enemy predators, hunting prey, and the long fairway shots necessary to get on the green over the early Pleistocene's tar pit hazards.

Hitting things with a stick is the cornerstone of civilization. Consider all the things that can be improved by hitting them with a stick: veal, the TV, Woody Allen. Having a dozen good sticks at hand, all of them well balanced and expertly made, is one reason I took up golf. I also wanted to show my support for the vice president. I now know for certain that Quayle is smarter than his critics. He's smart enough to prefer golf to spelling. How many times has a friend called you on a Sunday morning and said, "It's a beautiful day. Let's go spell potato"?

I waited until I was almost forty-five to hit my first golf ball. When I was younger I thought golf was a pointless sport. Of course all sports are pointless unless you're a professional athlete or a professional athlete's agent, but complex rules and noisy competition mask the essential inanity of most athletics. Golf is so casual. You just go to the course, miss things, tramp around in the briars, use pungent language, and throw two thousand dollars worth of equipment in a pond. Unlike skydiving or rugby, golf gives you leisure to realize it's pointless. There comes a time in life, however, when all the things that do have a point—career, marriage, exercising to stay fit—start turning, frankly, golflike. And that's when you're ready for golf.

The great thing about starting golf in your forties is that you *can* start golf in your forties. You can start other things in your forties but generally your wife makes you stop them, as Bill Clinton found out. Golf does not require tremendous strength or endurance. You can drive a little car around on the playing surface—something you can't do on a tennis court. Although, the way I play tennis, it wouldn't hurt.

Golf has gravitas. You play it with your pants on. There's nothing sadder than seeing a short, winded, aging ofay—me—on a basketball court. Although watching our presidential candidates out for a morning jog is close. Picture George Washington and Abraham Lincoln puffing around in their underwear. We'd be a slave-owning southernmost province of Canada except that King George and Jeff Davis would have laughed themselves to death.

I'm already a fool, I don't need to look the fool besides. I want my secretary to walk into my office and find me putting into an overturned highball glass. That's stylish. I don't happen to have an office. But I might get one and what would my secretary think if she walked in and found me batting grounders into the kneehole of my desk?

You can play golf first thing in the morning. I've noticed, for men my age, more and more of the important things happen at that hour of the day: golf, heart attacks, delivery of *The Wall Street Journal,* and—intermittently—erections and bowel movements.

You can smoke or drink on a golf course without interrupting the game, and you can take a leak—something you can't do on a squash court and shouldn't do in a swimming pool.

I wanted a sport with a lot of metaphors. I'm a journalist. We journalists like to draw upon the common fund of human experience when we express our many important ideas. And what's more common or better funded than sports? Sports metaphors are the bricks of journalistic prose. Sports similes are the mortar. Sports analogies are the trowel, or maybe the hod carrier . . . You get the idea. "Tinker to Evers to Chance." "Hang Time." "He shoots! He scores!" " 'Roid Rage." Without sports metaphors American journalism would experience, as it were, sudden death.

But I was running out of valuable athletic clichés. Would beach volleyball say much about proposals for federal health care reform? Could I use mumblety-peg comparisons to explain the North American Free Trade Agreement negotiations? Golf, however, is ideal for these purposes. "Christian fundamentalists put a wicked slice in the Republican party platform." "Somebody should replace the divot on the back of Al Gore's head." "Let's go hit Congress with a stick."

I also wanted a sport with a lot of equipment. All truly American sports are equipment intensive. Basketball was strictly for hoop-over-the-barn-door Hoosiers and Jersey City Y's until two-hundred-dollar gym shoes were invented. And synchronized swimming will never make it to network prime time because how often do you need new nose plugs? I'm an altruistic guy, in my own Reaganomics way. Sports gear purchases are about all that's keeping the fragile U.S. economy alive, and you'd have to get into America's Cup yachting or cross-country airplane racing to find a sport that needs more gear than golf. I've bought the shoes, hats, socks, pants, shirts, umbrellas, windbreakers, and plus fours—all in colors that Nirvana fans wouldn't dye their hair. Then there are the drivers, irons, putters, and the special clubs: parking-lot wedge, back-of-the-tree mashie, nearby highway niblick. MasterCard has installed a plaque on the wall of their headquarters office to commemorate my taking up golf.

Actually, I was forced to become a golfer. As a middle-aged affluent Republican, it was beginning to look weird that I didn't play. People were casting aspersions on my sex life. What with not being out on the golf course at the crack of dawn and not being soused at the nineteenth hole until all hours of the night—I might have one. Where I live in New Hampshire, if that kind of thing gets around, you can be drummed out of the local GOP and lose your Magic George Bush Decoder Ring.

Thus I prevailed upon a friend of mine to take me to his country club. There—once it was established that I'm not really Catholic and that, although my name technically ends in a vowel, it's silent—I was graciously allowed to play as a guest. This is another thing I like about golf, the exclusiveness. Of course most country clubs exclude the wrong kinds of people, such as me. But I hold out the hope that somewhere there's a club which bans first wives, people in twelve-step programs, Sting, the editorial board of *The Boston Globe,* and Ross Perot.

I played nine holes, and I must admit, for a complete tyro, I wasn't bad. I'll now proceed to tell you about every stroke on every hole. And that's one more swell thing about golf, it provides ammunition for the social bore. Who doesn't love cornering others with tales of action and adventure starring the self? But racquetball, for instance, has limits in this regard: "I hit it. She hit it. I hit it. She hit it really hard." And so on. Golf, on the other hand, is picaresque. A good golf bore can produce a regular *Odyssey* of tedium. And golf allows banal sports chitchat to be elevated to the plane of theoretical physics. An absolute lunkhead—the guy from work who files "The First National Bank" under *T* for "The" and thinks John Donne is a bathroom cleanser—turns into Stephen Hawking on the subject of golf. Note this passage from Jack Nicklaus's *Golf My Way:*

> When the club's face looks to the right of the direction in which the head is traveling, the ball spins around an equator tilted from left to right and thus curves to the right during flight.

I'll do you a favor and *not* tell you about every stroke. Or any stroke at all. Though I got off some very nice drives. True, they didn't land on the correct fairway, but that was due to wind. And I will stand mute on the subject of technique except to say I learned that many chip shots are best played with a sharp kick from the toe of a golf shoe. And if you cut a hole in your pants pocket you can drop a ball down your trouser leg and "discover" that your shot landed remarkably close to the green. And putting, for a person of my socioeconomic background, is best done by envisioning the cup as being behind a little windmill or inside the mouth of a cement whale. I also found out that all the important lessons of life are contained in the three rules for achieving a perfect golf swing:

1. Keep your head down.
2. Follow through.
3. Be born with money.

There's a fine camaraderie on a golf course—lumbering around with your fellow Republicans, encompassed by a massive waste of space and cash, bearing witness to prolific use of lawn chemicals and countenancing an exploitative wage scale for the maintenance employees.

Golf is the only sport known to have inspired an indignant left-wing poem. It was written by one Sarah Northcliffe Cleghorn in 1915:

> *The golf links lie so near the mill*
> *That almost every day*
> *The laboring children can look out*
> *And see the men at play.*

Just show me an indignant left-wing poem about softball or bungee jumping. And our local mill has been converted to a shopping mall, so the kids are still there.

Golf is also the only sport God is known to play. God and St. Peter are out on Sunday morning. On the first hole God drives into a water hazard. The waters part and God chips onto the green. On the second hole God takes a tremendous whack and the ball lands ten feet from the pin. There's an earthquake, one side of the green rises up, and the ball rolls into the cup. On the third hole God lands in a sand trap. He creates life. Single-cell organisms develop into fish and then amphibians. Amphibians crawl out of the ocean and evolve into reptiles, birds, and furry little mammals. One of those furry little mammals runs into the sand trap, grabs God's ball in its mouth, scurries over, and drops it in the hole.

St. Peter looks at God and says, "You wanna play golf or you wanna fuck around?"

And golf courses are beautiful. Many people think mature men have no appreciation for beauty except in immature women. This isn't true, and, anyway, we'd rather be playing golf. A golf course is a perfect example of Republican male aesthetics—no fussy little flowers, no stupid ornamental shrubs, no exorbitant demands for alimony, just acre upon acre of lush green grass *that somebody else has to mow.*

Truth, beauty, and even poetry are to be found in golf. Every man, when he steps up to the tee, feels, as Keats has it,

Like stout Cortez when with eagle eyes
  He star'd at the Pacific—and all his men
Look'd at each other with a wild surmise—
  Silent, upon a peak in Darien.

That is, the men were silent. Cortez was saying, "I can get on in two, easy. A three-wood drive, a five-iron from the fairway, then a two-putt max. But if I hook it, shit, I'm in the drink."